SHAMANISM

SHAMANISM
An Expanded View of Reality
compiled by Shirley Nicholson

A publication supported by
THE KERN FOUNDATION

Quest Books
Theosophical Publishing House

Wheaton, Illinois ◆ Madras, India

Quest Books
Theosophical Publishing House
P.O. Box 270
Wheaton, IL 60189-0270

www.questbooks.net

Library of Congress Cataloging-in-Publication Data

Shamanism.
(A Quest book)
"A Quest original"—T.p. verso.
Includes bibliographies.
1.   Shamanism.   2. Spiritual life.   I. Nicholson, Shirley J.
BL2370.S5S48   1987   291   85-40405
ISBN 978-0-8356-0617-2

Printed in the United States of America

Contents

Foreword
The Mind and Soul of the Shaman
Jean Houston vii

Acknowledgments xv

Contributing Authors xvii

I   The Shaman's Alternate Reality 1

   1   The Ancient Wisdom in Shamanic
      Cultures
      Michael Harner/Gary Doore 3

   2   Shamanism and Cosmology
      Mircea Eliade 17

   3   The Presence of Spirits in Magic and
      Madness
      Richard Noll 47

   4   Crazy Wisdom: The Shaman as
      Mediator of Realities
      Mary Schmidt 62

   5   Shamanism: An Archaic and/or Recent
      Belief System
      Mihály Hoppál 76

II   Shamanic States of Consciousness 101

   6   The Shaman: Master Healer in the
      Imaginary Realm
      Jeanne Achterberg 103

7 Dreams and Shamanism
   Stanley Krippner 125

8 Shamanism, ESP, and the Paranormal
   D. Scott Rogo 133

9 Rolling Thunder at Work
   Jim Swan 145

III Shamanic Traditions 159

10 The Tamang Shamanism of Nepal
    Larry G. Peters 161

11 Shamanism in the Jewish Tradition
    Rabbi Yonassan Gershom 181

12 The Way of the Adventurer
    Serge King 189

13 The Native American Prayer Pipe
    John Redtail Freesoul 204

IV Shamanism and the Perennial Philosophy 211

14 Shamanism, Mind, and No-Self
    Joan Halifax 213

15 The Dreamtime, Mysticism, and
    Liberation: Shamanism in Australia
    Ven. E. Nandisvara Nayake Thero 223

16 Transformation Process in Shamanism,
    Alchemy, and Yoga
    Ralph Metzner 233

17 Shamanism and Theosophy
    Robert Ellwood 253

V Shamanism in a Changing World 265

18 The Shaman Within
    David Feinstein 267

19 Lineage of the Sun
    Brooke Medicine Eagle 280

20 Black Elk: Then and Now
    William Lyon 285

Foreword

The Mind and Soul of the Shaman

JEAN HOUSTON

Why is there so great a renewal of interest in one of the oldest forms of the religious life—the practice of shamanism? I believe that a good part of its fascination lies in the fact that it is prepolitical, for all religions begin as spiritual experiences which then become politicized and bureaucratized. Shamanism, in both its most ancient and most modern forms, recalls the democratization of the spiritual experience, in which hierarchies are reserved for levels of experience rather than for priests and bishops. Each level and dimension of reality is available to the one who will make the effort to learn and practice the ways and means of the spiritual journey. Thus, in shamanic practice one can have one's spiritual experience and revelation direct and unmediated by structures ordained by church or doctrine. This appeals immensely to those who seek autonomy in the spiritual journey.

And what a journey it is! The shaman perceives a world of total aliveness, in all parts personal, in all parts sentient, in all parts capable of being known and being used. This pan-animism yields to the practicing shaman its powers and principalities, and these in turn can be used for healing, for renewal, and for bringing into the profane world the transformational powers of sacred time and space.

Additionally, the shaman's ability for self-orchestration on the continuum of states of consciousness enables him or her to serve as a bridge between ordinary reality and transpersonal realms. So different, however, is the shaman's practice of altered states of consciousness—whether induced by drumming, chanting, fasting, temperature regulation, sensory deprivation, or mind-altering substances—that some anthropologists such as Michael Harner refer to these states as shamanic states of consciousness (SSC) to distinguish them from the tamer altered states of consciousness (ASC). For indeed the way of the shaman calls for initial steps of radical disintegration and dissociation, as well as procedures for consciously entering into chaos. Living at his edges, standing outside and beyond himself, the shaman experiences ecstasy as a condition of his mastery, although the ordeals and voyages into shadow worlds bring with it a harrowing of the soul that few but the shaman could endure. In the shamanic journey, psyche and cosmos gain access to each other; the shaman becoming the channel for creatures and spirits, for the animates of nature and the designates of gods. The art and discipline needed for so special a relationship are enormous and do much to explain the reverence in which the shaman has been held for millennia.

The papers in this volume cover the field of shamanic practice and belief in as comprehensive a manner as has ever been presented to the general public. From the distant past to the emergent future, and across the boundaries of cultures, the depth culture of the shaman is shown to persist, curiously consistent in both method and metaphor.

The structure of the universe is conceived of in very similar ways by the shamanic consciousness, regardless of where or when the shaman dwells. The universe is thought to have three levels—sky, earth, and underworld—connected by a central axis. The shaman's knowledge and technique has to do with ways of journeying from one of these regions to another. His knowledge is especially resourceful when it comes to understanding the mystery of the breakthrough in plane; that is, passing through an opening or hole in reality (often designated as tent post or pillar) through which the gods descend to earth and the dead to the subterranean regions, and the soul of the shaman in ecstasy can fly up or down in the course of his journeys to heaven or hell. This axis of the world, known locally but representing the very center of things, is for the shaman the place through which sacred space and time become manifest. This is always the prerogative of shamans in archaic cultures. It is only they, in the words of Mircea Eliade, "who know how to make an ascent through the central opening; only tney transform a cosmo-theological concept into a concrete mystical experience." In other words, for the community, the central pillar of the house or the upper opening of the tent is a symbolic statement of the availability of local space and time for the entrance of sacred space and time. It is a site that permits one to send prayers and offerings to the Holy Ones. For the shaman, however, it is a mystical itinerary and the beginning place for the great journey.

Another aspect of relative consistency found in shamanic cultures is remembrance of what can only be called the "World Myth." Many so-called advanced cultures also remember fragments of this myth in both story and scripture, but the shamanic tradition preserves a remarkable similarity of narrative themes from the most disparate locales, races, and cultures. It is as if the shamanic myth carries the charge of a forgotten gnosis. As the cultural anthropologist and linguistic scholar Roger Westcott has noted:

> And what is striking about this worldwide narrative pattern is that it portrays an archaic world—or, more accurately, a se-quence of worlds—very different from those documented by historians or reconstructed by prehistorians. ("Minds Out of Uniform" in *The Forum for Correspondence and Contact*, 13:1, November, 1982, pp. 1-15)

As one looks at the phenomenology of this World Myth, one discovers the remarkable fact that most versions of it tell us that the earliest generally remembered stage of human life was a kind of golden age of light, abundance, harmony, and tenderness, with perpetual summer. The sky was always occupied by a huge and seemingly stationary object of light, variously known as the "cosmic egg" or the "sun of night," that served as a focus for human devotion and admiration. The planet was connected with the luminous object by means of a ladder, tree, mountain, stair-case, pillar, pole, or rope, thought to be the *axis mundi*, the center of the world. In many of these myths angels or special divine beings ascended and descended along this axis.

In most of these myths the story then changes and tells of the catastrophic end of the golden age, involving the disappearance of the great luminary, a worldwide flood or fire, violent earth tremors, boiling seas, deafening sounds, and prolonged darkness, followed by a series of protracted periods of quiesence between disasters, constituting a succession of world ages, each one harsher and less congenial to harmonious living than its predecessor.

In recent years aspects of this myth have apparently found growing scientific corroboration in catastrophe theory by scholars such as Immanuel Velikovsky to explain earth changes and their effects on consciousness. The critical issues of this evidence from science, shamanism, and myth has to do with the ultimate effects that these global cataclysms may have had on consciousness, on the fragmentation of consciousness, and the alienation of individual life from its source. The ancient gnostics speak with resentment of our having been hurled into a world that we never wanted to be in. The modern gnostic Heidegger speaks of our state as *entworfen*—our "throwness" in existence, and of course all existentialists speak of the resentful consciousness and of conscious alienation as being a primary condition of our humanity.

Cataclysms would presumably fracture collective consciousness in such a way that individual minds would, at least under norman circumstances, no longer have access to others' thoughts. Also it may have polarized differences and made them opposites, thus sharply accentuating emotional disparities between male and female, young and old, and one community and another. Additionally, and most critically, it would have accentuated the divided self. We ask ourselves why we are so blind and so given to gating in the mind, to the "isms" and "ologies" that force our thinking into narrow corridors. Somewhere we remember a mass trauma having to do with the splitting of our physical and spiritual perception. The ancients imputed mind to celestial bodies as well as to the forces of nature. We disclaim this and call it superstition or animistic thinking, or, if we are really being sophisticated, anthropomorphism. Perhaps what happened is that in the catastrophe we became morbidly cut off and thus anthropocentric, losing our communion with nature, with the planet, with the "gods," and with each other.

Indeed, the modern myth transmitters or channellers speak of the cataclysm as setting up a resentment to God, so that there was a consequent shift from God-centeredness to self-centeredness, from identity in God to identity in local form. The *Imago Dei* in which we were made became a less and less human image. The more the identification with local form, the more the need to defend this form, and the more the identification with cumbersome ego structures and experience.

Thus hard-wired patterns were set up, and we could not disidentify from our experience. Much of modern psychologizing is taken up with these issues of too rigid identification with experience and imprisoned thought structures. Unfortunately, too much of this psychologizing adjusts one to being happy in prison or in the creation of a more affable prison in which one at least learns to love the prisoner.

What also happened, of course, was the separation of the various levels of oneself and the loss of communication as an easy and natural and ordinary state of being. Deep communion became extraordinary and took extraordinary efforts to discover. These speculations concerning the World Myth, its consequences, and its importance to shamanic tradition justify in part the way and the genius of the shaman, for they assert that this deep communication was radically interrupted for all persons except for the shamans and mystics who are willing to do the enormous physical, spiritual, and psychological work of preparing themselves to break through the veils in body, mind, and spirit which were laid down so far in the past.

Consider, for example, the universality of the approach to time in shamanism, perhaps best typified by notions of dreamtime or suspended time. This kind of time is reached in part through the induction of shamanic states of consciousness which allow normal circadean time to be suspended and durative time to become available. In this durative, amplified sacred time, the everpresent Origin is always there, the time before the catastrophe, or the time of Creation. Time becomes a force which can break through the planes of the worlds to whatever realm or dimension the shaman wishes to visit.

To permit visiting these realms, there occurs in all shamanic cultures one of the most critical aspects of shamanic training—

activation of the capacity for inner imageries and visions. In altered states the neophyte shaman practices mental and physical imagery so vivid that it blocks out the awareness of normal perception and bodily feeling. For example, so bright can these internal images be that the shaman is temporarily blinded. So developed can the shamanic imaginal or secondary body be that it seems he or she is actually having a full physical experience of another place or dimension.

Once the novice can experience such lifelike imagery, the second phase of training begins, aimed at teaching him to orchestrate and control inner imagery and visionary content. In this way, he can evoke spirits and inner allies, can know how to come into contact with the right guides and helpers—those who will be his protectors and givers of power—and to avoid demonic and debilitating spirits.

Among the Australian Aborigines such training is aimed at the development of what they call the "strong eye." The gaze of shamans all over the world is often described as being uncomfortably intense, burning through the culturally acquired veils of others, shocking them into a remembrance of who and what they really are. This "lightening" or even enlightenment is wonderfully well portrayed in the explorer Knud Rasmussen's account of shamanic initiation among the Inuit of the Hudson Bay. He is describing the novice acquiring the spiritual sight for the first time:

> It consists of a mysterious light that the shaman suddenly feels in his body, inside his head, within the brain, an inexplicable searchlight, a luminous fire, which enables him to see in the dark, both literally and metaphorically speaking, for he can now, even with closed eyes, see through darkness and perceive things and coming events which are hidden from others; thus he looks into the future and into the secrets of others.
>
> The first time a young shaman experiences this light...he sees far ahead of him, through mountains, exactly as if the earth were one great plain, and his eyes could reach to the end of the earth. Nothing is hidden from him any longer; not only can he see things far away, but he can also discover souls, stolen souls, which are either kept concealed in far, strange lands or have been taken up or down to the Land of the Dead. (K. Rasmussen, *Intellectual Culture of the Iglulik Eskimos.* Report of the Fifth Thule Expedition, 1921-1924.)

The granting of reality to a geopsychic realm perceived in an altered state of consciousness has an ancient and honorable tradition. The Sufi mystics, for example, speak of the *alam al-mithal* or *mundus imaginalis,* an intermediate universe that is thought to be as ontologically real as the sensory empirical world and the noetic world of the intellect. It exists in metageography that possesses extension and dimension, as well as figure, color, and other features perceived by the senses. However, this world can be experienced only by those who, like the shamans, exercise their psychospiritual senses, and through this special form of imaginal knowing gain access to a visionary world that is not unlike the *mundus archetypus* of Carl Jung. There shamans, dreamers, and visionaries return again and again, extending consciousness and reality at the source level of *gnosis* and creative process, a place where the self moves freely amid archetypes and universals, listening to the pulse and dynamic transforming patterns of the Universal Dance.

For the shaman, however, the vision is never the goal. He or she *must* bring back from this other reality knowledge and power to heal the body and regenerate the social order. Without this humane and practical application, the shaman is merely crazy at best or unworthy at worst. Indeed, we might consider that there are many natural shamans who are haunting the corridors of asylums, inmates who, under other circumstances and with different training, could have been ecstatics and visionaries, evokers of the sacred in society, instead of maimed and miserable spirits.

This book asks us to take seriously the way of the shaman. It is my hope that, by virtue of its scope and depth, it will cause us to rethink our tendency to label and pathologize that which may be one of the most valuable and courageous forms of our human condition. The shamanic promise is again being heard in the words of the chant that is rising in many of the trainings offered in new and very, very old ways of being:

> We are a new people
> We are an old people
> We are the same people
> Deeper than before.

Acknowledgments

The American Theosophist published eight of the articles in this book in its Special Issue "Ancient Wisdom in Shamanic Cultures," Fall, 1985 (Harner/Doore, Achterberg, Brooke Medicine Eagle, Freesoul, Halifax, Peters, Thero, King). The publishers wish to thank Gary Doore, former managing editor of *The American Theosophist,* for his help in acquiring and selecting additional articles in the early stages of the anthology. Also thanks to Michael Harner for supplying names of potential contributors.

"The Shaman: Master Healer in the Imaginary Realm" is from *Imagery in Healing* by Jeanne Achterberg, © 1985. Reprinted by arrangement with Shambhala Publications, Inc., P.O. Box 308, Boston, MA 02117.

"Shamanism and Cosmology" is from Mircea Eliade, *Shamanism: Archaic Techniques of Ecstasy,* trans. Willard R. Trask, Bollingen Series LXXVI. Copyright © 1964 by Princeton University Press. Chapter 8 is reprinted with permission of Princeton University Press.

"The Native American Prayer Pipe" is adapted from a chapter of John Redtail Freesoul's book *Breath of the Invisible: the Way of the Pipe* (Wheaton, IL: Theosophical Publishing House, 1985).

"Shamanism: An Archaic and/or Recent Belief System" by Mihály Hoppál is reprinted with permission of the copyright owners of the *Ural-Altaische Jahrbücher/Ural-Altaic Yearbook,* Bloomington, Indiana.

An earlier version of "Dreams and Shamanism" by Stanley Krippner appeared in *The Dream Network Bulletin,* vol. 3, no. 4 (March-April, 1984) and is published with permission.

The poem at the end of "Black Elk Then and Now" by William Lyon is from "airborne, down to earth; words of wallace black elk," published by Charles Cameron in *The Greenfield Review*, vol. 9, nos. 3-4, winter 81/82.

"The Tamang Shamanism in Nepal" by Larry Peters is reproduced by permission of the American Anthropological Association from *American Ethnologist* 9:1, pp 21-30, 1982. It is not for further reproduction.

"Shamanism, ESP, and the Paranormal" by D. Scott Rogo appeared in a somewhat altered form in the September, 1983, issue of *Fate* magazine.

"Rolling Thunder at Work" by Jim Swan was first published in *Shaman's Drum*, no. 3, Winter 1985, and is reprinted by permission of the author.

In "The Shaman Within" by David Feinstein, the author uses the terms "the shaman within" and "personal mythology" as well as other definitions and statements that appear in the book *Personal Mythology* by Stanley Krippner and David Feinstein, to be published by J. P. Tarcher, Inc.

Contributing Authors

Jeanne Achterberg, Ph.D., is associate professor and director of research in the Department of Rehabilitation Science, and clinical professor of Psychology and Physical Medicine at the University of Texas Health Science Center. She is co-author of *Imagery of Cancer, Bridges of the Bodymind*, and author of *Imagery in Healing: Shamanism and Modern Medicine*.

Brooke Medicine Eagle holds an M.A. in counseling psychology and is a Feldenkrais practitioner. Her work draws heavily from her Native American background as well as from numerous other spiritual sources. Her visions and spiritual journeys have been documented in Joan Halifax's *Shamanic Voices*. A forthcoming book, *Bringing Gold to the House of Silverado*, will further delineate her Earth-centered teachings.

Gary Doore, Ph.D., has a doctorate from the University of Oxford. His articles on ethics and the philosophy of religion have appeared in *Mind, Philosophy*, and *Religious Studies*, among other journals. He was formerly managing editor of *The American Theosophist*.

Mircea Eliade (1907-1986) served as chairman of the department of history of religions at the University of Chicago, and after his retirement from that post was Sewell L. Avery Distinguished Service Professor in the Divinity School and professor in the Committee on Social Thought. A native of Romania, he formerly lectured in the École des Hautes-Études of the Sorbonne. He is author of some fifty books, including

such works as the three-volume *A History of Religious Ideas,
Yoga: Immortality and Freedom,* and *The Vanishing God,* and
he served as editor-in-chief for Macmillan's newly published
The Encyclopedia of Religion. His *Shamanism: Archaic Techniques of Ecstasy* is a seminal book in which, writing as a
historian of religion, he synthesizes the approaches of psychology, sociology, and ethnology.

Robert Ellwood is Bashford Professor of Oriental Studies in the
School of Religion at the University of Southern California.
He has fourteen publications to his credit, including *Religious
and Spiritual Groups in Modern America, Alternative Altars,
Mysticism and Religions, Theosophy: A Modern Expression
of the Wisdom of the Ages,* and two books on meditation, *Finding the Quiet Mind* and *Finding Deep Joy.* A native of Normal,
Illinois, he received his B.A. from the University of Colorado
and his Ph.D. in the history of religions from the University
of Chicago.

David Feinstein, Ph.D., is director of Innersource, Inc., in
Ashland, Oregon. Trained in both clinical and community
psychology, he has presented seminars and workshops internationally using personal mythology as a framework for individual psychological development. *Personal Mythology,* a
book on this topic which he co-authored with Stanley Krippner, is forthcoming from J. P. Tarcher, Inc., and Dr. Feinstein
has published numerous professional papers along this line.
Additionally, he served for seven years as a senior clinical
psychologist with the San Diego County Mental Health
Services.

John Redtail Freesoul is a Cheyenne-Arapahoe, an award-winning
artist, teacher, and professional therapist using both conventional and Native American methods. He is the pipeholder and
spokesman for the Redtail Hawk Medicine Society, an intertribal society for the perpetuation of Indian medicine as
religious and therapeutic tools, and is active in reviving and
performing original ceremonies and medicine for use in self-

realization, spiritual communion, and in coping sanely with modern life. He is author of *Breath of the Invisible: the Way of the Pipe.*

Rabbi Yonassan Gershom is a Jewish spiritual teacher in the traditional mode of *maggid* (storyteller/preacher). He received his ordination from Rabbi Zalman Schachter-Shalomi, the B'nai Or Rebbe, and currently serves as spiritual director of Twin Cities B'nai Or (Disciples of Light) Jewish Fellowship in Minneapolis, Minnesota. Rabbi Gershom is also a practicing shaman, utilizing techniques from Jewish mysticism for counseling and psychological healing, and also offers workshops on kabbalah and Hassidic philosophy.

Joan Halifax, Ph.D., medical anthropologist and director of the Ojai Foundation, has worked with healers and shamans worldwide. In addition to her research at Columbia and Miami Universities, the Musée de l'Homme, and the Maryland Psychiatric Research Center, she assisted Joseph Campbell on his *Historical Atlas of World Mythology.* A Harvard faculty member, she is co-author of *The Human Encounter with Death,* and author of *Shamanic Voices* and *Shaman, The Wounded Healer.*

Michael Harner, Ph.D., is a professor and former chairman of the Anthropology Department of the Graduate Faculty at the New School for Social Research in New York. He is also co-chairman of the Anthropology Section of the New York Academy of Sciences. He has been visiting professor at Columbia, Yale, and the University of California, Berkeley, where he received his Ph.D. and served as assistant director of the Lowie Museum of Anthropology. In addition to his academic work, Michael Harner is the founder of the Center for Shamanic Studies in Connecticut. He also travels worldwide doing research and teaching shamanism and shamanic practice. His books include *The Jivaro, Hallucinogens and Shamanism, The Way of the Shaman* (a guide to basic shamanic practice), and a novel, *Cannibal,* which he co-authored.

Mihály Hoppál, Ph.D., is a senior research associate with the Folklore Research Team of the Hungarian Academy of Sciences in Budapest. He is a student of the internationally known Hungarian folklorist Gyula Ortutay. He has traveled extensively in the USSR doing field work and came to the USA in 1984 on a study trip.

Jean Houston, Ph.D., is an internationally renowned psychologist, teacher, and workshop leader. She and her husband Robert Masters are among the founders of the human potential movement. Dr. Houston is past president of the Association for Humanistic Psychology and is now director of the Foundation for Mind Research in Pomona, New York. Among the many books she has authored or co-authored are *Mind Games, Listening to the Body, Life Force,* and *The Possible Human.*

Serge King, Ph.D., was initiated by his father into an esoteric order of kahunas at the age of fourteen and has studied under masters of psychospiritual knowledge from Africa to Hawaii. Among his books are *Imagineering for Health, Kahuna Healing,* and *Mastering Your Hidden Self,* and he has written many articles and courses and lectured widely. A member of Phi Beta Kappa, he holds Master's and Ph.D. degrees. He is director of the Order of Huna International, and lives in Malibu, California.

Stanley Krippner, Ph.D., is a psychologist and director of The Center for Consciousness Studies at Saybrook Institute in San Francisco. In a dozen volumes and over 500 articles in scientific and educational publications, he has investigated and reported on the forefront of developments in consciousness research, education, and healing. Among the books he has authored or co-authored are *Human Possibilities, Dream Telepathy, The Song of the Siren,* and *The Realms of Healing.* He has served as president of several national organizations including the Association for Humanistic Psychology, the Parapsychological Association, and the American Psychological Association's Division of Humanistic Psychology. He served as Director of the Dream Laboratory at Maimonides Medical Center in New York City for ten years, and in 1976 gave the first invited address on the topic of parapsychology to the Soviet Academy of Pedagogical Sciences, one of the most prestigious institutions in the Soviet Union.

William S. Lyon, Ph.D., is currently a research associate in the Department of Anthropology at the University of California, Berkeley, where he is conducting cross-cultural studies on shamanism. Formerly professor of anthropology at Southern Oregon State College, he has published professional and popular papers on shamanism and participated in professional conferences on the topic. For the past nine years he has worked in close association with Wallace Black Elk, and a course they worked out was chosen by the North American Association of Summer Session as the most innovative course for North America. Dr. Lyon has been invited to act as translator and organizer for Wallace's current developmental goals.

Ralph Metzner, Ph.D., obained a B.A. in philosophy and psychology at Oxford University, and a Ph.D. in clinical psychology at Harvard University, where he also did post-doctoral research in psychopharmacology. He worked with Timothy Leary and Richard Alpert on psychedelic research, edited the *Psychedelic Review*, and co-authored *The Psychedelic Experience*, is author of *Maps of Consciousness*, *Know Your Type*, and recently *Opening to Inner Light*. Currently, he is professor of East-West psychology as well as academic dean at the California Institute of Integral Studies in San Francisco, and is also in private practice as a psychotherapist.

Shirley Nicholson is senior editor for the Theosophical Publishing House, in charge of Quest Books. She is author of *Ancient Wisdom—Modern Insight* and of a children's book, *Nature's Merry-Go-Round*, as well as of many articles in *The American Theosophist* and other journals. For many years she has been a student of esoteric philosophy and theosophical thought, including such topics as altered states of consciousness.

Richard Noll, M.A., is a doctoral candidate in clinical psychology at the New School for Social Research in New York City and serves as psychologist at Ancora Psychiatric Hospital in Hammonton, New Jersey. He has published articles on shamanism in major national and international journals and presented papers on the topic at international conferences. Besides research on the phenomenology of shamanism, he has investigated altered states of consciousness, mental imagery, hallucinations, and the clinical manifestations of dissociative disorders, particularly multiple personality disorder.

Larry G. Peters, Ph.D., conducted anthropological field research on the psychological and sociological aspects of shamanism in Nepal, summarized in his book *Ecstasy and Healing in Nepal*. Dr. Peters is currently Assistant Professor of Psychology at The California Graduate Institute, Graduate School of Psychology in Westwood, California, and is also a psychotherapist in private practice.

D. Scott Rogo currently serves on the graduate faculty of John F. Kennedy University in California. He is author of over twenty-five books on the paranormal, and has held research positions with the Psychical Research Foundation (formerly in Durham, North Carolina) and with the Maimonides Medical Center's former Division of Parapsychology and Psychophysics in Brooklyn. He serves on the editorial staff of *Fate* magazine and was formerly a columnist for *Human Behavior* magazine.

Mary Schmidt, M.A., is a doctoral candidate in symbolic anthropology at the University of Western Ontario in London (Canada) and holds a B.A. in philosophy. She has studied the psychological possibilities of altering perceptions of reality in order to effect change. She plans to pursue her interest in applying new findings to psychological health.

Jim Swan, Ph.D., is an environmental psychologist, writer, and media producer. He has special expertise in environmental perception, educational program and methods design, and evaluation. He is one of the originators of the division of environmental and population psychology of the American Psychological Association, and his work has received special recognition from organizations such as the American Public Health Association and UNESCO. Working with traditional peoples, he organized the first Medicine Wheel Gathering for Sun Bear and toured with Rolling Thunder.

Venerable E. Nandisvara Nayake Thero, Ph.D., is the Chief Sanghanayaka of the Theravada Order of Buddhist monks in India. He is a former professor of comparative religion at Madras University, as well as director of the Maha Bodhi Society of Sri Lanka and secretary general of the World Sangha Council. A writer, lecturer, and editor of *The Maha Bodhi* journal, Dr. Nandisvara has for many years traveled widely in Asia, Europe, and Australia as an instructor in Vipassana Meditation. He recently returned from a research expedition with an anthropological team in Australia, where he lived for some time with the native Aboriginal community.

I
The Shaman's Alternate Reality

One of the outstanding characteristics of shamans is their familiarity with realities other than those of three-dimensional space and linear time known to our usual waking consciousness. While the articles in this section address many aspects of shamanism, they all have some bearing on the shaman's access to non-ordinary reality.

All researchers seem to agree that shamans deal with a realm where spirit beings can offer wisdom and help, and one where such beings might be mischievous and threatening. In his classic chapter reprinted here, Eliade has mapped these realms into the zones of the sky, earth, and underworld, which are joined by an axis or central opening through which the shaman can communicate with all the zones. Harner explains that in this view of reality everything is connected at a deep level. This gives shamans the ability to draw on a power greater than themselves. They take care of the spiritual as well as the material condition of their patients, who like shamans have a higher component or spirit or vital soul. The shaman is the mediator between the ordinary world and an alternate reality.

In the altered state that shamans use for such work, they are fully in control of their journeys to other realms and are conscious of everything that transpires. They enter those realms only for the purpose of being effective in the everyday world, to heal and help others. Hoppál stresses the shamans' cultural role of preserving the past for their people, and he connects shamanic functions with shamanic belief systems. Schmidt, on the other hand, believes that shamans experience

1

an ultimate undifferentiated reality which they distinguish from cognitive structures of their culture, and they restructure reality for themselves and for those around them, thus effecting change in individuals and in their society.

Are the spirit helpers and other worlds of the shaman projections from their own unconscious minds, or do these have objective reality? Harner holds that the shaman "does not view these non-ordinary phenomena as mental in the sense that they are regarded as a projection of one's own mind. Rather, the mind is being used in order to gain access, to pass through a door into another reality, which exists independently of that mind." As for himself, Harner is "inclined to think that there is more to the universe than the human mind." Noll defines "spirit" as "transpersonal forces that we experience as moving in us or through us but are not entirely moved by us." Imagery enhancement among shamans facilitates dialogue with these spirits. Noll quotes Jung's remarks about his own guardian spirit who provided crucial insight to him: "There are things in the psyche which I do not produce, but which produce themselves and have their own life," and "there is something in me which can say things that I do not know and do not intend." It seems evident that it is possible to experience and get help from levels of reality quite different from that of our common everyday awareness.

1

The Ancient Wisdom in Shamanic Cultures

AN INTERVIEW WITH MICHAEL HARNER
CONDUCTED BY GARY DOORE

Gary Doore: What are the distinguishing features of a shaman?

Michael Harner: I think we are on safe ground if we use the kind of definition employed by Mircea Eliade in his classic book *Shamanism,* which is the kind of definition used by anthropologists who study this phenomenon worldwide. The main defining characteristic of a shaman is that he or she is someone who enters an altered state of consciousness (which I have called the *shamanic state of consciousness,* or SSC), usually induced by monotonous drumming or other percussion sound, in order to make journeys for a variety of purposes in what are technically called the Lower and Upper Worlds. These other worlds accessible to the shaman in the SSC are regarded as an alternate reality, and the shaman's purpose in journeying to it in the SSC is to interact consciously with certain guardian powers or spirits there, which are usually perceived as power animals. The shaman solicits the friendship and aid of such power animals in order to help other people in various ways, and he or she may also have spiritual teachers in this hidden reality who give advice, instruction, and other forms of assistance.

Many of the so-called medicine men, medicine women, and priests of Native North American cultures also do work of immense value, but what they do is often not strictly speaking shamanism if they do not make journeys to the Lower and Upper Worlds.

G.D.: Does the shaman regard this other world entered in the SSC as a mental or imaginal world as opposed to the "material" world of ordinary experience?

M.H.: Views on the nature of reality differ from culture to culture. For example, an extreme position is taken by the Jivaro of South America, where they say that the only reality is that which is accessible in the SSC, and that our ordinary state of consciousness is just an illusion, or "lies." They maintain that any significant event in this world is the result of hidden events in that other dimension.

The position I prefer when introducing people to shamanism is characterized in terms of Carlos Castaneda's distinction between ordinary reality and non-ordinary reality. It is useful because it does not introduce the concepts of mental and material. In shamanic experience, when one is in non-ordinary reality things will seem quite as material as they are here. One feels the coldness or warmth of the air, the hardness or smoothness of a rock; one perceives colors, sounds, odors, and so forth. All the phenomena that characterize the so-called material world will appear just as real and material there as they do here if it is an extremely clear shamanic journey. But the shaman does not view these non-ordinary phenomena as mental in the sense that they are regarded as a projection of one's own mind. Rather, the mind is being used in order to gain access, to pass through a door into another reality which exists independently of that mind.

G.D.: What is the typical shamanic conception of the ultimate basis of these different realities? Is there, for instance, an absolute spiritual power or principle "behind" the universe, so to speak, as its fundamental reality?

M.H.: Usually the shaman views the universe itself as the ultimate reality. In many shamanic cultures there is no preoccupation with the idea that there is some spiritual being who is either in charge of the whole show, or who once was but is now on permanent vacation. Most shamans seem to believe that this universe is "just the way things are." We are given the fact that there is a universe where everything is alive, that there is an interconnectedness of all things, and that there are hidden purposes which we can attempt to investigate to some extent through shamanic methods. But shamanism ultimately is only a method, not a religion with a fixed set of dogmas. Therefore people arrive at their own experience-derived conclusions about what is going on in the universe, and about what term, if any, is most useful to describe ultimate reality.

G.D.: You said that shamanism is not a religion, but what is its relation to religion?

M.H.: Yes, I characterized it as a method rather than a religion. It is a method which is often associated with the religion known as animism, but distinct from it. Animism is basically the belief in spirits, and spirits are defined in shamanism simply as those things or beings which are normally not seen by people in an ordinary state of consciousness, but are seen by the shaman in the SSC. Moreover, they are entities that the shaman respects, having some sort of integrity or power.

So, as one gets involved in shamanism and thus keeps seeing, interacting, and talking with spirits, one quite naturally tends to believe in their existence. And those who continue doing shamanism will most likely also start to believe in the existence of the human soul. That is another step. But animism is in many ways the "bottom line" of any religion that considers the existence of spirits. Of course, more supposedly "sophisticated" religions may then be built upon that base.

I think it is noteworthy that modern physics seems to have elements of animism. Some physicists today are like animists in that they believe everything which exists is alive. It is the sense of our unity with a living universe, the feeling that we are all just parts of that greater life, which is basic to animism.

G.D.: Do you find in shamanism the concept of a higher component of the individual that is somehow in close contact or at one with the ultimate reality?

M.H.: Yes, this component is called simply the spirit or vital soul of the person, and it is definitely in contact with that reality. Moreover, it is believed that at death it becomes even more closely in contact.

G.D.: Doesn't the shamanic journey in fact begin with experiences that are very much like what have been described recently as near-death experiences?

M.H.: Yes. The shaman's journey starts with an experience of going through a tunnel of some kind, usually with a light at the end, and this is very similar to descriptions of the so-called near-death experiences. But the shaman goes all the way through the tunnel and explores the world into which it opens at the end, the world that people feel themselves passing into at the time of death. So, when one is ready for death, or preparing for it, it is a good idea to have explored the region in question beforehand by shamanic means, since then one will not be so surprised by what happens in the post-mortem state. The geography will be known to some extent.

G.D.: It is interesting that Socrates defined philosophy as the preparation for death. And there are well-known stories about him standing for hours in what appeared to be an altered state of consciousness, which he explained in terms of a communion with his guardian spirit or "daemon." Is there evidence for shamanic influence in ancient Greece, perhaps through the Orphic/Pythagorean mystery schools?

M.H.: Yes, Orpheus does seem to have been a shaman. He was called a "doctor of souls," and the Greek Orpheus myth is a version of the same myth found in a variety of shamanic cultures all over the world. It is basically the story of a shaman who performs the typical shamanic activity of journeying to the Lower World in search of the soul of a person who has died. Usually this means that the person is comatose by Western standards. But he gets into trouble on the return journey because he is emotionally attached to the person in question. This myth constitutes some of the strongest evidence we have that shamans were known very anciently in Greece.

G.D.: Does the shaman attempt to help others in the process of actually dying?

M.H.: Yes, but beyond this, after they have died he continues to assist them in terms of getting located in the afterlife in circumstances where they will be happier. He is the psychopomp or conductor of souls to the other world. So it is very much an applied skill; applied to help others. But it also has the result of helping oneself, because as one works with power in attempting to help others, one tends to receive help; whereas those who are greedy with power, or who use it for bad purposes, tend to get the negative consequences for themselves that they intended for others.

G.D.: Many anthropological studies and films seem to emphasize the use of shamanism for sorcery. Are you suggesting that its use for destructive purposes is not as widespread as it has often been portrayed?

M.H.: There are, of course, people that stray from good purposes with shamanism. But, as I have seen in the upper Amazon, they do not last very long, and they usually come to a very grievous end. Sorcery is extremely self-destructive, and this is common folk knowledge all over the world. Naturally this does not mean that people never practice sorcery. Such things do exist in many tribal groups, but they are very much a function of the social, economic, and political problems of a particular society—problems of how power is used—which is true of any kind of power in any society.

I was in one upper Amazon tribe of thousands of people where no one had been murdered for twenty years, and the tribe was very shamanic. Another tribe, also very shamanic, had murders occurring constantly. So shamanism is not the problem. The problem is how this knowledge is used.

G.D.: Then it is very important for would-be shamans to have a strong sense of ethical responsibility.

M.H.: Certainly. One of the things I have noticed is that people in general have shamanic abilities, whether they are conscious of them or not. The basic forces of anger and love, for instance, have a tremendous influence in the world on many levels of reality of which we are ordinarily unaware. Thus, when one person gets angry at another it is not just an exchange of words and emotions; because from a spiritual point of view anger is terribly destructive, both for the person who is giving it as well as for the one receiving it. I submit that not knowing what spiritual damage we may do to others in anger is not a good thing; and therefore I think that one of the biggest dangers connected with shamanism is to be ignorant about the unconscious shamanic abilities we all have. For this reason I do not subscribe to the argument that shamanic practices should not be taught because the knowledge might be dangerous. Ignorance is far more dangerous, because those who are unaware of the existence of these powers are more likely to endanger others than those who have shamanic knowledge. Anything people can learn from the wisdom of shamanism about the effects of our thoughts and feelings at those hidden levels can be beneficial, and therefore should be available.

G.D.: Do you find in shamanism the idea that one of the purposes of life is to unfold the latent powers of consciousness?

M.H.: Most shamans of my acquaintance in tribal cultures are not too preoccupied with that question. They do know, however, that we are here, that we are going to die someday, and that we have various difficulties to face in our daily lives. Therefore, the focus is on what we can do to help each other with the problems of existence, of life and death.

G.D.: In other words it is much more of a practical discipline than a speculative enterprise?

M.H.: Yes. People seek help from a shaman for all sorts of problems, about very practical matters such as the location of food resources needed for the tribe, or today about some question in their lives such as whether to change a career or move to a new location. But classically, perhaps because health problems are the most common and serious, they tend to come up very frequently.

G.D.: What are the main methods of shamanic healing?

M.H.: Shamanic healing is done basically in two ways. These involve either putting something which is lacking back into the person who is ill, or removing something that does not belong in the person's body. The latter kind of healing, usually employed for more localized illnesses, does not involve the shamanic journey, but consists of working here in the Middle World, using divination techniques and moving back and forth from ordinary to nonordinary reality in order to see the illness and to remove it by certain methods. The other technique, restoring something that is lost or lacking, does involve the journey. This might be the restoration of the simple vital soul of the individual, typically in cases where someone is at death's door or suicidal. In such cases the shaman can move in search of the lost soul in the other world, and can find it and restore it to the person.

G.D.: How does the shaman restore lost power?

M.H.: This is a more common practice than bringing back a lost soul, and the shaman's client does not by any means have to be in dire straits for this method to be used. The technique is to make a journey to the other world to search for the lost power, which is usually perceived in the form of a guardian animal. The journey to restore such a power animal is undertaken in order to help energize the person in question, to strengthen resistance to illness, dispiritedness, and so forth, and generally to help him or her lead a good, successful life. In this kind of work the shaman does not need to know the specific nature of the illness in order to go out and search for a power connection to the universe, because protective power fights illness in general.

G.D.: Does the shaman ever search for power animals in order to heal himself or herself?

M.H.: The search for power animals is generally done for others. One of the reasons that shamanism is a powerful tool is that it is the intercession of one human being on behalf of another in a spiritual quest. If you intercede merely on behalf of yourself you are less likely to get results. This is why most shamans have at least one partner. They help each other. It is important to keep in mind that in shamanic work one is primarily engaged in helping others.

A comparison can be made between shamanic methods and certain visualization techniques as they are used today in trying to heal oneself. Thus, in some native South American tribes the shaman is the one who takes a pharmaceutical (usually a strong psychedelic) for the patient's illness, and it is the shaman who then makes the visualizations which are instrumental in the healing. It is not the patient who visualizes. We might contrast this with something like the Simontons' methods of working with cancer patients, where the person who is ill is asked to visualize his or her illness and then to work on it. Visualization of illness is a shamanic method independently discovered by the Simontons. But if it were even more shamanic, there would be a shaman present visualizing the illness more intently than the patient.*

G.D.: Is the idea of self-healing then entirely foreign to shamanism?

M.H.: There is indeed something that might be described as "self-healing" in shamanism—or rather, something that looks like self-healing but really is not. I refer to the experience of drawing on a power greater than oneself. For example, if a shaman does

---

* Cf. Jeanne Achterberg, *Imagery in Healing* (Boston & London: Shambhala, 1985.)

need personal help, it is possible for him or her to make a journey to visit a healer in non-ordinary reality and to ask for assistance. The healer may then work on the shaman, who may get well without appearing to have received any outside aid. Observers might then describe this as self-healing. But if you take the whole thing seriously, "self-healing" is not an accurate description. It merely looks like self-healing from the standpoint of ordinary reality.

G.D.: Will you explain the other method of healing you mentioned: taking something away that does not belong in the patient?

M.H.: We all know how, in ordinary reality terms, infections can exist in the body, or some malfunction can take place. The shaman sees the spiritual nature of such localized problems in the body and extracts them, much as someone might do a surgical removal of a tumor or suck out poison from a snakebite. In the same way, the shaman removes what is undesirable or "dirty" from the person. But this is all done in non-ordinary reality, on a spiritual level.

G.D.: When you say that the shaman sees the spiritual nature of illnesses, you do not mean seeing with the physical eyes.

M.H.: That's right. What is called in some traditions the "third eye" is referred to, for instance, by the Australian shamans as the "strong eye." But it is the same thing. Or they may refer to "seeing with the heart." In other words, it is a type of "vision" which can be done with the eyes closed. It is not seeing in the way that people ordinarily understand it.

G.D.: Does this type of *seeing* involve the clairvoyant or psychic observation of the energy field or so-called aura of the patient?

M.H.: Those would commonly be observed, but usually the shaman is *seeing* the illness itself. This is often perceived in the form of some creature which, at a "gut level," the shaman just knows does not belong in a human being. He usually sees something which, merely aesthetically and emotionally, should not be present. It is very similar to the forms visualized by the Simontons' cancer patients mentioned earlier. The same kind of repulsive and disgusting creatures emerge. The aura you refer to may also be seen, but shamanic work with illness does not typically involve aura-cleansing.

G.D.: Is the shamanic approach to disease compatible with Western medicine?

M.H.: Yes, it is definitely compatible. Not a single shaman of my acquaintance ever denigrated other effective methods of working on the body in a material, ordinary way, whether this involved taking plant substances or modern pharmaceuticals, doing mechanical manipulations, or performing surgery. In other words, shamanism has always been, so far as I can tell, holistic in its approach.

G.D.: The reverse is not true, however, is it? There are probably not many modern physicians in our culture who would approve of shamanic techniques as part of a patient's course of treatment.

M.H.: This is very curious, because in the modern world people seem to set the autonomy of one particular system of health care above the integrity of the universe, and somehow feel that a single man-made system is the total approach to healing. In shamanism there is no such problem. It is understood that one has to take care of the spiritual as well as the material condition of the patient.

G.D.: Does the patient necessarily have to believe that the shaman can help? Can healing take place in spite of a patient's disbelief?

M.H.: The received wisdom in the academy, of course, is that it is completely a matter of belief, in other words, that it will tend to work for those who believe but not for those who disbelieve. Now this so-called "placebo effect" in itself is a powerful tool, even if that were all that takes place. And you might say that shamanism produces the *real* placebo effect, because if it can be produced by physicians 25 percent of the time using only sugar pills, you can imagine how much more powerful it will be with the drum and the altered state of consciousness. Thus at the minimum in shamanism the placebo effect is very much amplified. But there is more to it than this. To get back to your question about what the patient believes, my conclusion is that the patient does not really know what he or she believes. Belief with the conscious mind and belief with the powerful unconscious mind are two entirely different things; and in shamanism we are dealing with the latter. People are healed for reasons that are not at all clear in terms of modern psychological models. I have seen people express skepticism on a conscious level when it was very obvious that on some deeper level they were not skeptical at all. The conscious mind is just the tip of the iceberg. So people often really do not know that they believe at that deep level. And it seems to me the reason they believe at that level is because they are tapping into the same hidden universe in which the shaman operates; that shamanism works precisely because we are all somehow connected in that dimension.

G.D.: Perhaps one reason that current psychological models do not easily explain why shamanism works is because modern empirical psychologists have too narrow a definition of what constitutes empirical evidence. It could be argued that observations of the geography of non-ordinary reality in the SSC can count as scientific because they can be repeated and independently verified in many cases.

M.H.: Exactly. One of the things that has most impressed me, as well as many anthropologists who have attended some of my sessions, is how people who were completely ignorant of the basic principles and practices of shamanism at a conscious level were able, in just a few journeys, to bring back things from that other reality which one would expect to find in the classical ethnological literature for, say, Siberia. So we are dealing with something which, at the very least, is important to know about the human mind. But it goes far beyond that, because we get such incredible synchronicities involving people being healed who have no physical contact, sometimes thousands of miles away from each other. There is no presently existing model to account for that in the empirical psychology of the academic world. There are, of course, no clinical studies or tests with laboratory animals on this sort of thing. And yet, by studying shamanism at the practical level, by learning how to do it, one is forced to the conclusion that something very powerful and significant is going on. In fact, I would say that this type of research is (or anyway ought to be) one of the new frontiers of psychology. Psychologists up to this point have generally avoided contact with it. Jung showed them a door that most did not choose to enter because things inside seemed vague and unfamiliar in terms of the methodology to which they were accustomed. But once they open the door experimentally and start going inside that other dimension in order to explore and map the terrritory, it is really going to be an extraordinary and revolutionary development.

G.D.: Would you say a bit more about shamanic drumming and its role in producing the SSC?

M.H.: Yes. It is important to emphasize the central role of drumming in shamanism in general, and to be clear about the distinctive features of shamanic drumming. Although in a few parts of the world, such as the upper Amazon, the SSC is entered primarily through the use of strong psychedelic drugs, in most of the world the method employed is percussion sound. This is a very monotonous sound, very regular, at a specific number of beats per second, and is normally produced by drums or other percussion instruments. It has the remarkable effect of creating a rapid change to another state of consciousness, and is also very safe. One can remember what happens while journeying to the beat of the drum, for there is no amnesia, no harmful physical side-effects exist, and one can control the length of time of the journey in a way that is not possible with strong psychedelics. Using percussion, one just goes through a different door, so to speak, and the technique is amazingly effective. The use of monotonous percussion sound is found all over the world among shamans, except sometimes in the regions where they rely on psychedelics. So this is a key aspect of shamanism.

G.D.: Why do you think that monotonous percussion sound has the effect of altering one's state of consciousness? Is there any scientific explanation?

M.H.: I do not think there are adequate scientific explanations yet, although there may be some forthcoming. My own opinion is that part of the answer may be that the drum activates the brain on wave-lengths similar to those of the EEG corresponding to altered states. For instance, the deerskin drum used shamanically among the Coast Salish Indians of Western Canada has been found to emit primarily a frequency of 4 to 7 cycles per second, and that corresponds to the theta range of the EEG—a rather interesting "coincidence." There has been some suggestive research on this by Neher.*

G.D.: Do you regard yoga as an outgrowth of shamanism?

M.H.: Yes, that is my view. It is a hypothesis suggested by something I have seen happen with drumming in our culture when people are attempting to do shamanic work. The shamanic drum is used among groups of people that are sparsely distributed, where the sound will not disturb others. But the drum is not a suitable

---

*Cf. Jeanne Achterberg's article, in this volume, p. 119.

tool in cities because it tends to irritate one's neighbors. And since the first cities and states were in the Near and Far East, I think there was a very good reason to substitute methods of silent meditation for drumming to induce an altered state of consciousness. Also, the state religions from ancient times had dogmas revealed by particular prophets. Since every shaman is, in effect, his or her own prophet, you can see that it then becomes a bit of a heresy to be engaged in shamanism as the citizen of such a state. So not only would beating the drums upset the neighbors; it could also bring the attention of the state ecclesiastical authorities. Therefore, I personally think that shamanism, using the drum, is the original meditation or meditative technique, and that with growth of city-states, and through great effort and study, people had to develop silent methods of meditation. These are excellent, but actually they involve immeasurably more time and discipline than using the old-fashioned drum. In fact, I sometimes think that the ease and effectiveness of shamanic drumming is almost embarrassing!

G.D.: What is the role of reason and rationality—or, to put it another way, the function of the left hemisphere of the brain—in shamanic practice?

M.H.: It is a very significant role. The shaman is not only trying to experience non-ordinary reality, but also to codify what is being experienced so that the information can be brought back and communicated to others. So the shaman in fact has to think about what is being seen and otherwise experienced, and perhaps also silently talk to himself or herself about what is happening on the journey so that the knowledge can be recovered. Therefore, entering the shamanic state of consciousness (SSC) does not at all involve paralyzing the left brain and the rational faculties. For example, in the upper Amazon the shaman very often sings while he or she is on the journey, describing to the village what is being experienced in that other reality. In my own work I often recommend to those who use cassette tapes of shamanic drumming for their journeys that they talk softly into a recorder about what is occurring during the journey at the time that it is happening. This amplifies the experience rather than detracts from it, and obviously requires left-brain activity.

G.D.: Is it incorrect to call the SSC a *trance?*

M.H.: A trance in Western culture is often associated with a mediumistic performance, which in turn is often characterized by amnesia. The medium speaking during mediumistic trance commonly does not recollect later what he or she said or experienced. And a mediumistic trance involves a takeover of control of the medium's faculties by some spiritual entity. But this is not at all what occurs during the SSC because one can remember what happened later, and in most cultures where shamanism is practiced there is no loss of control of one's faculties as in so-called possession by an outside entity.

Shamanic work is typically different, then, from the so-called possession cults such as are found in West Africa, Brazil or the Caribbean, because there the gods come and "ride" the dancer, who feels their power but does not remember afterwards what happened. In some parts of the world shamanism overlaps with such possession cults, for instance, in the Himalayas. But where you have pure shamanism you generally do not find this. Instead, the shaman is the "master of spirits." The spirits work for the shaman; he or she possesses them, rather than the reverse. Hence, the shaman typically has a number of power animals or spirit helpers at his or her disposal, since animals are the form in which the spirits usually appear in non-ordinary reality.

G.D.: Would you say that such spirits or power animals are actually forces or faculties within the human psyche? Or are they really "out there"?

M.H.: As a person who has followed the path of shamanism for a long time, I am inclined to think that there is more to the universe than the human mind.

G.D.: You mentioned earlier that every shaman is in effect his or her own prophet. Some people might consider this a rather dangerous idea.

M.H.: If a state political organization is founded in part upon a state religion with a dogma based on one or a few "official" prophets, then shamanism, where every shaman is her or his own prophet, is dangerous to the state. In my opinion, the real problem is not too many prophets, but too few.

Shamanism, as I said, is not a religion. The spiritual experience usually becomes a religion after politics has entered into it. So the renewed interest in shamanism today can be viewed as democratization, returning to the original spiritual democracy of our ancestors in ancient tribal societies where almost everyone had some access to spiritual experience and direct revelation. We are now restoring ancient methods to get our own direct revelations, without the need of ecclesiastical hierarchies and politically-influenced dogma. We can find things out for ourselves.

G.D.: Would you like to say something about your vision of the future of our Western society and what place the shaman might have in that future?

M.H.: I think that almost everybody is potentially a shaman. What is needed is to wake up that potential and begin to explore experientially one's spiritual relationship to the universe, to other forms of life on the planet, and to each other. The more people there are who have the experiences we have been discussing—whether they get them through shamanism or other means—the more we will have a population that is more respectful of other species and members of our own species.

Respect is a key word in this regard because the experiences that come from shamanism tend to foster a great respect for the universe, based on a feeling of oneness with all forms of life. By getting into harmony one has much more power available to help others, because harmony with the universe is where the true power comes from. Then one is much more likely to lead a life that emphasizes love rather than hatred, and which promotes understanding and optimism. With this kind of work there is no end. And to my mind this is a beautiful thing, a very beautiful thing.

2

Shamanism and Cosmology

MIRCEA ELIADE

The Three Cosmic Zones and the World Pillar

The pre-eminently shamanic technique is the passage from one cosmic region to another—from earth to the sky or from earth to the underworld. The shaman knows the mystery of the breakthrough in plane. This communication among the cosmic zones is made possible by the very structure of the universe. As we shall see presently, the universe in general is conceived as having three levels—sky, earth, underworld—connected by a central axis. The symbolism employed to express the interconnection and intercommunication among the three cosmic zones is quite complex and not without contradictions. For it has had a "history" and has been frequently contaminated and modified, in the course of time, by other more recent cosmological symbols. But the essential schema is always to be seen, even after the numerous influences to which it has been subjected; there are three great cosmic regions, which can be successively traversed because they are linked together by a central axis. This axis, of course, passes through an "opening," a "hole"; it is through this hole that the gods descend to earth and the dead to the subterranean regions; it is through the same hole that the soul of the shaman in ecstasy can fly up or down in the course of his celestial or infernal journeys.

Before examples of this cosmic topography are cited, a preliminary remark is in place. The symbolism of the "Center" is not

17

necessarily a cosmological idea. In the beginning, "Center" or site of a possible break-through in plane, was applied to any sacred space, that is, any space that had been the scene of a hierophany and so manifested realities (or forces, figures, etc.) that were not of our world, that came from elsewhere and primarily from the sky. The idea of a "Center" followed from the experience of a sacred space, impregnated by a transhuman presence: at this particular point something from above (or from below) has manifested itself. Later, it was supposed that manifestation of the sacred in itself implied a break-through in plane.[1]

The Turko-Tatars, like a number of other peoples, imagine the sky as a tent; the Milky Way is the "seam"; the stars, the "holes" for light.[2] According to the Yakut, the stars are the "windows of the world"; they are openings provided for ventilating the various celestial spheres (usually 9 in number, but sometimes also 12, 5, or 7).[3] From time to time the gods open the tent to look at the earth, which accounts for meteors.[4] The sky is also conceived as a lid; sometimes it is not perfectly fitted to the edges of the earth, and then the great winds blow in through the crack. It is likewise through this narrow crack that heroes and other privileged beings can squirm to enter the sky.[5]

In the middle of the sky shines the Pole Star, holding the celestial tent like a stake. The Samoyed call it the "Sky Nail"; the Chukchee and the Koryak the "Nail Star." The same image and terminology are found among the Lapps, the Finns, and the Estonians. The Turko-Altaians conceive the Pole Star as a pillar; it is the "Golden Pillar" of the Mongols, the Kalmyk, the Buryat, the "Iron Pillar" of the Kirgiz, the Bashkir, the Siberian Tatars, the "Solar Pillar" of the Teleut, and so on.[6] A complementary mythical image is that of the stars as invisibly linked to the Pole Star. The Buryat picture the stars as a herd of horses, and the Pole Star (the "Pillar of the World") is the stake to which they are tethered.[7]

As we should expect, this cosmology has found an exact replica in the microcosm inhabited by mankind. The Axis of the World has been concretely represented, either by the pillars that support the house, or in the form of isolated stakes, called "World Pillars." For the Eskimo, for example, the Pillar of the

Sky is identical with the pole at the center of their dwellings.[8] The Tatars of the Altai, the Buryat, and the Soyot assimilate the tent pole to the Sky Pillar. Among the Soyot the pole rises above the top of the yurt and its end is decorated with blue, white, and yellow cloths, representing the colors of the celestial regions. This pole is sacred; it is regarded almost as a god. At its foot stands a small stone altar, on which offerings are placed.[9]

The central pillar is a characteristic element in the dwellings of the primitive peoples[10] of the Arctic and North America; it is found among the Samoyed and the Ainu, among the tribes of Northern and Central California (Maidu, Eastern Pomo, Patwin) and among the Algonkin. Sacrifice and prayer are conducted at the foot of the pillar, for it opens the road to the celestial Supreme Being.[11] The same microcosmic symbolism has been preserved among the herdsmen-breeders of Central Asia, but since the form of the dwelling has changed (there is a transition from the conical-roofed hut with central pillar to the yurt), the mythico-religious function of the pillar has passed to the upper opening, through which the smoke escapes. Among the Ostyak this opening corresponds to the similar orifice in the "Sky House," and the Chukchee have assimilated it to the "hole" made in the celestial vault by the Pole Star. The Ostyak also speak of the "golden flues of the Sky House" or the "seven flues of the Sky God."[12] The Altaians also believe that it is through these "flues" that the shaman passes from one cosmic zone to another. So too the tent put up for the Altaic shaman's ascension ceremony is assimilated to the celestial vault, and like it, has a smoke hole.[13] The Chukchee hold that the "hole in the sky" is the Pole Star, that the three worlds are connected by similar "holes," and that it is through them that the shaman and the mythical heroes communicate with the sky.[14] And among the Altaians—as among the Chukchee—the road to the sky runs through the Pole Star.[15] The *udesi-burkhan* of the Buryat open the road to the shaman as one opens doors.[16]

This symbolism, of course, is not confined to the Arctic and North Asian regions. The sacred pillar, rising in the center of the house, is also found among the Hamitic Galla and Hadia herdsmen, the Hamitoid Nandi, and the Khasi (Assam).[17] Everywhere, sacrificial offerings are brought to the foot of this pillar.

Sometimes they are oblations of milk to the celestial God (as among the African tribes cited above); in some cases, even blood sacrifices are offered (for example, among the Galla of Kenya).[18] The World Pillar is sometimes represented apart from the house—as among the ancient Germans (*Irminsūl*, an image of which Charlemagne destroyed in 772), the Lapps, the Ugrian peoples. The Ostyak call these ritual posts "The Powerful Posts of the Center of the City"; the Ostyak of Tsingala know them under the name of "Man-Pillar of Iron," invoke them in their prayers as "Man" and "Father," and offer them blood sacrifices.[19]

The symbolism of the World Pillar is also familiar to more developed cultures—Egypt, India,[20] China, Greece, Mesopotamia. Among the Babylonians, for example, the link between heaven and earth—a link symbolized by a Cosmic Mountain or its replicas (ziggurat, temple, royal city, palace)—was sometimes imagined as a celestial column. We shall see before long that the same idea is also expressed in other images: Tree, Bridge, Stair, and so on. This whole complex forms part of what we have called the symbolism of the "Center," which appears to be of considerable antiquity, for it is found in the most "primitive" cultures.

At this point we wish to emphasize the following fact: Although the shamanic experience proper could be evaluated as a mystical experience by virtue of the cosmological concept of the three communicating zones, this cosmological concept does not belong exclusively to the ideology of Siberian and Central Asian shamanism, nor, in fact, of any other shamanism. It is a universally disseminated idea connected with the belief in the possibility of direct communication with the sky. On the macrocosmic plane this communication is figured by the Axis (Tree, Mountain, Pillar, etc.); on the microcosmic plane it is signified by the central pillar of the house or the upper opening of the tent—which means that *every human habitation is projected to the "Center of the World,"*[21] or that every altar, tent, or house makes possible a break-through in plane and hence ascent to the sky.

In the archaic cultures communication between sky and earth is ordinarily used to send offerings to the celestial gods and not for a concrete and personal ascent; the latter remains the prerogative of shamans. Only they know how to make an ascent through the "central opening"; only they transform a cosmo-theological concept into a *concrete mystical experience*. This point is important. It explains the difference between, for example, the religious life of a North Asian people and the religious experience of its shamans; the latter is a *personal and ecstatic experience*. In other words, what for the rest of the community remains a cosmological ideogram, for the shamans (and the heroes, etc.) becomes a mystical itinerary. For the former, the "Center of the World" is a site that permits them to send their prayers and offerings to the celestial gods, whereas for the latter it is the place for beginning a flight in the strictest sense of the word. Only for the latter is *real communication* among the three cosmic zones a possibility.

In this connection the reader will remember the previously cited myth of a paradisal age in which human beings could easily go up to the sky and maintained familiar relations with the gods. The cosmological symbolism of the dwelling and the experience of shamanic ascent confirm, though in another aspect, this archaic myth. They do so in this way: After the interruption of the *easy communications* that, at the dawn of time, existed between mankind and the gods, certain privileged beings (and first of all the shamans) preserved the power to actualize, for their own persons, the connection with the upper regions; similarly, the shamans have the power to fly and to reach the sky through the "central opening," whereas for the rest of mankind the opening serves only for the transmission of offerings. In both cases alike, the shaman's privileged status is due to his faculty for ecstatic experiences.

We have had to emphasize this point—of primary importance, in our view—a number of times in order to bring out the universal character of the ideology implied in shamanism. The shamans did not create the cosmology, the mythology, and the theology of their respective tribes; they only interiorized it, "experienced" it, and used it as the itinerary for their ecstatic journeys.

The Cosmic Mountain

Another mythical image of the "Center of the World" that makes connection between earth and sky possible is that of the

Cosmic Mountain. The Tatars of the Altai imagine Bai Ülgän in the middle of the sky, seated on a golden mountain.[22] The Abakan Tatars call it "The Iron Mountain"; the Mongols, the Buryat, the Kalmyk know it under the names of Sumbur, Sumur, or Sumer, which clearly show Indian influence (= Mount Meru). The Mongols and the Kalmyk picture it with three or four storeys; the Siberian Tatars, with seven; in his mystical journey the Yakut shaman, too, climbs a mountain with seven storeys. Its summit is in the Pole Star, in the "Navel of the Sky." The Buryat say that the Pole Star is fastened to its summit.[23]

The idea of a Cosmic Mountain as Center of the World is not necessarily of Oriental origin, for, as we have seen, the symbolism of the "Center" seems to have preceded the rise of the paleo-Oriental civilizations. But the ancient traditions of the peoples of Central and North Asia—who doubtless knew the image of a "Center of the World" and of the Cosmic Axis—were modified by the continual influx of Oriental religious ideas, whether Mesopotamian in origin (and disseminated through Iran) or Indian (disseminated through Lamaism). In Indian cosmology Mount Meru rises at the "Center of the World" and above it shines the Pole Star.[24] Just as the Indian gods grasped this Cosmic Mountain (= World Axis) and stirred the primordial ocean with it, thus giving birth to the universe, so a Kalmyk myth relates that the gods used Sumer as a stick to stir the ocean, thus creating the sun, moon, and stars.[25] Another Central Asian myth shows the penetration achieved by Indian elements: The Mongolian god Ochirvani (= Indra), taking the form of the eagle Garide (= Garuda), attacked the snake Losun in the primordial ocean, wound it three times around Mount Sumeru, and finally crushed its head.[26]

There is no need to cite all the other Cosmic Mountains of Oriental or European mythologies—Haraberezaiti (Elbruz) of the Iranians, for example, Himingbjörg of the ancient Germans, and so on. In Mesopotamian beliefs a Central Mountain joins heaven and earth; it is the "Mount of the Lands," which connects the territories.[27] But the very names of the Babylonian temples and sacred towers bear witness to their assimilation to the Cosmic Mountain: "Mount of the House," "Mount of the Mountains of All Lands," "Mount of Storms," "Link between Heaven and

Earth,'' and the like.[28] The ziggurat was, properly speaking, a Cosmic Mountain, a symbolic image of the Cosmos; its seven storeys represented the seven planetary heavens (as at Borsippa) or bore the colors of the world (as at Ur).[29] The temple of Borobudur, a veritable *imago mundi,* was built in the form of a mountain.[30] Artificial mountains are attested in India, and are also found among the Mongols and in Southeast Asia.[31] It seems probable that Mesopotamian influences reached India and the Indian Ocean, although the symbolism of the "Center" (Mountain, Pillar, Tree, Giant) is an organic part of the most ancient Indian spirituality.[32]

Mount Tabor, in Palestine, might signify *tabbūr,* that is, "navel," omphalos. Mount Gerizim, at the center of Palestine, was doubtless invested with the prestige of the "Center," for it is called "navel of the earth."[33] A tradition preserved by Petrus Comestor says that at the summer solstice the sun casts no shadow on "Jacob's Fountain" (close to Gerizim). And he goes on: "Sunt qui dicunt locum illum esse umbilicum terrae nostrae habitabilis" ("Some say that place is the navel of our habitable earth").[34] Palestine, being the highest land—since it lay close to the summit of the Cosmic Mountain—was not covered by the Flood. A rabbinical text says: "The land of Israel was not submerged by the Deluge."[35] For the early Christians, Golgotha was at the "Center of the World," for it was the summit of the Cosmic Mountain and at the same time the place where Adam was created and buried. Thus the Saviour's blood falls on Adam's skull, buried exactly at the foot of the Cross, and redeems him.[36]

We have shown elsewhere how frequent and essential this symbolism of the "Center" is both in the archaic ("primitive") cultures and in all the great civilizations of the East.[37] To summarize very briefly: palaces, royal cities,[38] and even simple houses were believed to stand at the "Center of the World," on the summit of the Cosmic Mountain. We have already seen the deeper meaning of this symbolism; it is at the "Center" that the break-through in plane, that is, communication with the sky, becomes possible.

It is such a Cosmic Mountain that the future shaman climbs in dream during his initiatory illness and that he later visits on his ecstatic journeys. Ascending a mountain always signifies a journey to the "Center of the World." As we have seen, this "Center" is made present in many ways, even in the structure of the human dwelling place—but it is only the shamans and the heroes who *actually scale* the Cosmic Mountain, just as it is primarily the shaman who, climbing his ritual tree, is really climbing a World Tree and thus reaches the summit of the universe, in the highest sky. For the symbolism of the World Tree is complementary to that of the Central Mountain. Sometimes the two symbols coincide; usually they complete each other. But both are merely more developed mythical formulations of the Cosmic Axis (World Pillar, etc.).

The World Tree

There is no occasion to review the extensive documentation on the World Tree here.[39] We will confine ourselves to citing the themes most frequently found in Central and North Asia, and indicating their role in the shamanic ideology and experience. The Cosmic Tree is essential to the shaman. From its wood he makes his drum;[40] climbing the ritual birch, he effectually reaches the summit of the Cosmic Tree; in front of his yurt and inside it are replicas of the Tree, and he depicts it on his drum.[41] Cosmologically, the World Tree rises at the center of the earth, the place of earth's "umbilicus," and its upper branches touch the palace of Bai Ülgän.[42] In the legends of the Abakan Tatars a white birch with seven branches grows on the summit of the Iron Mountain. The Mongols imagine the Cosmic Mountain as a four-sided pyramid with a Tree in the center; the gods use it as a hitching post for their horses, as they do the Pillar of the World.[43]

The Tree connects the three cosmic regions.[44] The Vasyugan-Ostyak believe that its branches touch the sky and its roots go down to the underworld. According to the Siberian Tatars, a replica of the Celestial Tree stands in the underworld; a fir with nine roots (or, in other variants, nine firs) rises before the palace of Irle Kan; the King of the Dead and his sons hitch their horses to its trunk. The Goldi reckon three Cosmic Trees: the first is in the sky (and the souls of men perch on its branches like birds, waiting to be carried down to earth to bring infants to birth), the second on earth, and the third in the underworld.[45] The Mongols know the tree *Zambu* whose roots plunge to the base of Mount Sumer and whose crown spreads over its summit; the gods *(Tengeri)* feed on the fruits of the Tree, and the demons *(asuras),* hidden in the gorges of the Mountain, watch them enviously. A similar myth is found among the Kalmyk and the Buryat.[46]

Several religious ideas are implied in the symbolism of the World Tree. On the one hand, it represents the universe in continual regeneration,[47] the inexhaustible spring of cosmic life, the paramount reservoir of the sacred (because it is the "Center" for the reception of the celestial sacred, etc.); on the other, it symbolizes the sky or the planetary heavens.[48] We shall return later to the Tree as symbol of the planetary heavens, since this symbolism plays an essential role in Central Asian and Siberian shamanism. But it is important to remember at this point that in a number of archaic traditions the Cosmic Tree, expressing the sacrality of the world, its fertility and perenniality, is related to the ideas of creation, fecundity, and initiation, and finally to the idea of absolute reality and immortality. Thus the World Tree becomes a Tree of Life and Immortality as well. Enriched by innumerable mythical doublets and complementary symbols (Woman, the Wellspring, Milk, Animals, Fruits, etc.), the Cosmic Tree always presents itself as the very reservoir of life and the master of destinies.

These ideas are sufficiently old, for they are found among numerous "primitive" peoples, incorporated in a lunar and initiatory symbolism.[49] But they have been frequently altered and developed, the symbolism of the Cosmic Tree being almost inexhaustible. There is no doubt that southeastern influences contributed greatly toward the present physiognomy of the mythologies of the Central and North Asian peoples. In particular, the idea of the Cosmic Tree, reservoir of souls and "Book of Fate," seems to have been imported from more developed civilizations. For the World Tree is a Tree that *lives and gives life.* The Yakut believe that at the "golden navel of the Earth" stands a tree with eight branches; it rises in a sort of primordial paradise, for there the first man was born and he feeds on the milk of a woman who half emerges from the trunk of the tree.[50] As Harva remarks,[51] it is hard to believe that such an image was invented by the Yakut in the bitter climate of northern Siberia. The prototypes are found in the ancient East, as well as in India (where Yama, the first man, drinks with the gods beside a miraculous tree[52]) and Iran (where Yima on the Cosmic Mountain imparts immortality to man and animals[53]).

The Goldi, the Dolgan, and the Tungus say that, before birth, the souls of children perch like little birds on the branches of the Cosmic Tree and the shamans go there to find them.[54] This mythical motif, which we have already encountered in the initiatory dreams of future shamans,[55] is not confined to Central and North Asia; it is attested, for example, in Africa and Indonesia.[56] The cosmological schema Tree—Bird (= Eagle), or Tree with a Bird at its top and a Snake at its roots, although typical of the peoples of Central Asia and the ancient Germans, is presumably of Oriental origin,[57] but the same symbolism is already formulated on prehistoric monuments.[58]

Another theme—clearly of exotic origin—is that of the Tree-Book of Fate. Among the Osmanli Turks the Tree of Life has a million leaves, on each of which a human fate is written; each time a man dies, a leaf falls.[59] The Ostyak believe that a goddess, seated on a seven-storey celestial mountain, writes a man's fate, as soon as he is born, on a tree with seven branches.[60] The same belief is found among the Batak;[61] but as both the Turks and the Batak acquired writing only comparatively late, the Oriental origin of the myth is obvious.[62] The Ostyak also believe that the gods look for the child's future in a Book of Fate; according to the legends of the Siberian Tatars, seven gods write the destiny of newborn infants in a "Book of Life."[63] But all these images derive from the Mesopotamian concept of the seven planetary heavens regarded as a Book of Fate. We have mentioned them in this context because the shaman, when he reaches the summit of the Cosmic Tree, in the last heaven, also in a manner asks the "future" of the community and the "fate" of the "soul."

The Mystical Numbers 7 and 9

The identification of the seven-branched Cosmic Tree with the seven planetary heavens is certainly due to influences originally from Mesopotamia. But, to repeat, this does not mean that the idea of the Cosmic Tree = Axis of the World was conveyed to the Turko-Tatars and other Siberian peoples by Oriental influences. Ascent to the sky along the Axis of the World is a universal and archaic idea, much earlier than the idea of traversing the seven celestial regions (= seven planetary heavens), which could only have spread through Central Asia long after the Mesopotamian speculations on the seven planets. It is known that the religious value of the number 3—symbolizing the three cosmic regions[64]—preceded the value of the number 7. We also hear of 9 heavens (and of 9 gods, 9 branches of the Cosmic Tree, etc.), a mystical number probably explicable as 3 × 3 and hence to be regarded as forming part of a more archaic symbolism than that depending on the number 7, of Mesopotamian origin.[65]

The Altaic shaman climbs a tree or a post notched with seven or nine *tapty*, representing the seven or nine celestial levels. The "obstacles" *(pudak)* that he must overcome are really, as Anokhin remarked,[66] the heavens that he must enter. When the Yakut make blood sacrifices, their shamans set up a tree with nine notches outdoors and climb it to carry the offering to the celestial god Ai Toyon. The initiation of shamans among the Sibo (related to the Tungus) includes, as we have seen, the presence of a tree with steps; another, smaller tree notched with nine *tapty* is kept in his yurt by the shaman.[67] It is one more indication of his ability to journey ecstatically through the celestial regions.

We have seen that the Cosmic Pillars of the Ostyak have seven incisions.[68] The Vogul believe that the sky is reached by climbing a stairway of seven stairs. The conception of seven heavens is general throughout southeastern Siberia. But it is not the only one found; the image of nine celestial levels, or of sixteen, seventeen, and even thirty-three heavens, is not less widespread. As we shall see presently, the number of heavens does not correspond to the number of gods; the correlations between the pantheon and the number of heavens sometimes seem quite forced.

Thus the Altaians speak of seven heavens, but also of twelve, sixteen, or seventeen;[69] among the Teleut the shamanic tree has sixteen incisions, representing as many celestial levels.[70] In the highest heaven dwells Tengere Kaira Kan, "The Merciful Emperor Heaven"; on the three lower levels are the three principal gods brought forth by Tengere Kaira Kan through a sort of emanation: Bai Ülgän sits in the sixteenth on a golden throne on top of a golden mountain; Kysugan Tengere, "The Very Strong," in the ninth (no information is given as to the inhabitants of the fifteenth to tenth heavens); Mergen Tengere, "The All-Knowing," in the seventh, where the Sun also resides. The other lower levels are populated by the rest of the gods and a number of semidivine figures.[71]

Among the same Tatars of the Altai, Anokhin found an entirely different tradition.[72] Bai Ülgän, the Supreme God, inhabits the highest heaven—the seventh; Tengere Kaira Kan does not figure at all (we have already observed that he is in the process of disappearing from the current religion); Ülgän's seven Sons and nine Daughters live in heavens, but in which ones is not stated.[73]

The group of seven or nine Sons (or Servants) of the celestial god is frequently found in Central and North Asia, both among the Ugrians and the Turko-Tatars. The Vogul know seven Sons of God, the Vasyugan-Ostyak speak of seven Gods inhabiting the seven levels: in the highest is Num-tôrem, the other gods are called the "Guardians of the Sky" (Tôrem-karevel) or the "Interpreters of the Sky."[74] A group of seven Supreme Gods is also found among the Yakut.[75] Mongolian mythology, on the contrary, speaks of "nine Sons of the God" or "Servants of the God," which are at once tutelary gods (sulde-tengri) and warrior gods. The Buryat even know the names of these nine Sons of the Supreme God, but they vary from one region to another. The number 9 also appears in the rituals of the Chuvash of the Volga and of the Cheremis.[76]

In addition to these groups of seven or nine gods, and the respective images of seven or nine heavens, more numerous groups are found in Central Asia—such as the thirty-three gods (tengri) who inhabit Sumeru and whose number may be of Indian origin.[77] V. L. Verbitsky found among the Altaians the idea of thirty-three heavens, and N. V. Katanov found the same conception among the Soyot.[78] This number, however, appears very infrequently, and it may be considered a recent importation, presumably of Indian origin. Among the Buryat the number of gods is three times as great: ninety-nine gods, divided into good and evil and distributed by regions—fifty-five good gods in the southwestern regions and forty-four evil ones in the north-eastern. These two groups of gods have been fighting each other for a very long time.[79] The Mongols, too, knew ninety-nine *tengri* in times past.[80] But neither the Buryat nor the Mongols can say anything definite about these gods, whose names are obscure and artificial.

It should, however, be remembered that belief in a celestial Supreme God is autochthonous and very ancient in Central Asia and the Arctic.[81] No less ancient is the belief in the Sons of God, though the number 7 represents an Oriental, and hence recent, influence. It is probable that the shamanic ideology has played a part in the dissemination of the number 7. A. Gahs considers the mythico-cultural complex of the lunar Ancestor related to the idol with seven gashes and the Tree-Mankind with seven branches, as well as to the periodical and "shamanistic" blood sacrifices, of southern origin, that have taken the place of the bloodless sacrifices (offerings of the head and bones to the celestial Supreme Gods).[82] However this may be, among the Yurak-Samoyed the Earth Spirit has seven sons and the idols *(sjaadai)* have seven faces, or a face with seven gashes, or simply seven incisions; and these *sjaadai* are related to the sacred trees.[83] We have seen that the shaman has seven bells on his costume, representing the voices of the seven celestial maidens.[84] Among the Ostyak of the Yenisei the future shaman withdraws into solitude, cooks a flying squirrel, divides it into eight parts, eats seven, and throws away the eighth. After seven days he returns to the same place and receives a sign that determines his vocation.[85] The mystical number 7 apparently plays an important role in the shaman's technique and ecstasy, for among the Yurak-Samoyed the future shaman lies unconscious for seven days and seven nights, while the spirits dismember and initiate him;[86] the Ostyak and Lapp shamans eat mushrooms with seven spots to enter into trance;[87] the Lapp shaman is given a mushroom with seven spots by his master;[88] the Yurak-Samoyed shaman has a glove with seven fingers;[89] the Ugrian shaman has seven helping spirits;[90] and so on. In the case of the Ostyak and the Vogul it has been shown that the importance of the number 7 is due to definite influences from the ancient East[91]—and it is beyond doubt that the same phenomenon has occurred in the rest of Central and North Asia.

What is significant for our study is that the shaman appears to have more direct knowledge of all these heavens, and hence, of all the gods and demigods inhabiting them. For his ability to enter the celestial regions one after the other is due in part to the help their inhabitants give him; before he can address Bai Ülgän, he converses with the other celestial figures and asks their support and protection. The shaman displays a like experiential knowledge of the subterranean regions. The Altaians conceive the entrance to the underworld as a "smoke hole" of the earth, located, of course, at the "Center" (situated, according to the myths of Central Asia, in the North, which corresponds to the Center of the Sky;[92] for, as we know, the "North" is assimilated to the "Center" through the whole Asian area, from India to Siberia). By a sort of symmetry, the underworld has been imagined to have the same number of levels as the sky: three, among the Karagas and the Soyot, who reckon three heavens; seven or nine for most of the Central and North Asian peoples.[93] We have seen that the Altaic shaman successively passes through the seven underworld "obstacles" *(pudak)*. Indeed it is he, and he alone, who commands experiential knowledge of the underworld, for he enters it as a living man, just as he mounts and descends through the seven or nine heavens.

Shamanism and Cosmology in the Oceanian Region

Without undertaking to compare two phenomena as complex as Central and North Asian shamanism on the one hand and the shamanism of Indonesia and Oceania on the other, we will rapidly review certain data from the Southeast Asian area in order to demonstrate two points: (1) the presence, in these regions, of the archaic symbolism of the three cosmic zones and the World Axis; (2) the Indian influences (recognizable especially from the cosmological and religious role of the number 7) that have been superimposed on the substratum of the autochthonous religion. For, in our opinion, the two cultural units, Central and North Asia on the one hand and Indonesia and Oceania on the other, display common characteristics in this respect, due to the fact that both have seen their religious traditions definitely modified by the radiation of higher cultures. It is not our intention to enter upon a historico-cultural analysis of the

Indonesian and Oceanian area; such a study would go far beyond the limits of this book.[94] We wish only to set up a few signposts to show from what ideologies and by virtue of what techniques shamanism could develop there.

Among one of the most archaic peoples of the Malay Peninsula, the Semang Pygmies, we find the symbol of the World Axis; an immense rock, Batu Ribn, rises at the "Center of the World"; below it is the underworld. Formerly, a tree trunk rose from Batu Ribn into the sky.[95] According to the data collected by Evans, a stone pillar, Batu Herem, supports the sky; its top passes through the celestial vault and comes out above the heaven of Tapern, in a region called Ligoi, where the Chinoi live and amuse themselves.[96] The underworld, the center of the earth, and the "gate" of the sky are situated on the same axis, and in past times it was by this axis that passage from one cosmic region to another was effected. One would hesitate to credit the genuineness of this cosmological schema among the Semang Pygmies, if there were not reason to believe that a similar theory had already been outlined in prehistoric times.[97]

When we come to examine the beliefs held regarding the Semang healers and their magical techniques, we shall note certain Malayan influences (for example, the power to take the form of a tiger). Such influences can also be discerned in these Pygmies' ideas (given below) concerning the destiny of the soul in the beyond. At death the soul leaves the body through the heel and sets off eastward to the sea. For seven days the dead souls can return to their village; after that, those who have led a good life are guided by Mampes to a miraculous island, Belet; to reach it they go over a switchbacked bridge, which crosses the sea. The bridge is called Balan Bacham; Bacham is a kind of fern that grows at the further end of the bridge; there they encounter a Chinoi woman, Chinoi-Sagar, who decks her head with Bacham ferns, and the dead must do likewise before setting foot on the island of Belet. Mampes is the guardian of the bridge, and he is imagined as a gigantic Negrito; it is he who eats the offerings for the dead. Arrived in the island, the dead go to the Mapic Tree (presumably the tree stands in the center of the island), where all the other dead are assembled. But the new arrivals may not wear flowers from the tree or taste of its fruits until the dead who have preceded them have broken all their bones and reversed their eyes in the sockets, so that they look inward. When these conditions have been duly fulfilled, the newly deceased become real spirits *(kemoit)* and may eat the fruits of the tree.[98] This, of course, is a miraculous tree and the source of life; for at its roots are breasts heavy with milk, and there too are the spirits of infants[99]—presumably the souls of the yet unborn. Although the myth obtained by Evans is silent on this point, probably the dead become infants again, thus preparing themselves for another life on earth.

Here we find the idea of the Tree of Life, in whose branches the souls of infants are perched, which seems to be a very old myth, although belonging to a different religious complex from that which centers on the god Ta Pedn and the symbolism of the World Axis. For in this myth we discern, on the one hand, the mystical solidarity between man and plant and, on the other, some traces of a matriarchal ideology, both of which are foreign to the archaic complex: uranian Supreme God, symbolism of the three cosmic zones, myth of a primordial time when there were direct and easy communications between earth and heaven (myth of the "Lost Paradise"). In addition, the detail that the dead can return to their village for *seven* days shows an Indo-Malayan influence that is still more recent.

Among the Sakai such influences become still more marked. They believe that the soul leaves the body through the back of the head and sets off westward. The dead man attempts to enter the sky through the same gate by which the souls of Malays go in, but, failing, starts over a bridge, Menteg, across a caldron of boiling water (this idea is of Malayan origin[100]). The bridge is really a tree trunk stripped of its bark. The souls of the wicked fall into the caldron. Yenang seizes them and burns them to dust; then he weighs them; if the souls have become light, he sends them to the sky; otherwise, he continues burning them to purify them by fire.[101]

The Besisi of the Kuala Langat district of Selangan, like those of Bebrang, speak of a Fruit Island to which the souls of the dead go. The island is comparable to the Mapic Tree of the Semang. There, when men reach old age they can become children and begin to grow again.[102] According to the Besisi conception, the universe is divided into six upper regions, the earth, and six underground regions;[103] this shows a mixture of the old tripartite conception with Indo-Malayan cosmological ideas.

Among the Jakun[104] a post five feet high is set up on the grave; it has fourteen notches, seven running up one side and seven down the other; the post is called the "soul ladder."[105] We shall return to this ladder symbolism;[106] for the present, we may note the presence of the seven incisions, which, whether the Jakun are aware of it or not, represent the seven celestial levels that the soul must pass through—which proves the penetration of ideas of Oriental origin even among peoples as "primitive" as the Jakun.

The Dusun[107] of North Borneo picture the road of the dead as mounting a hill and crossing a stream.[108] The role of the mountain in funerary mythologies is always explained by the symbolism of ascent and implies a belief in a celestial dwelling place for the dead. We shall see elsewhere that the dead "cling to the mountains," just as the shamans or heroes do in their initiatory ascents. What it is important to note at this point is that, among all the peoples whom we are passing in review, shamanism shows the closest dependence on funerary beliefs (mountain, paradisal island, Tree of Life) and cosmological concepts (World Axis, Cosmic Tree, three cosmic regions, seven heavens, etc.). In exercising his profession of healer or psychopomp, the shaman employs the traditional details of infernal topography (be it celestial, marine, or subterranean), details that are finally based on an archaic cosmology, though one that has frequently been enriched or altered by exotic influences.

The Ngadju Dyak of South Borneo have a peculiar conception of the universe: although they know an upper and a lower world, they do not regard our world as a third one but as the sum of the two others, for it at once reflects and represents them.[109] All this, however, forms part of the archaic idea that the things of the earth are only a replica of the exemplary models that exist in the sky or the beyond. We may add that the concept of three cosmic zones does not contradict the idea of the unity of the world. The numerous symbolisms that express the likeness between the three worlds and the means of communication between them are at the same time an expression of their *unity*, their integration in a single cosmos. The tripartition of the cosmic zones—a motif that, for reasons set forth above, we must emphasize—excludes neither the profound unity of the universe nor its apparent "dualism."

The mythology of the Ngadju Dyak is quite complicated, but a dominant can be discerned in it; and this is precisely a "cosmological dualism." The World Tree precedes this dualism, for it represents the cosmos in its totality;[110] it even symbolizes the unification of the two supreme divinities.[111] The creation of the world is the result of a conflict between two gods representing two polar principles: feminine (cosmologically lower, represented by the waters and the snake) and masculine (the upper region, the bird). During the struggle between these two antagonists, the World Tree (= the primordial totality) is destroyed.[112] But its destruction is only temporary; archetype of all creative human activity, the World Tree is destroyed only that it may be reborn. In this myth we are inclined to see both the ancient cosmological schema of the hierogamy between heaven and earth (a schema also expressed, on another plane, by the symbolism of the complementary opposites bird-snake) and the "dualistic" structure of the ancient lunar mythologies (opposition between contraries, alternate destructions and creations, the eternal return). In any case, it is incontestable that Indian influences were later imposed on the ancient autochthonous material, though they were often confined to the nomenclature of the gods.

What must be noted as of particular importance is the presence of the World Tree in every Dyak village and even in every Dyak house.[113] And the Tree is represented with seven branches. That it symbolizes the World Axis and hence the road to the sky is proved by the fact that a similar World Tree is always found in the Indonesian "ships of the dead," which are believed to transport the deceased to the celestial beyond.[114] This Tree, represented with six branches (seven including the tufted top) and with the sun and moon on either side, sometimes takes the form of a lance decorated with the same symbols that serve to designate the "shaman's ladder," by which he climbs to the sky to bring back the patient's fugitive soul.[115] The tree-lance-ladder represented in the "ships of the dead" is only the replica of the miraculous tree that stands in the beyond and to which souls come on their journey to the god Devata Sangiang. The Indonesian shamans (for example, among the Sakai, the Kubu, and the Dyak) also have a tree that they use as a ladder to reach the world of the spirits in seeking the souls of patients.[116] We shall realize the role played by the tree-lance when we examine the technique of Indonesian shamanism. Let us note in passing that the shamanic tree of the Dusun Dyak, which serves in healing ceremonies, has seven branches.[117]

The Batak, most of whose religious ideas derive from India, conceive the universe as divided into three regions: sky, with seven storeys, inhabited by the gods; earth, occupied by mankind; and underworld, the home of the demons and the dead.[118] Here too we find the myth of a paradisal time, when the sky was nearer to earth and there was continuous communication between gods and men; but, because of man's pride, the road to the celestial world was blocked. The Supreme God, Mula djadi na bolon ("He who has his beginning in himself"), the creator of the universe and of the other gods, inhabits the most distant heaven and seems to have become—like all the Supreme Gods of "primitives"—a *deus otiosus;* no sacrifices are offered to him. A cosmic snake lives in the subterranean regions and will finally destroy the world.[119]

The Menangkabau of Sumatra have a hybrid religion, based on animism but strongly influenced by Hinduism and Islamism.[120] The universe has seven levels. After death the soul must cross the edge of a razor that extends over a fiery underworld; sinners fall into the flames, the good go up to the sky, where there is a great tree. There souls remain until the final resurrection.[121] It is easy to perceive the mixture of archaic themes (the bridge, the Tree of Life as receptacle and nurse of souls) with exotic influences (underworld fire, the idea of a final resurrection).

The Niassans know the Cosmic Tree that gave birth to all things. To go up to the sky, the dead pass over a bridge; under the bridge is the abyss of the underworld. A guardian with shield and lance is posted at the entrance to the sky; a cat throws guilty souls into the infernal waters for him.[122]

So much for Indonesian examples. We shall return to all these mythical motifs (funerary bridge, ascent, etc.) and the shamanic techniques that are in one way or another connected with them.

For the moment, it is enough to have shown the presence, at least in part of the Oceanian area, of a cosmological and religious complex of very great antiquity, variously modified by successive influences from Indian and Asian ideas.

Notes

1. On this whole problem of the sacred space and the "Center," see Eliade: *Patterns in Comparative Religion*, pp. 367 ff.; *Images and Symbols*, pp. 27 ff.; "Centre du Monde, Temple, Maison."
2. U. Harva, *Die religiösen Vorstellungen der altaischen Völker*, pp. 178 ff., 189 ff.
3. W. Sieroszewski, "Du chamanisme d'apres les croyances des Yakoutes," p. 215.
4. Harva, *Die religiösen Vorstellungen*, pp. 34 ff. Similar ideas prevailed among the Hebrews (Isa. 40), etc.; cf. Robert Eisler, *Weltenmantel und Himmelszelt*, II, 601 ff., 619 ff.
5. Holmberg (Harva): *Der Baum des Lebens*, p. 11; *Die religiösen Vorstellungen*, p. 35. P. Ehrenreich *(Die allgemeine Mythologie und ihre ethnologischen Grundlagen*, p. 205) remarks that this mythico-religious idea dominates the whole of the Northern Hemisphere. It is yet another expression of the widespread symbolism of ascent to the sky through a "strait gate"; the aperture between the two cosmic planes widens for only a moment and the hero (or the initiate, the shaman, etc.) must take advantage of this paradoxical instant to enter the beyond.
6. Cf. Holmberg (Harva): *Der Baum des Lebens*, pp. 12 ff.; *Die religiösen Vorstellungen*, pp. 38 ff. The *Irminsül* of the Saxons is termed by Rudolf of Fulda *(Translatio S. Alexandri)* "universalis columna, quasi sustinens omnia." The Lapps of Scandinavia received this idea from the ancient Germans; they call the Pole Star the "Pillar of the Sky" or "Pillar of the World." The *Irminsül* has been compared to the pillars of Jupiter. Similar ideas still survive in Southeast European folklore; cf., for example, *Coloana Ceriului* (the Sky Pillar) of the Romanians (see A. Rosetti, *Colindele Românilor*, pp. 70 ff.).
7. The idea is common to the Ugrian and Turko-Mongol peoples; cf. Holmberg (Harva): *Der Baum des Lebens*,, pp. 23 ff.; *Die religiosen Vorstellungen*, pp. 40 ff. Cf. also Job 38:31; the Indian *skambha* *(Atharva Veda*, X, 7, 35; etc.).

8. W. Thalbitzer, "Cultic Games and Festivals in Greenland," pp. 239 f.
9. Harva, *Die religiösen Vorstellungen*, p. 46. Cf. the cloths of various colors, used in shamanic ceremonies or sacrifices, which always indicate the symbolic traversal of the celestial regions.
10. The "Urkultur" of the school of Graebner-Schmidt.
11. Cf. the material assembled by W. Schmidt, *Der Ursprung der Gottesidee*, VI, pp. 67 ff., and the same author's remarks, "Der heilige Mittelpfahl des Hauses," p. 966; id *Der Ursprung*, XII, 471 ff.
12. Cf., for example, K. F. Karjalainen, *Die Religion der Jugra-Völker*, II, 48 ff. The entrance to the subterranean world is, of course, directly below the "Center of the World"; cf. Holmberg, *Der Baum des Lebens*, pp. 30-31 and fig. 13 (Yakut disk with central hole). The same symbolism is found in the ancient East, India, the Greco-Roman world, etc,; cf. Eliade, *Cosmologie si alchimie babiloniana*, pp. 35 ff.; A. K. Coomaraswamy, "Svayamatrnna: Janua Coeli."
13. Harva, *Die religiösen Vorstellungen*, p. 53.
14. W. G. Bogoras, *The Chukchee*, p. 331; W. I. Jochelson, *The Koryak*, p. 301. The same idea is found among the Blackfoot Indians: cf. H. B. Alexander, *North American [Mythology]*, pp. 95 ff. See also the comparative data for North Asia and North America in Jochelson,, *The Koryak*, p. 371.
15. A. V. Anokhin, *Materialy po shamanstvu u altaitsev*, p. 9.
16. Harva, *Die religiosen Vorstellungen*, p. 54.
17. W. Schmidt, "Der heilige Mittelpfahl," p. 967, citing his *Der Ursprung*, VII, 53, 85, 165, 449, 590 ff.
18. The question of the empirical "origin" of such conceptions (for example, the structure of the cosmos conceived in accordance with certain material elements of the dwelling, which in turn are explicable by the necessity of adaptation to the milieu, etc.) is wrongly posed and hence fruitless. For, for "primitives" in general, there is no clear difference between "natural" and "supernatural," between empirical object and symbol. An object becomes "itself" (that is, the carrier of a value) in so far as it participates in a "symbol"; an act acquires meaning in so far as it repeats an archetype, etc. In any case, this problem of the "origin" of values belongs rather to philosophy than to history. For, to cite but one example, it scarcely seems that the fact that the first discovery of geometrical laws was due to the empirical necessities of irrigating the Nile delta can have any bearing on the validity or invalidity of those laws.

19. Karjalainen (Die Religion der Jugra-Völker, II, 42 ff.) supposes, erroneously, that the role of these posts is to hold the sacrificial victim. Actually, as Holmberg (Harva) has shown, this pillar is called the "Seven-divided high man-father," just as Sanke, the celestial god, is invoked as "Seven-divisioned high man, Sanke, my father, my three-directions-watching man father," etc. (Finno-Ugric [and] Siberian [Mythology], p. 338). The pillar was sometimes marked with seven notches; the Ostyak of Salym, when they offer blood sacrifices, make seven incisions in a post (ibid., p. 339). This ritual post corresponds to the "Seven-divided pure silver holy pillar" of Vogul tales, to which the sons of the god tie their horses when they visit their father (ibid., pp. 339-40). The Yurak also offer blood sacrifices to wooden idols (sjaadai) with seven faces or seven gashes; according to Lehtisalo (Entwurf einer Mythologie der Jurak-Samojeden, pp. 67, 102, etc.), these idols are related to "sacred trees" (that is, to a degradation of the Cosmic Tree with seven branches). Here we see a process of substitution well known in the history of religions and which is also confirmed by other cases in the Siberian religious complex. So, for example, the pillar that originally served as the offering place for the celestial god Num becomes, among the Yurak-Samoyed, a sacred object to which blood sacrifices are offered: cf. A. Gahs, "Kopf-, Schädel- und Langknochenopfer bei Rentier- völkern," p. 240. On the cosmological meaning of the number 7 and its role in shamanic rituals, see below, pp. 274 ff.

20. See, for example, Rg-Veda, X, 89, 4; etc.

21. See Eliade: Patterns in Comparative Religion, pp. 379 ff.; The Myth of the Eternal Return, pp. 76 ff.

22. W. Radlov, Aus Sibirien, II, 6.

23. Holmberg (Harva): Der Baum des Lebens, pp. 41, 57; Finno-Ugric [and] Siberian [Mythology], p. 341; Die religiösen Vorstellungen, pp. 58 ff.

24. W. Kirfel, Die Kosmographie der Inder, p. *15.

25. Harva, Die religiösen Vorstellungen, p. 63.

26. G. N. Potanin, Ocherki severo-zapadnoi Mongolii, IV, 228; Harva, Die religiösen Vorstellungen, p. 62. On Greek coins a snake twines three times around the omphalos (ibid., p. 63).

27. A Jeremias, Handbuch, p. 130; cf. Eliade, The Myth of the Eternal Return, pp. 13 ff. For the Iranian data, see A. Christensen,

Les Types du premier homme et du premier roi dans l'histoire légendaire des Iraniens, II, 42.

28. T. Dombart, *Der Sakralturm. I: Ziqqurat*, p. 34.

29. Id., *Der babylonische Turm*, pp. 5 ff. Eliade, *Cosmologie si alchimie babiloniana*, pp. 31 ff. On the symbolism of the ziggurat, cf. A. Parrot, *Ziggurats et Tour de Babel*.

30. P. Mus, *Barabudur. Esquisse d'une histoire du Bouddhisme fondee sur la critique archeologique des textes*, I, 356.

31. Cf. W. Foy, "Indische Kultbauten als Symbole des Götterbergs," pp. 213-16; Harva, *Die religiösen Vorstellungen*, p. 68; R. von Heine-Geldern, "Weltbild und Bauform in Südostasien," pp. 48 ff; cf. also H. G. Quaritch Wales, *The Mountain of God: a Study in Early Religion and Kingship*, passim.

32. Cf. Mus, *Barabudur*, I, 117 ff., 292 ff., 351 ff., 385 ff., etc.; J. Przyluski, "Les Sept Terrasses de Barabudur," pp. 251-56; Coomaraswamy, *Elements of Buddhist Iconography*, passim; Eliade, *Cosmologie*, pp. 43 ff.

33. *Tabbūr eres;* cf. Judges 9:37: "...See there come people down by the middle [Heb., navel] of the land..."

34. Eric Burrows, "Some Cosmological Patterns in Babylonian Religion," pp. 51, 62, n. 1.

35. Cited by A.J. Wensinck, *The Ideas of the Western Semites concerning the Navel of the Earth*, p. 15; Burrows (p. 54) mentions other texts.

36. Wensinck, p. 22; Eliade, *Cosmologie*, pp.34 ff. The belief that Golgotha is at the "Center of the World" has been preserved in the folklore of the eastern Christians (for example, among the Little Russians; cf. Holmberg, *Der Baum des Lebens*, p. 72).

37. Eliade: *Cosmologie*, pp. 31 ff.; *Patterns*, pp. 367 ff.; *The Myth of the Eternal Return*, pp. 12 ff.

38. Cf. Mus, *Barabudur*, I, 354 ff. and passim; Jeremias, *Handbuch*, pp. 113, 142, etc.; M. Granet, *La Pensée chinoise*, pp. 323 ff.; Wensinck, *Tree and Bird as Cosmological Symbols in Western Asia*, pp. 25 ff.; Birger Pering, "Die geflugelte Scheibe"; Burrows, "Some Cosmological Patterns," pp. 48 ff.

39. The essential elements and bibliographies will be found in Eliade, *Patterns*, pp. 273 ff., 327 ff.

40. See above, pp. 169 f.

41. See, for example, the drawing on the drum of an Altaic shaman,

in Harva, *Die religiösen Vorstellungen*, fig. 15. The shamans sometimes use an "inverted tree," which they set up near their house, which it is believed to protect; cf. E. Kagarow, "Der umgekehrte Schamanenbaum." The "inverted tree" is, of course, a mythical image of the cosmos; cf. Coomaraswamy, "The Inverted Tree," which contains an abundant Indian documentation; Eliade, *Patterns*, pp. 274 ff., 327. The same symbolism is preserved in Christian and Islamic traditions: cf. ibid., p. 274; A. Jacoby, "Der Baum mit den Wurzeln nach oben und den Zweigen nach unten"; Carl Martin Edsman, "Arbor inversa."

42. Radlov, *Aus Sibirien*, II, 7.

43. Cf. Holmberg (Harva): *Der Baum des Lebens*, p. 52; *Die religiösen Vorstellungen*, p. 70. In the same way, Odin hitches his horse to Yggdrasil (Eliade, *Patterns*, p. 277). On the mythical complex horse-tree (post) in China, see C. Hentze, *Frühchinesische Bronzen und Kultdarstellungen*, pp. 123-30.

44. Cf. H. Bergema, *De Boom des Levens in Schrift en Historie*, pp. 539 ff.

45. Harva, *Die religiösen Vorstellungen*, p. 71.

46. Holmberg (Harva): *Finno-Ugric [and] Siberian [Mythology]*, pp. 356 ff.; *Die religiösen Vorstellungen*, pp. 72 ff. We have already referred to a possible Iranian model: the tree Gaokērēna which grows on an island in Lake Vourukasha and beside which lurks the monstrous lizard created by Ahriman (cf. above, p. 122, n. 27). As for the Mongol myth, it is, of course, Indian in origin: *Zambu* = *Jambū*. Cf. also the Tree of Life (Cosmic Tree) of Chinese tradition, growing on a mountain and sending its roots down to the underworld (Hentze: "Le Culte de l'ours et du tigre et le t'ao-t'ié," p. 57; *Die Sakralbronzen und ihre Bedeutung in den frühchinesischen Kulturen*, pp. 24 ff.).

47. Cf. Eliade, *Patterns*, pp. 273 ff.

48. Or sometimes the Milky Way; cf., for example, Y. H. Toivonen, "Le Gros Chêne des chants populaires finnois."

49. Cf. Eliade, *Patterns*, p. 275.

50. Harva (Holmberg): *Die religiösen Vorstellungen*, pp. 75 ff.; *Der Baum des Lebens*, pp. 57 ff. For the paleo-Oriental prototypes of this mythical motif, see Eliade, *Patterns*, pp. 283 ff. Cf. also Gertrude R. Levy, *The Gate of Horn*, p. 156, n. 3. On the theme Tree—Goddess (= First Woman) in the mythologies of America, China, and Japan, cf. Hentze, *Frühchinesische Bronzen*, pp. 129 f.

51. *Die religiösen Vorstellungen*, p. 77.
52. *Rg-Veda*, X, 135, 1.
53. *Yasna*, 9, 4 f.; *Vidēvdat*, 2, 5.
54. Harva, *Die religiösen Vorstellungen*, pp. 84, 166 ff.
55. See above, pp. 39 f.
56. In the sky there is a tree on which there are children; God picks them and throws them down to earth (H. Baumann, *Lunda. Bei Bauern und Jägern in Inner-Angola*, p. 95). On the African myth of the origin of man from trees, cf. id., *Schöpfung und Urzeit des Menschen im Mythus der afrikanischen Völker*, pp. 224 f.; for comparative material, see Eliade, *Patterns*, pp. 300 ff. The Dyak believe that the first pair of ancestors was born from the Tree of Life (H. Schärer, *Die Gottesidee der Ngadju Dajak in Süd-Borneo*, p. 57; see also below, pp. 352 f.). But it should be noted that the image of soul (child)-bird-World Tree is peculiar to Central and North Asia.
57. Harva, *Die religiösen Vorstellungen*, p. 85. On the meaning of this symbolism, see Eliade, *Patterns*, pp. 290 ff. Documentation: A. J. Wensinck, *Tree and Bird as Cosmological Symbols in Western Asia*. Cf. also Hentze, *Frühchinesische Bronzen*, p. 129.
58. See Georg Wilke, "Der Weltenbaum und die beiden kosmischen Vögel in der vorgeschichtlichen Kunst."
59. Harva, *Die religiösen Vorstellungen*, p. 72
60. Ibid., p. 172
61. J. Warneck, *Die Religion der Batak*, pp. 49 ff. On the symbolism of the tree in Indonesia, see below, pp. 284 ff., 357 f.
62. Cf. G. Widengren: *The Ascension of the Apostle of God and the Heavenly Book; The King and the Tree of Life in Ancient Near Eastern Religion*.
63. Harva, *Die religiösen Vorstellungen*, pp. 160 ff.
64. On the antiquity, consistency, and importance of cosmological conceptions based on a tripartite schema, see Coomaraswamy, "Svayamātrnnā: Janua Coeli," passim.
65. On the religious and cosmological implications of the numbers 7 and 9, cf. W. Schmidt, *Der Ursprung*, IX, 91 ff., 423, etc. Harva (*Die religiösen Vorstellungen*, pp. 51 f., etc.), on the contrary, considers the number 9 more recent. He also thinks that the nine heavens are a late idea explained by the concept of the nine planets, which, though also attested in India, is of Iranian origin (ibid., p. 56). In any case, two different religious complexes are involved.

Obviously, in contexts where the number 9 clearly shows multiplication of the number 3, one is justified in considering it earlier than the number 7. See also F. Röck, "Neunmalneun und Siebenmalsieben," passim; H. Hoffmann, *Quellen zur Geschichte der tibetischen Bon-Religion*, pp. 150, 153, 245; A Friedrich and G. Buddruss, *Schamanengeschichten aus Sibirien*, pp. 21 ff., 96 ff., 101 ff., etc.; W. Schmidt, *Der Ursprung*, XI, 713-16.

66. *Materialy po shamanstvu u altaitsev*, p. 9.

67. Harva, *Die religiösen Vorstellungen*, p. 50.

68. Above, pp. 263-64, n. 19

69. W. Radlov, *Aus Sibirien*, II, 6 ff.

70. Harva, *Die religiösen Vorstellungen*, p. 52.

71. Radlov, pp. 7 f.

72. *Materialy*, pp. 9 ff.

73. See the analysis of these two cosmological conceptions in W. Schmidt, *Der Ursprung*, IX, 84 ff., 135 ff., 172 ff., 449 ff., 480 ff., etc.

74. In all probability, as Karjalainen has shown *(Die Religion der Jugra-Völker*, II, 305 ff.), these names were borrowed from the Tatars, together with the conception of seven heavens.

75. Harva, *Die religiösen Vorstellungen*, p. 162 (after V. L. Priklonsky and N. V. Pripuzov). Sieroszewski says that Bai Baianai, Yakut god of the chase, has seven companions, of whom three are favorable and two unfavorable to hunters ("Du chamanisme," p. 303).

76. Harva, *Die religiösen Vorstellungen*, pp. 162 f.

77. Ibid., p. 164

78. Ibid., p. 52.

79. G. Sandschejew, "Weltanschauung und Shamanismus der Alaren-Burjaten," pp. 939 ff.

80. Harva, *Die religiösen Vorstellungen*, p. 165.

81. Eliade, *Patterns* pp. 60 ff.

82. "Kopf-, Schadel- und Langknochenopfer bei Rentiervölkern," p. 237; "Blutige und unblutige Opfer bei den altaischen Hirtenvölkern," pp. 220 ff.

83. T. Lehtisalo, *Entwurf einer Mythologie der Jurak-Samojeden*, pp. 67, 77 ff., 102. On these seven-faced idols, see also Kai Donner, *La Sibérie*, pp. 222 ff.

84. Cf. Mikhailowski, "Shamanism in Siberia," p. 84.

85. Donner, p. 223.
86. Lehtisalo, *Entwurf,* p. 147.
87. Karjalainen, *Die Religion der Jugra-Völker,* II, 278; III, 306; T. I. Itkonen, *Heidnische Religion und späterer Aberglaube bei den finnischen Lappen,* p. 149. Among the Ostyak of Tsingala the patient sets a loaf of bread with seven gashes on a table and sacrifices to Sänke (Karjalainen, III, 307).
88. Itkonen, p. 159.
89. Lehtisalo, p. 147.
90. Karjalainen, III, 311.
91. Josef Hackel, "Idolkult und Dualsystem bei den Ugriern (zum Problem des eurasiatischen Totemismus)," p. 136.
92. Harva, *Die religiösen Vorstellungen,* p. 54.
93. Among the Ugrians the underworld always has seven levels, but the idea seems not to be native; cf. Karjalainen, II, 318.
94. The essentials will be found in Pia Laviosa-Zambotti's brief and daring synthesis, *Les Origines et la diffusion de la civilisation,* pp. 337 ff. On the earliest history of Indonesia, see G. Coèdes, *Les États hindouisés d' Indochine et d' Indonésie,* pp. 67 ff.; cf. also H. G. Quaritch Wales, *Prehistory and Religion in South-East Asia,* especially pp. 48 ff., 109 ff.
95. P. Schebesta, *Les Pygmees,* pp. 156 ff.
96. Ivor H. N. Evans, *Studies in Religion, Folk-Lore & Custom in British North Borneo and the Malay Peninsula,* p. 156. The Chinoi (Schebesta: cenoi) are at once souls and nature spirits, which serve as intermediaries between God (Tata Ta Pedn) and men (Schebesta, pp. 152 ff.; Evans, pp 148 ff.) On their role in healing, see below, pp. 337 ff.
97. Cf., for example, W. Gaerte, "Kosmische Vorstellungen im Bilde prahistorischer Zeit: Erdberg, Himmelsberg, Erdnabel und Weltströme." As for the problem of the authenticity and archaism of the Pygmies' culture, stoutly maintained by W. Schmidt and O. Menghin, it is not yet solved; for a contrary view, cf. Laviosa-Zambotti, *Les Origines,* pp. 132 ff. However this may be, there is no doubt that the Pygmies of the present day, though affected by the higher culture of their neighbors, still preserve many archaic characteristics; this conservatism is found especially in their religious beliefs, so different from those of their neighbors, which

are more developed. Hence we believe we are justified in classing
the cosmological schema and the myth of the World Axis among
the genuine survivals of the Pygmies' religious tradition.

98. The breaking of bones and reversal of the eyes suggest the initiatory
rites intended to transform the candidate into a "spirit." On the
paradisal Fruit Island of the Semang, Sakai, and Jakun, cf. W. W.
Skeat and C. O. Blagden, *Pagan Races of the Malay Peninsula*,
II, 207, 209, 321. See also below, pp. 282-83, n. 102.

99. Evans, *Studies*, p. 157; Schebesta: *Les Pygmées*, pp. 157-58;
"Jenseitsglaube der Semang auf Malakka."

100. Evans, *Studies*, p. 209, n. 1.

101. Ibid., p. 208. The weighing of the soul and its purification by fire
are Oriental ideas. The underworld of the Sakai shows strong and
probably recent influences that have replaced the autochthonous
conceptions of the beyond.

102. This is the widespread myth of the "paradise" where life flows
on endlessly, in an eternal recapitulation. Cf. Tuma, the island of
spirits (= the dead) of the Melanesians of the Trobriands:
"...when they [the spirits] find themselves old, they slough off
the loose, wrinkled skin, and emerge with a smooth body, dark
locks, sound teeth, and full of vigor. Thus life with them is an eternal recapitulation of youth with its accompaniment of love and
pleasure." (B. Malinowski, *The Sexual Life of Savages in NW
Melanesia*, p. 435.) The same idea is expressed in id., *Myth in
Primitive Psychology*, pp. 80 ff. ("Myth of Death and the Recur-
rent Cycle of Life").

103. Evans, *Studies*, pp. 209-10.

104. According to Evans (ibid., p. 264), they are of Malay race but represent an earlier wave (coming from Sumatra) than the Malays proper.

105. Ibid., pp. 266-67.

106. Cf. below, pp. 487 ff.

107. Of Proto-Malayan race and the aboriginal inhabitants of the island
(Evans, *Studies*, p. 3).

108. Ibid., pp. 33 ff.

109. Cf. H. Schärer: "Die Vorstellungen der Ober- und Unterwelt bei
den Ngadju Dajak von Süd-Borneo," especially p. 78; *Die Gottesidee der Ngadju Dajak in Süd-Borneo*, pp. 31 ff. Cf. also W.
Münsterberger, *Ethnologische Studien an Indonesischen Schöp-
fungsmythen. Ein Beitrag zur Kulturanalyse Südostasiens*, especially

pp. 143 ff. (Borneo); J. G. Roder, *Alahatala. Die Religion der Inlandstämme Mittelcerams*, pp. 33 ff., 63 ff., 75 ff., 96 ff. (Ceram).
110. Scharer, *Die Gottesidee*, pp. 35 ff.
111. Ibid., pp. 37 f.
112. Ibid., p. 34.
113. Cf. ibid., pp. 76 f. and Pls. I-II.
114. Alfred Steinmann: "Das kultische Schiff in Indonesien," p. 163; "Eine Geisterschiffmalerei aus Südborneo" (offprint), p. 6.
115. Id., "Das kultische Schiff," p. 163.
116. Ibid. In Japan, too, the mast and the tree are still believed today to be the "road to the gods"; cf. A. Slawik, "Kultische Geheimbünde der Japaner und Germanen," pp. 727-28, n. 10.
117. Steinmann, "Das kultische Schiff," p. 189.
118. But, as we should expect, many of the dead reach the sky (E. M. Loeb, *Sumatra*, p. 75). On the plurality of funerary itineraries, see below, pp. 355 ff.
119. Loeb, *Sumatra*, pp. 74-78.
120. As we have noted before, and shall show in more detail later, this phenomenon is general throughout the Malay world. Cf., for example, the Mohammedan influence in Toradja, Loeb, "Shaman and Seer," p. 61; complex Indian influences on the Malays, J. Cuisinier, *Danses magiques de Kelantan*, pp. 16, 90, 108, etc.; R. O. Winstedt, *Shaman, Saiva and Sufi: a Study of the Evolution of Malay Magic*, especially pp. 8 ff., 55 ff., and passim (Islamic influences, pp. 28 ff. and passim); id., "Indian Influence in the Malay World"; Munsterberger, *Ethnologische Studien*, pp. 83 ff. (Indian influences in Indonesia); Hindu influences in Polynesia, E. S. C. Handy, *Polynesian Religion*, passim; H. M. and N. K. Chadwick, *The Growth of Literature*, III, *303 ff.*; W. E. Mühlmann, *Arioi und Mamaia. Eine ethnologische, religionssoziologische und historische Studie uber polynesische Kultbünde*. pp. 177 ff. (Hindu and Buddhist influences in Polynesia). But we must not lose sight of the fact that these influences have usually altered only the *expression* of magico-religious life; that, in any case, they have not *created* the great mystico-cosmological schemas with which we are concerned in this study.
121. Loeb, *Sumatra*, p. 124.
122. Ibid., pp. 150 ff. The author notes (p. 154) the similarity between this complex of Niassan infernal mythology and the ideas of the

Indian Naga peoples. The comparison could be extended to other aboriginal peoples of India; we are dealing with vestiges of what has been called the Austroasiatic civilization, shared by the pre-Aryan and pre-Dravidian peoples of India and the majority of the aboriginal peoples of Indochina and the Indian Archipelago. On some of its characteristics, cf. Eliade, *Yoga: Immortality and Freedom,* pp. 344 ff.

3

The Presence of Spirits in Magic and Madness

RICHARD NOLL

> Everyone may educate and regulate his imagination so as
> to come thereby into contact with spirits, and be taught
> by them.
>
> Paracelsus, *Philosophia sagax*

One of the most common mistakes that many people make about shamanism is to regard it as a rare, exotic, perhaps even endangered species of human endeavor: an archaic anomaly, a vestige of the silent, ancient origins of our sacred life. Shamanism is often grandiosely imagined as a freak of cultural evolutionary history, a one-of-a-kind phenomenon, totally unlike other sacred traditions of humankind. It is written about as if it exists in some magical space outside of time, a realm of human experience not directly accessible to the "civilized" individual of today. Nothing could be farther from the truth.

Shamanism shares certain core characteristics with esoteric traditions throughout history. These have appeared in all known societies, including ours today. The distinguished scholar of comparative religions, Mircea Eliade, had this in mind when he wrote that "shamanism is the most archaic and most widely distributed occult tradition" (Eliade 1976:56). Shamans are, and always have been, human beings, and no matter how "simple" or "primitive" their society compared to ours, no matter how bizarre or magical their exploits, there is no essential experience of these men and women that has not been reported by individuals in our own Western European culture at one time or another. Nor, for that matter, is there any experience of shamans that cannot be taught to individuals such as you and me through careful training, if we are willing.

An example of such a universal human experience that is central to the practice of shamanism is the one that Paracelsus wrote about in the 16th century—contacting and engaging in dialogues with "spirits." This is a common experience, so widespread that it is perhaps fundamental in some way to what it means to be a human being. Every culture generates its own folklore about encounters between humans and extramundane entities (whether called "spirits," "gods," "deities," "angels," "demons," "ghosts," "apparitions," "fairies," or whatever). In fact, most people will find that someone among their relatives or ancestors has had a personal encounter with spirits, even if they themselves have not been jolted in the stillness of the night by such an experience.

What, then, are "spirits"? Cross-culturally, "spirits" are subjectively described as those transpersonal forces that we experience as moving in us or through us but are not entirely moved *by* us. This means that these (usually) personified forces or agencies are autonomous entities with their own agendas. Generally they cannot be contacted and engaged while we are in an ordinary state of waking consciousness, but are more clearly seen when we are in altered states. Dreams are the most common altered state in which they appear. How many of us have been visited by images of the dead in our dreams, or by mythological figures who have come to show us new paths?

Spirits are an incontestable part of humankind's "experienced reality," and, regardless of what their "ultimate reality" is, cross-culturally they seem to represent *the forces of transformation* that can either enhance growth or inflict illness or even death. Therefore, they are by their very nature both good and evil, both guides and deceptors, both healers and destroyers, the creators of life and the servants of death. To seek out these transformative powers willingly, as the shaman does, brings one into intimate contact with the secrets of existence itself. To open one's soul to these double-edged forces is thereby to transform oneself. Thus, "spirits" can be thought of as ego-alien energy currents that step forward from the shadows of the "not-I" to introduce new information to the individual who cannot access this information while in an ordinary state of waking consciousness.

The shaman intentionally induces these altered states called "ecstasies," "trances," or "visions" in order to contact and manipulate spirits for distinct purposes. Shamans are therefore known as both "masters of trance" and "masters of spirits." Spirits are employed to effect changes in the shaman himself or in others (as in healing), or to make changes in or receive information about the outer physical world. This latter function of spirits is a common characteristic of *magic* (Mauss 1972 [1950]). A more formal definition of shamanism is an ecstatic healing tradition which at its core is concerned with the techniques for inducing, maintaining, and interpreting the vivid experiences of enhanced mental imagery that occur in the deliberately induced altered states of consciousness in the shaman.

The key to the esoteric training of the novice shaman—and, as we shall see, of the novices of many magico-religious traditions worldwide—is the development of enhanced skills in mental imagery. There are many self-help books on "creative visualization" on the market today, and some of these offer tips to entering the imaginal realm. In shamanism, the development of visual imagery seems to be of particular importance, although there is an auditory component developed as well.

Shamanic training in such "vision cultivation" is a two-phase process. First, the neophyte is trained to increase the *vividness* of his internal visual imagery through various psychological and physiological techniques. Many of them are considered extreme by our culture's standards: pain stimulation, hypoglycemia and dehydration, forced hypermotility such as long periods of dancing, acoustic stimulation (particularly drumming), seclusion and restricted mobility, sleep deprivation, hyperventilation, and the ingestion of hallucinogens. Practicing any of these techniques would induce an alteration in one's state of consciousness. Experimental studies in psychology have shown that mental imagery can become so vivid that it can block out the awareness of normal visual perception. It is almost as if the vibrant world within becomes so bright that it blocks out the light from the world around one.

Once the novice can experience vivid "life-like" imagery, a

second phase of training begins, aimed at increasing control over internal imagery. Shamans engage and interact with the visionary contents and learn to master spirits in this way. As the ethnologist Czaplicka (1914:179) notes in a study of Siberian shamanism, "the mental part of the training consists in coming into contact with the right spirits, i.e., with the spirits who are to be the shaman's protectors in his shamanistic practice."

There are numerous reports of the transformation of the shaman's eyes, or of the development of an "inner" or "spiritual sight," which comes as a result of the imagery enhancement training. Among the Australian Aborigines such training is aimed at the development of the "strong eye." The anthropologist A.P. Elkin (1977 [1945]:49) reveals that, "an important faculty which the 'clever men' possess and which is assiduously trained, is the 'strong eye'. . . . to possess the 'strong eye' is to have the faculty of seeing spirits, of the living and of the dead." A Nganasan Samoyed shaman of Siberia reports that in his initiatory vision a spirit "blacksmith" dismembered him and also "changed his eyes; and that is why, when he shamanizes, he does not see with these bodily eyes but with these mystical eyes" (Siikala 1978:184). The gaze of a shaman's eyes is often described as uncomfortably intense, almost as if a focused inner fire within the shaman is directed from his eyes and pierces the shadowy depths of others.

An impressive account of shamanic initiation among the Iglulik Inuit of the Hudson Bay area is found in the Arctic adventures of the explorer Knud Rasmussen (1929). To become a shaman *(angakok)*, one must first acquire the experience of "lightening" or "enlightenment," which gives the novice an inner or spiritual sight that he did not have before.

> It consists of a mysterious light which the shaman suddenly feels in his body inside his head, within the brain, an inexplicable searchlight, a luminous fire, which enables him to see in the dark, both literally and metaphorically speaking, for he can now, even with closed eyes, see through darkness and perceive things and coming events which are hidden from others: thus they look into the future and into the secrets of others.
> The first time a young shaman experiences this light. . . . he sees far ahead of him through mountains, exactly as if the

earth were one great plain, and his eyes could reach to the end of the earth. Nothing is hidden from him any longer; not only can he see things far, far away, but he can also discover souls, stolen souls, which are either kept concealed in far, strange lands or have been taken up or down to the Land of the Dead (Rasmussen 1929:112-113).

Michael Harner (1980:22-24), in his fascinating guidebook to shamanic practice for members of our own culture, describes this kind of vision as "shamanic enlightenment."

It is clear from the above passage, as in others, that besides the development of the ability to see spirits, an ability for clairvoyance is also strengthened by learning to use one's own vivid internal mental imagery. This talent of shamans is now being verified in parapsychological experiments, which seem to indicate that individuals can score higher on clairvoyant tasks if they are in a relaxed, slightly altered state of consciousness that is conducive to increasing the vividness of one's own internal mental imagery (George and Krippner 1984). Are modern scientists finally catching up with the ancient shamans?

Guardian Powers and Spirit Teachers

Spiritual guides and teachers, imaginal gurus who appear to the spiritual seeker—these are ancient human experiences that have endured the span of centuries and are the legacy of every society known to man. The shamans certainly know them. Paracelsus seemed to know them, as have many other seekers in Western European culture, as we shall see.

Humankind has traditionally consulted extramundane entities for expanded knowledge and empowerment, for they are traditionally considered "sources of wisdom" (see Achterberg 1985) that are transpersonal and able to convey crucial information beyond the normal constraints of space and time. Guardian spirits, angels, deceased ancestors, natural deities have all been contacted through the occult rituals of many traditions. The practitioner usually initiates dialogues with spiritual entities by first inducing an altered state of consciousness, which allows these "invisible guests" to be seen and heard (see Watkins 1986). However, in some instances it is *they* who knock first on the doors of imaginal perception. Called or not called, they offer symbolic potential for transformation, whether for oneself, for others, or for desired changes in the physical environment.

Thus, instruction from spirits can facilitate spiritual transformation, and such "guardian spirits" or "spirit guides and teachers" are invoked by the shaman/practitioner, who believes he is tapping into the collective repository of the wisdom of our species. These beings are not imaginary in the sense of being not real, pure fantasy, or artificially made up. They are *imaginal*, existing in a realm of experience in which they inhabit a reality of their own, a *mundus imaginalis* or "imaginal world," as Henri Corbin (1972) deems it, which is co-existent with the mundane experiential world of our ordinary state of waking consciousness. Imaginal beings are part of our experienced reality and have probably been so since the birth of human consciousness.

The transmission of cultural tradition and other practical guidance from master shamans is a necessary component of the training of the apprentice in many cultures. However, almost universally the most important teachings are considered to come from spirit guides and teachers. In Siberian shamanism "according to the shamanic view the novice acquires knowledge from the spirits. Thus during the period of initial contacts the spirits function above all as teachers" (Siikala 1978:228). During his travels in Siberia at the turn of the century, the ethnographer Jochelson (1905:47) met two Koryak shamans who reported that, while in solitude, "the spirits appear to them in visible form, endow them with power, and instruct them." Michael Harner (1980:96) gives a good phenomenological account of how such guardian spirits or "power animals" have traditionally been consulted by shamans for healing and divinatory purposes, and he provides detailed instructions for those who are interested in following the way of the shaman on how we may be able to do the same.

The novice shaman draws upon the power of his protective guardian spirit whom he meets, either in animal or human form, in his initiatory visions. This spirit helps him gain access to the power of other "helping" or "tutelary" spirits whom he commands to help him in healing and divinatory rituals. These tutelary spirits are believed to be necessary for the successful accomplishment of magical procedures; without these spirit-assistants, the shaman can do nothing.

In many initiatory visions, a common theme is the narrative of how the novice shaman enters an altered state and begins a visionary journey after meeting his guardian spirit in human or animal form. He is led by this guardian spirit through the imaginal "lower world" in order to learn the arcane arts of shamanism. Often the novice is shown or given items, and new imaginal terrains are revealed. An example of such an account (and they are rare) can be found in the Siberian Nganasan shaman Sereptie Dyarouskin's initiatory visions as reported to the Soviet ethnographer A.A. Popov (which has been reprinted in full by Siikala [1978:175-183] in her book *The Rite-Technique of the Siberian Shaman*).

According to the report, the young aspirant slides down the roots of a sacred tree and follows his guardian spirit (who is in human form) into the lower world. The novice is then literally led by the hand of his guardian spirit from tent to tent in the spirit world, in order to learn about the particular "spirits" in each that cause the diseases of humankind. If we remember that "spirits" represent the forces of transformation, we can see how important it is for the shaman to become acquainted with these transpersonal powers. The young shaman saw a tent tied with rope:

> "And what is this tent tied around with a rope?" asked my companion. And I said, "When men go mad and become shamans, they are tied with this rope." (I was quite unconscious and tied up too.)

He becomes very frightened and questions whether he had been led to the right place. His guardian admonishes him:

> If I do not lead you to see the spirits, how could you make magic for the insane? If you find the spirit madness, you will begin to shamanize, initiating new shamans. You must be shown the ways of all diseases.

After leading his charge to the last of the nine tents, the guardian leaves the novice to journey alone, for he must now put the knowledge he has gained to use and prove that he is a true shaman.

Sometimes the spiritual guides and teachers sought for knowledge are dead ancestors. This was true of the Ghost Dance revitalization movement among the American Indians in the 1890s in which rituals involving visionary journeys to the Upperworld were conducted for the purpose of consulting with spiritual ancestors. In another chapter in this anthology, the anthropologist Larry Peters recounts how the Tamang shaman Bhirendra of Nepal was visited in his dreams by his deceased grandfather, who later became an "internal guru" for him when he underwent the shamanic initiation process.

Madness

Until recently, it had long been believed by many scholars that shamans suffered from chronic mental illness. That is, that the bizarre experiences that they report were nothing more than the ravings of florid psychotics, and that the "primitive" societies in which they lived were too ignorant to recognize such psychopathology and instead institutionalized it into a religious social role. I demonstrated in an earlier paper (Noll 1983) that this "schizophrenia metaphor" of shamanism is unfounded. Scholars were viewing human experience narrowly through what I call the "abnormal/normal dichotomy," the "either/or" box into which every human experience had to neatly fit.

Harner (1980:48) reports that among people in shamanic cultures there is an implicit understanding in everyday conversation of the types of experiences that can occur in the ordinary state of consciousness and those that can occur only in the "shamanic state of consciousness." Western interpreters' misunderstanding of this "given" often saw shamanic accounts as similar to the hallucinations and delusions of schizophrenics. Devoid of the personal experiences of altered states, yet quite familiar with the altered states of the diagnostic manual, interpreters of the incredible sagas of shamans must indeed have seen them as psychotic, for they considered only experiences in an ordinary state of consciousness to be valid and mentally healthy. Yet the shaman exists in two worlds, and the validity of both is acknowledged by the shaman, whose mastery derives from his ability not to confuse the two.

Shamans "see" and "talk" to spirits; schizophrenics and other psychotics "hear voices" of spirits and sometimes "see" or "feel" them when they "shouldn't." What's the difference?

For the past several years I have been employed as a staff clinical psychologist in a state psychiatric hospital where I have daily contact with large numbers of both chronic and acute schizophrenics. For me, the psychiatric hospital is equivalent to the tent with the rope tied around it that Sereptie Dyarouskin's guardian spirit led him to. It is the place where I have been led in my apprenticeship to learn the origins and ways of the spirits of madness. From this experience I can say without any reservations whatsoever that the transformational processes in shamans and psychotics are clearly not the same.

Volition is the key difference: the shaman actively seeks out the spirits in deliberately induced altered states of consciousness, which is only a part-time activity, as he must maintain full social and occupational functioning. The person undergoing a psychosis is victimized by the voices, usually mercilessly criticized and mocked by them. Sometimes they tell the unfortunate person to commit suicide. Although, as Eugen Bleuler observed in his classic work *Dementia Praecox; or the Group of Schizophrenias* (1911), schizophrenics can temporarily stop or block out the voices by shouting or clapping their hands, they inevitably return to haunt the patient.

This leads to the question of whether these "voices" that plague the mentally ill are the handiwork of malevolent spirits. From the shamanic point of view, they undoubtedly are. However, from the psychological point of view they are "splinter psyches," as C.G. Jung would call them, dissociated bits of the personality. Each has an allotment of consciousness all its own which serves particular functions. The assumption is that the disunity of consciousness is not inconsistent with the unity of self.

One interesting finding to ponder is a hypnosis study of 45 psychiatric patients (Bliss, Larson and Nakashima 1983) reporting auditory hallucinations in an acute ward. It was determined that 60 percent of the sample experienced auditory hallucinations after hypnotic inductions based upon the presence of "personalities." Many of these "personalities" even had names, and they were found to vary in numbers within each individual. "In hypnosis the 'voices' could be contacted, engaged in conversation, and would readily admit to being the culprit. Personalities included those bent on suicide and homicide, an assortment of friends and foes—even the Devil" (Bliss, et al. 1983:30). The shamanic and the psychological viewpoints would offer different causal explanations for this, but the phenomenology is familiar terrain for both the shaman and the psychologist and is beyond dispute.

Further Dialogues with Spirits:
Some "Civilized" Examples

Individuals within our own culture have employed techniques similar to those of the shamans in order to "see spirits" and establish dialogues with them. What is astonishing is how similar the experiences of these individuals have been to those in shamanic cultures.

"Spirit mastery" through learning to see and then command spirits is an ancient activity of our cultural ancestors. The earliest accounts of such activity are in Babylonian oil magic recipes in which a thumbnail or whole hand would be covered in oil so that the spirits could appear in the gloss. Plato records long conversations between Socrates and his *"daimon,"* an imaginal being who was his guardian spirit and teacher. The Spanish-born Arab theologian Ibn 'Arabi (1165-1240) "was, and never ceased to be, the disciple of an invisible master" named Khadir (Corbin 1969:32). Even Jesus was considered to "command spirits" by his contemporaries and was considered a magician, but this early image of "Jesus the magician" was apparently lost to us through the centuries until very recently (Smith 1978).

Shamanism is related to two Western occult traditions, alchemy and ritual or ceremonial magic, in that they, too, cultivate mental imagery in order to contact imaginal beings. Alchemy contained two distinct practices through which the alchemist could transmute base substances into "noble" ones, and thereby analogously transform his own inner nature as well. These were called the *meditatio* and the *imaginatio.* "Meditation" for the alchemists was the practice of imaginal dialogues with one's invisible guests. A "Lexicon of Alchemy" from the year 1622 defines the *meditation* as follows:

> Meditation: The name of an Internal Talk of one person with another who is invisible, as in the invocation of the Deity, or

communion with one's self, or with one's Good Angel (cited in Jung 1970 [1955]:497).

The ancient alchemists called their brand of mental imagery cultivation the *imaginatio*. European alchemical texts speak of "seeing with the eyes of the spirit or the understanding" (Jaffee 1971:58), which seems to indicate that the eyes of the alchemists, like the shamans, were "changed" in some way too, or that an inner or spiritual sight was developed. Through dreams and visions, the alchemists could study the vital transformative processes first hand and thereby quicken and perfect the work of nature, as well as transform themselves. The *imaginatio* also meant meeting spirit guides during visionary journeys. For example, notice how similar the account of Zosimos, a Gnostic alchemist of the 3rd century A.D., is to shamanic accounts. In his vision-dream Zosimos climbs up a lofty staircase and has the following experiences:

> And again I beheld the divine and holy bowl-shaped altar, and I saw a priest clothed in a white robe reaching to his feet, who was celebrating these terrible mysteries, and I said: "Who is this?" And the answer came: "This is the priest of the inner sanctuaries. It is he who changes the bodies into blood, makes the eyes clairvoyant, and raises the dead" (cited in Jung 1967 [1954]:63).

Ritual or ceremonial magic is a Western occult tradition which utilizes visions to contact and manipulate "spirits" for divinatory and psychokinetic purposes and empowerment. Although its roots extend far back into pagan antiquity, it reached its ascendancy in classical, medieval, and Renaissance Europe, only to virtually disappear for several centuries. The present popularity of ritual magic can be traced to its rebirth in the French occult revival of the mid-1800s and to the founding of the Hermetic order of the Golden Dawn in Britain in the 1880s.

In ritual magic, imaginal beings are summoned when the ritual magician or *magus* enters a visionary altered state induced by elaborate rituals which conjure or invoke "spirits," "gods," "demons," or "apparitions." Our familiar image of Faust standing within the protection of his magic circle, adorned in a robe covered with apotropaic symbols to keep the conjured entity safely beyond the circle, a book of spells in one hand and a sword or magic wand in the other, is based upon the ritual magician or magus. Again, notice the similarity between ritual magic and shamanism in this discussion of spirit mastery from a Renaissance *grimoire* or magical "book of experiments":

> Yet if, however, the Inferior Spirits be disobedient, you shall call their supervisors, and remind them of the oaths which they have taken unto you, and of the chastisement which awaiteth the breaking of such vows.
>
> And immediately, on beholding your steadfastness, they will obey you; but should they not, you ought then to invoke your Guardian Angel, whose chastisement they will quickly feel (Mathers 1974:102).

Both magus and shaman consult the spirits of the dead in visionary states for divinatory and other purposes. However, during the Middle Ages this exercise was called "necromancy" and was a heretical crime punished by death.

Freud and Jung as Shamans/Magicians

A curious fact has recently emerged about Sigmund Freud, the father of the great 20th century system of magical healing—psychoanalysis. Freud owned a large collection of classical Greek, Roman, Oriental, and Egyptian antiquities. On his desk were arranged three rows of statuettes, including a tiny toy porcupine, all of whom stared at Freud with ancient eyes while he wrote at his desk. On a small table to the right of the desk sat an antique statue of a Chinese scholar. According to the Freud family's housekeeper Paula, Freud—the paragon of the triumph of reason over the irrational—would greet this Chinese statue each day when he came into his study to write (Engleman 1976:64). Furthermore, a Freud family associate recently revealed a more intimate relationship between Freud and his statuettes:

> "The artificats weren't only decorative. He used some of them to help him to write," [the associate] explained in hushed tones as he stood near the desk. "He used to hold one in his hand and sometimes, when it was time to go and eat dinner, he would take the artifact with him to the table. He used it as an inspiration, to help him develop and retain a train of thought" (reported in *The Philadelphia Inquirer*, 2 August 1986).

What Freud may have been practicing—consciously or unconsciously—was an ancient form of magic in which consecrated statues representing spirits or transpersonal powers would engage the magician in imaginal dialogues and supply him with invaluable knowledge. Such magical practices were well known in ancient Egypt, Greece, and Rome, and the very statuettes that Freud owned may have been used for such practices by their contemporaries.

C.G. Jung met with a guardian spirit in visionary states who supplied him with insights, and in this regard "he was like a shaman who, having been given a special vision, translated it into terms meaningful for his tribe" (Staude 1981:60). The guardian's name was Philemon—an ancient Gnostic figure who appeared to Jung as an old man with a long white beard, the horns of a bull, and the wings of a kingfisher. Jung painted a portrait of him, with wings spread, on the wall over his bed in the austere tower he built in Bollingen, his home. In his autobiography, Jung writes:

> Philemon and the other figures of my fantasies brought home to me the crucial insight that there are things in the psyche which I do not produce, but which produce themselves and have their own life. Philemon represented a force which was not myself. In my fantasies I had conversations with him, and he said things which I had not consciously thought. For I observed clearly that it was he who spoke, not I. He said I treated thoughts as if I generated them myself, but in his view thoughts were like animals in the forest, or people in a room, or birds in the air, and added, "If you should see people in a room, you would not think that you had made those people, or that you were responsible for them." It was he who taught me psychic objectivity, the reality of the psyche. Through him the distinction was clarified between myself and the object of my thought. He confronted me in an objective manner, and I understood that there is something in me which can say things that I do not know and do not intend, things which may even be directed against me.
>
> Psychologically, Philemon represented superior insight. He was a mysterious figure to me. At times he seemed quite real, as if he were a living personality. I went walking up and down the garden with him, and to me he was what the Indians call a guru (Jung 1963:183).

Jung recognizes the psychotherapeutic implications of contact with the imaginal world—whatever the ultimate reality of its beings. In a letter to the Adlerian psychotherapist Fritz Künkel, he writes:

> In actual practice one finds oneself again and again in the position of having to make do with the terminological crudities of science. I would like to draw a radical distinction between psychology as a science and psychology as a technique. In practice I have no compunction, if the case seems to be sufficiently certain, in speaking simply of spirits. (Jung 1973:II, 432-433).

And so, Jung and the shamans speak the same universal language.

References

Bleuler, E. 1930 [1911]. *Dementia praecox, or the group of schizophrenias.* New York: International Universities Press.

Bliss, E.L.; M.D. Esther; and S. R. Nakashima. 1983. Auditory hallucinations and schizophrenia. *Journal of Nervous and Mental Disease* 171:30-33.

Corbin, H. 1969. *Creative imagination in the Sufism of Ibn 'Arabi.* Translated by R. Mannheim. Princeton: Princeton University Press.

Corbin, H. 1972. *Mundus imaginalis,* or The imaginary and the imaginal. *Spring: An annual of archetypal psychology and Jungian thought,* pp. 1-19.

Czaplicka, M.A. 1969 [1914]. *Aboriginal Siberia: A study in social anthropology.* Oxford: Clarendon Press.

Eliade, M. 1964. *Shamanism: Archaic techniques of ecstasy.* Princeton: Princeton University Press.

Eliade, M. 1976. "The occult and the modern world," in *Occultism, witchcraft and cultural fashions.* Chicago: University of Chicago Press.

Elkin, A.P. 1977 [1945]. 2nd edition. *Aboriginal men of high degree.* New York: St. Martin's Press.

Engleman, E. 1976. *Berggasse 19: Sigmund Freud's home and office, Vienna 1938.* Chicago: University of Chicago Press.

George, L. & S. Krippner. 1984. "Mental imagery and psi phenomena: a review," in *Advances in parapsychological research, vol. 4.* Edited by S. Krippner. Jefferson, N.C.: McFarland.

Harner, M. 1980. *The way of the shaman: A guide to power and healing.* New York: Harper and Row.

Jaffe, A. 1971. "Alchemy," in *From the life and work of C.G. Jung*. New York: Harper Colophon.

Jochelson, W. 1905. *The Koryak*. Memoirs of the American Museum of Natural History 10.

Jung, C.G. 1963. *Memories, dreams, reflections*. Recorded and edited by A. Jaffe. Translated by R. and C. Winston. New York: Vintage Books.

Jung, C.G. 1967 [1954]. "The visions of Zosimos," in *The collected works of C.G. Jung*, vol. 13, *Alchemical Studies*. Edited by H. Read, M. Fordham, G. Adler, and W. McGuire. Translated by R.F.C. Hull. Princeton: Princeton University Press.

Jung, C.G. 1970 [1955]. *The collected works of C.G. Jung*, vol. 14, *Mysterium Coniunctionis: An inquiry into the separation and synthesis of psychic opposites in alchemy*.

Jung, C.G. 1973. *Letters, II:1951-1961*. Edited by G. Adler. Translated by R.F.C. Hull.

Mathers, S.L. 1974. *The sacred book of Abre-melin the Mage*. Hyde Park, N.Y.: University Books.

Mauss, M. 1971 [1950]. *A General theory of magic*. Translated by R. Brain. London: Routledge and Kegan Paul.

Noll, R. 1983. Shamanism and schizophrenia: A state-specific approach to the "schizophrenia metaphor" of shamanic states. *American Ethnologist* 10:443-459.

Noll, R. 1985. "Mental imagery cultivation as a cultural phenomenon: The role of visions in shamanism." *Current Anthropology* 26:443-461.

Rasmussen, K. 1929. *Intellectual culture of the Iglulik Eskimos*. Report of the Fifth Thule Expedition, 1921-1924. (7) 1.

Siikala, A.L. 1978. *The rite-technique of the Siberian shaman*. Helsinki: Suomalainen Tiedeakatemia.

Smith, M. 1978. *Jesus the magician*. San Francisco: Harper & Row.

Staude, J.R. 1981. *The adult development of C.G. Jung*. Boston: Routledge and Kegan Paul.

Watkins, M. 1986. *Invisible guests: The development of imaginal dialogues*. Hillsdale, N.J.: The Analytic Press.

4

Crazy Wisdom: The Shaman as Mediator of Realities

MARY SCHMIDT

I have seen things as if someone opens a door and the door is closed. I have had nightmares, but not ordinary ones. I have seen myself introduced through a hole in the air, and I went through an immense, immense void. I have felt numbness in all my body as if my hands were huge but I could not grasp; I could not hold up my hand.

Eduardo, a Peruvian curandero

Anthropologists, mental health practitioners, and shamans themselves have contributed heavily to the literature describing and explaining shamanism. I wish to add my speculative analysis to the group, dealing with the shaman as a member of a special population of category makers and breakers. Ideally, the spiritual and cognitive combine in these men and women to render them powerful healers of their society. Shamans become epistemological mediators; that is, as they discover their art, they learn how to bridge different realms of reality.

To most of us, there exists a clear distinction between products that we make (equipment, books) and those that exist in the world (human nature, gods). But as the anthropologist Michael Taussig (1980) wisely notes, "time, space, matter, cause, relation, human nature, and society itself are social products, created by man just as are the different types of tools, farming systems, clothes, houses, monuments, languages, myths, and so on, that mankind has produced since the dawn of human life" (Taussig

1980, 4). But to their participants, all cultures tend to present these categories as if they were not social products but elemental and immutable "givens." Anthropologists like Mary Douglas (1979) have noted that those things which seem to sit on the grey space between "made" and "found" are the subject of taboo and repressed from memory. When presented with something we believe to be unreal, we doubt our senses or our sanity.

Against the backdrop we call "normal" comes an uneasy growth. In early youth a budding shaman differs from his or her peers in certain general ways. Although the shaman's designated role differs across cultures, there is a group of family resemblances that seems ubiquitous. In the tribes I have examined, one aspect receives consensus, that shamans "are the unusually gifted or perceptive members of their communities" (Sharon 1978, 16). Not everyone can be a shaman, and not everyone would want to be because some of the things common to shamans' experiences are at least initially unpleasant. For one thing, odd or deformed children—like those born with teeth or with six fingers (Dioszegi 1960, 64)—often become shamans. Those who by nature are set apart from their peers may receive the shamanic calling: tormented by nightmares and possibly by others' cruelty, the shaman stands alone.

Spirits recognize these people as shamans even in their youth: Vilmos Dioszegi (1960) writes of how the spirits of dead shamans called "black spirits" (p. 57) mark a child for the profession. A budding Blackfoot shaman would be visited by "Always Visible" (an old man, the sun) along with the Moon Woman and the child Morningstar (Wissler 1911, 76). Often these visitations badly frighten the child. Even more unpleasantly, one could receive the calling through a particularly pernicious disease. Yet the spirits, if they spare the person's life, might decide the brush with death earns him or her a position analogous to theirs.

Even though the path is tortuous, some do wish to become shamans. Ironically, there seems to be no refusing if one is called. The words of a young Karagasy shaman from Siberia provide eloquent testimony:

> The little one, the little spirit used to come to me. He had flown into my mouth and then I used to recite shaman songs.

> When I had no more strength left to suffer, finally I agreed to
> become a shaman. And when I became a shaman, I changed
> entirely (Dioszegi 1960, 143).

No doubt the calling alarms a child, and many would be reluctant
to shoulder this demanding gift. Social isolation, a plague of odd
thoughts, and the likelihood of personality alteration all characterize the fledgling shaman's experience, yet there is an inevitability about the movement. Shamans-to-be encounter raw
glimpses of something numinous and demanding, some threat or
promise in their own landscape of dreams.

Then comes the initiation ceremony around the child's pre-teen
or early teen years. I speak here specifically of the male rite,
though there are rites for girls, and thus I will use the masculine
pronoun throughout. This ritual transition itself represents a liminal moment in the child's life, when he is separated from the
normal and enters a space of "anti-structure." Prior to initiation,
the shaman-child's potential accumulates, and he, much like his
peers, is full of unformed energy. Here, between childhood and
adulthood, things begin to change.

Victor Turner (1974) emphasizes the all-important liminal
stage of initiation, elaborating on the phenomenon outlined by
Van Gennep. During this period, the neophyte experiences separation from structure and stands in the bewildering space "betwixt and between the categories of ordinary social life. Symbols
and metaphors found in abundance in liminality represent various dangerous ambiguities of this ritual stage, since the classifi-
cations on which order normally depends are annulled or
obscured" (p. 273). For example, the frightened boys in initiation ceremonies are not only beaten and kept awake for days but
they are also presented with odd sights, like people wearing
animal heads and men dressed as women. The familiar categories
for organizing experience have broken down and do not fit the
situation.

Turner (1979) writes that liminality is the stage of reflection:

> Much of the grotesqueness and monstrosity of liminal *sacra*
> [culturally essential knowledge] may be seen to be aimed not
> so much at terrorizing or bemusing neophytes into submission
> or out of their wits as at making them vividly and rapidly
> aware of what may be called "factors" of their culture (p.
> 240).

In my mind, these basic "factors" or knowledge from one's culture are analogous to Levi-Strauss's (1979b) "gross constituents" of myth. In the liminal state, such social categories are juxtaposed in odd ways so that the child initiate becomes aware of them as merely mental constructs.

Any child encountering a confusion of his familiar order would emerge changed, but the shaman-to-be, I believe, might change in a unique sense. Let me use an example: Say society's "gross constituents" or basic categories of reality are like the cards of a tarot deck; each figure is charged with a meaning which shifts or reverses as its relation to other cards varies. Before initiation, an average child would probably see the more predictable arrangement of cards—the emperor and empress enthroned, the major arcana following each other in prescribed sequence. He would likely perceive only predictable and orderly reshuffling of these positions. But during the confused liminal stage, the emperor becomes dethroned, cups and swords take on their own bizarre life, familiar and comforting figures play bewildering roles. All is chaos and dismaying juxtaposition. Everything that the child holds to be true and natural is transformed. From this experience, gradual realization emerges for the future shaman. Because he is able to abstract the cultural elements in the confusion, the child learns to read the arrangement of his world. The final step—reintegration—comes when the child learns that the way his society lays out the deck is the "right" way, the way that best describes the real world for his people. For instance, I can remember being taught, like most Western children, that tiny germs cause diseases; this teaching, which rests on the implicit basis that mind and matter are separate, may explain why some have such difficulty accepting the idea that we shape our own health through imagery. Achterberg (1985) describes how a person translates a harmless sore throat into abscessed tonsils using dire mental imagery (pp. 76-77).

The shaman-to-be starts from a position similar to that of most children: the emperor and empress may be throned. But there are vivid dreams, premonitions of alternatives which haunt the child. Perhaps he keeps silent, as did the Peruvian shaman Eduardo:

> Eduardo did not know where to turn in coping with his unusual experiences. He was afraid people would think he was crazy if he confided in them. So he learned to keep his inner world

to himself, handling these frightening events to the best of his ability, alone and unsupported'' (Sharon 1979, 11).

This gifted child enters the liminal stage and is presented with the same sort of juxtapositions but, perhaps, he takes away something from the experience that is unlike other children's interpretations. When he sees a person's head poised on an animal's body, perhaps something familiar stirs. He begins to look not so much at the *thing* presented but at the underlying *process* of trying to identify it. He has had dreams about the undifferentiated nebula of existence (Deikman 1972). When he sees things that do not fit into familiar categories, he may make the conceptual leap to abstracting the process by which categories are made. That is, he may come to know that through differentiation (and suppression of such hybrids as are paraded around during initiation rites), the undifferentiated realm he has dreamt of is split to form society's "gross constituents" or "factors" of essential knowledge.

He has just witnessed his elders lifting the boundaries, which are so often taken as immovable, and putting them elsewhere. Other children, upon reintegration into society, forget the nature of that restructuring of categories and remember only their contents. But the shaman may take this knowledge of the continuum-division back with him. Here he makes a quantum leap and sees how arbitrary cultural distinctions are: he understands then that he may not only *read,* but also *write* society. He can enter the amorphous realm beyond categories and emerge with a structure different from his culture's conventional one.

When the time comes to reintegrate into society, the shaman takes this knowledge and uses it to direct his visions. As Sharon (1978) so eloquently writes, his "epistemological touchstone for reality was direct personal psychical experiences of the forces of nature" (p. 38), but that touchstone needs to be refined by knowledge of his surrounding culture's epistemology. The shaman's frightening experience, when coupled with his new knowledge of the arbitrariness of reality, becomes something different and more rewarding. He has the ability to take a magical flight, just as he did before; but now he can handle it. He knows how to come back from the intense liminality of the interstice and how to reintegrate his comprehension into his culture. He is a person who has been tested and then rewarded, as so many aboriginal images prove. For example, a Blackfoot shaman relates this tale:

> When I was a young man, I went up on Heart Butte and fasted and prayed for seven days. I was dressed in very old clothes and continually called upon the sun to have pity on me. At last, the sun appeared before me as a very old man, gave me a drum and one song (Wissler 1911, 72).

In sum, shamans earn the wings they need to return from their involuntary spiritual flights—the wings which allow them to make that journey at will. They achieve this through some revelation, most likely gained through initiation, of their society's methods of abstraction.

There is an interesting graphic analogy to the process of liminal separation and subsequent reintegration in the literature of Siberian shamans. Nachtigall (1970) writes of how a fledgling shaman is dismembered and his flesh cut into tiny pieces which are distributed among the spirits of sickness. "All must have their share because the future shaman can heal only the diseases caused by the spirits who have eaten parts of his body." The spirits come to reassemble his body and cover the skeleton with new flesh "and transform the candidate into a new shaman" (p. 318). The spirits destroy and break the shaman, yet he is reborn and returns to earth with the power to heal. No longer just torn, he becomes reintegrated, and is more powerful for his experience.

The shaman takes power from the undifferentiated realm and brings it back. Sharon (1978) writes,

> Probably the central concept of shamanism, wherever in the world it is found, is the idea of power. Simply stated, this is the notion that underlying all the visible forms in the world, animate and inanimate, there exists a vital essence from which they emerge and by which they are nurtured. Ultimately everything returns to this ineffable, mysterious, impersonal unknown. The varied religious expressions of humanity are attempts to develop a meaningful and/or practical relationship with this power (p. 49).

Richard Shweder (1979) has performed some thought-provoking experiments with Zinacanteco shamans of Chiapas, Mexico.

He presented shamans and others with a set of Rorschach-type blurry photos and told them that they may label the pictures according to the experimenter's categories (e.g., "this is: a shoe, a flower, a man") or may say "I don't know" if there is the slightest doubt. The shamans, unlike the control group, made up their own answers and refused to admit the defeat of not knowing. Shweder writes, "Shamans seem to have available to themselves their own construction categories, and remain relatively insensitive to the alternative categories provided by the experimenter" (p. 329). The shaman appears as an inner-directed individual, able to control his or her situation.

A person who has hallucinations and visions, and is torn and taken into the depths uncontrollably, may be classified loosely as schizophrenic. While a shaman is a person characterized by ecstasy—which the *Oxford Dictionary* defines as a "person out of his senses or place"—he has the ability to control himself. A shaman understands that real and unreal are not differences in kind but of degree, and therefore he can relate to his hallucinations without feeling his mind split. His category divisions are not as brittle as those of most people, who, when presented with something they "know" to be unreal, doubt their sanity. Nevill Drury (1978) writes,

> The shaman, confronted with the spectacle of a transcendental cosmic drama, could well be expected to lose complete control of his perceptive faculties, and be overcome by awe. However, it is precisely his ability to remain composed, even in his mythological confrontations, which distinguishes him from the schizophrenic. As Eliade says, the shaman is the *technician of the sacred*. His mystical journey is subject to will (p. 17).

So a shaman must tear insight from the spirits who have torn him, must demand a passage back through glory.

It is not enough to recognize that the way culture has its categories arranged is arbitrary; one must be psychologist or philosopher enough to recognize that the *process* of arranging is necessary. Undifferentiated reality is not a place in which anyone can survive for long. Even if one can conceptualize relativity, one must be strong willed, inner directed, and free enough to compose a life, and then trust that it is feasible. To have only half of this awareness, the awareness of relativity, is to be in psychological danger.

I have noted, so far, that the shaman comes to know ultimate undifferentiated reality through his ecstatic experience and to know cultural differentiation through his analytic ability; further, he understands the need to arrange the world. Now he gathers this knowledge and begins to work. As Turner (1974) writes, "Only those who know how to build know how to collapse what has been built" (p. 297). The shaman begins by collapsing his own structures, aiming for controlled rebirth, and then goes on to rearrange the mental surety of those around him in order to effect social cures.

Often the shaman goes through a vision-quest, seeking contact with his mythic ancestors. Ingestion of hallucinogens, sleep or food deprivation, and physical pain are all used to induce visions (Jilek 1982). The shaman utilizes these techniques, as Deikman (1972) phrases it, to "deautomatize." He writes, "Deautomatization may be conceptualized as the undoing of automatization, presumably by reinvesting actions and precepts with attention" (p. 33). Those visions the youth may have tried to ignore are invited back; he relinquishes his grip on solid "reality" and begins to work with his visions. Noll (1985) describes the shaman's training as mental imagery cultivation; the shaman is trained to increase first the vividness and then the controlledness of his visions, for these are his vehicles to the sacred.

Another way to characterize deautomatization is, as Castaneda's (1977) Don Juan says, as a method of "stopping the world." You must learn to "not-do," or conversely, must unlearn what to do. This practice proves a nice solid metaphor for focusing on the inter-categorical realms: Castaneda relates that Don Juan

> repeated over and over in a whisper in my right ear that 'to not do what I knew how to do' was the key to power. In the case of looking at a tree, what I knew how to do was to focus immediately on the foliage. The shadows of the leaves or the spaces in between the leaves were never my concern...but I became so immersed in the shadows of the leaves that by the time Don Juan stood up I could almost group the dark mass of shadows as effectively as I normally grouped the foliage. The total effect was startling (pp. 180-181).

Startling indeed, for young Carlos was getting a taste of anti-structure, the space where shamans work. These methods are employed so the shaman may cultivate ecstasy. As the Chukchee of Siberia poetically phrase it, shamanic ecstasy or *an.na'arkin,* means "he sinks" (Bogoras 1979). The shaman must learn how to sink without drowning.

Although he chases ecstasy in a seemingly methodical way, the shaman must embrace it emotionally and experientially. He is like a Zen monk who tries to break into a koan with intellectual tools, but finally, through mental exhaustion, realizes that thought is "an interference with the direct contact that yields essential knowledge through perception alone" (Deikman 1972, 29). The shaman has progressed from a child plagued by night terrors to a more analytically minded youth. In the final synthesis through deautomatization, he must fuse the spontaneity of his early visions with the control of his subsequent training.

The shaman must render his visions themselves into culturally utilizable form, partaking, as Drury (1978) holds, "of the cosmic dream of his own mythical heritage" (p. 27). In order to bring his power home to his people, he must become part of their mythology. Even while understanding the inchoate, undifferentiated cosmos, he must manipulate his people's familiar heavens. He should have one foot firmly in the here-and-now or he cannot act as a mediator between the two realms, for he will be lost in that one. He must combine the wild insanity of extra-mythos existence with the sane calmness of conformity. In Chogyam Trungpa's phrase, he should have "crazy wisdom." Trungpa (1981) writes:

> Crazy wisdom is absolute perceptiveness, with fearlessness and bluntness. Fundamentally, it is being wise, but not holding to particular doctrines or disciplines or formats. There aren't any books to follow. Rather, there is endless spontaneity taking place. There is room for being blunt, room for being open. That openness is created by the environment itself. In fact, at the level of crazy wisdom, all activity is created by the environment. The crazy wisdom person is just an activator, just one of the conditions that have evolved in the environment (p. 140).

As the quotation attests, a shaman type will know that his environment or society is invented and that he must become a creative force in this humanly created cosmology.

So he begins to mediate, to lay himself as a bridge between the here and the there. Another good visual metaphor arises: the shape of the shaman's tools indicates his position in cultural cosmology. For example, Eduardo works his healing and divination by means of a *mesa* or group of sacred objects, which he arranges in a specific way. He sets up these artifacts on a board, and then divides the board into different categories or realms. The person requiring his aid sits in front of the board across from Eduardo and the healer reads what the mesa is "saying." Sharon explicitly calls this mesa a "microcosm," and notes that Eduardo aims for creating equilibrium by maneuvering this small cosmos. He is the step between ultimate reality and social reality. "Oneness of the cosmos is achieved and Eduardo becomes the manifest 'center' by transcending the opposites at work in the cosmos and within his own being" (p. 64). The shaman himself may represent the cosmos: a Blackfoot shaman wears a robe embellished with the sun, moon and stars, much like a medieval wizard, and he is reputed to control weather (Wissler 1911:76). He may become the very image of his activity, the distilled essence of liminality, with his face hidden in a wilderness of hair and his clothes unkempt.

The shaman cures his people by taking them out of themselves, making his ecstasy contagious; the shaman, "with his experience of flight, with his control, can guide patients and carry them, take them out of the evil in which they find themselves" (Sharon 1978, 114). Knowing the continuum is split by arbitrary boundaries, he lifts the divisions and puts them elsewhere, initiating his people into a changed state. They get a healthy change of perspective, seeing through his eyes for a time. He makes them remember their well-buried glimpses of inter-categorical anomalies; he makes them forget their carefully tended divisions.

The shaman leads his people to the edge of madness, but does so carefully. He usually effects his changes through percussion. The drum, Potapov (1967) says, is his mount to the spirits. Tricks and "sleight of hand" are also employed, but this does not make him a charlatan. As Begoras (1979) notes, "If he is a fraud then so are they [the ones he helps]" (p. 302). That is, all of his ventriloquism, singing, and drumming are used to alter his audience: anything that works is fair game. Aside from specific cures, trance states can prove beneficial. Wiltkower, (1970), writes that

> there can be no doubt in anybody's mind that trance and pos-
> session states in the countries in which they play an important
> part of religious rituals have an important distress-relieving,
> integrative, adaptive function. As far as mental illness is con-
> cerned, they may be of prophylactic value (p. 60).

Because he is inner-directed and can impose form, the shaman can create miracles, as this segment from the Siberian Buryat myth of the first shaman shows:

> The shaman went to the house of the rich man, and he began
> to charm and enchant, but not as he should have done, begging
> God or the spirits for a boy, but creating a boy himself. He
> made the bones from stone, the flesh from clay, and the blood
> from the water of the river, and then he undertook to make the
> soul. He gathered seventy kinds of flowers, and prepared the
> soul of the little boy from these. Some time elapsed and a boy
> child was born of the rich man." (Dioszegi 1960, 110).

Shamans effect miracles by changing the structure of cause and effect.

Also, as Levi-Strauss (1979a) contends, the shaman may cure people by providing them with a mythic language in which to express pain and confusion. He notes that "the cure would consist...in making explicit a situation originally existing on the emotional level and in rendering acceptable to the mind pains which the body refuses to tolerate" (p. 323). Just as the psychoanalyst does, the shaman acts as protagonist in the drama and as a sympathetic listener. In inducing the patient to live out the myth, he uses metaphor to tap deep problems and lighten the mental anguish. Myth itself, Levi-Strauss (1979b) says, works toward mediating oppositions and makes all things possible. The shaman acts as cosmic trickster, bringing the past into the present, shuffling cause and effect, and mediating life and death. Myth maps the distance between what *does* exist and what *can* exist and renders shamans powerful dealers of this game. The shaman doesn't "learn" so much as create images, shaping forceful metaphors from his people's experience in order to give them a handle for the numinous.

Perhaps, as I speculate, when he puts himself in the realm of the gods, they lose their awesomeness for him. He recognizes that their home is not entirely different from his, that he too can do what they do. He may, paradoxically, become like the hero of Miguel de Unamuno's (1956) story "Saint Emmanuel the Good, Martyr," who is the perfect priest, an uncanny Christ-like figure devoted to giving his small village the promise of absolute salvation, and yet who is himself secretly an atheist. When at Easter he cries, "My God, my God, why hast Thou forsaken me?" the irony is chilling.

If this analysis is true—even at a subconscious and unrevealed level—why would the shaman use the image and language of spirits? I believe he does so because it is not enough to go to the realm of the numinous; he must bring back the knowledge to his people, and in doing so must use their symbols. In most cases, those symbols involve spirits. Also, being trained within his cultural context, he must use its language to explain things to himself, and so in a way is the most faithful believer. Yet there is a tension, almost a contradiction, between the sense in which he believes in the spirits' ontological distinctness and the manner in which he manipulates them. This is an ambiguity, but a creative one. He must act 'as if' they exist, and to do so, paradoxically, he must believe that they *do* exist, even as he recognizes his role in creating them.

Shamans are people with the strength to become vulnerable, the will to impose form, and the wit to translate their treasure into an understandable dream. As Brooke Medicine Eagle (1985) writes:

> . . . The seer, man of many faces,
> Clown and fool and wise man,
> Relates to us in puns
> The spaces between the worlds.

References

Achterberg, Jeanne. 1985. *Imagery in Healing: Shamanism and Modern Medicine.* Boston: New Science Library.

Bogoras, Waldermar. 1979. "Shamanistic Performance in the Inner Room." In *Reader in Comparative Religion.* Ed. W. Lessa and E. Vost. New York: Harper and Row.

Castaneda, Carlos. 1972. *Journey to Ixtlian: the Lessons of Don Juan.* New York: Pocket Books.

Deikman, Arthur J., 1972. "Deautomatization and the Mystic Experience." In *Altered States of Consciousness.* Ed. Charles Tart. New York: Anchor Books.

Dioszegi, Vilmos. 1960. *Tracing Shamans in Siberia: the Story of an Ethnographical Research Expedition.* Trans. A. J. Babo. New York: Humanities Press Inc.

Douglas, Mary. 1979. "The Abominations of Leviticus." In *Reader in Comparative Religions.* Ed. W. Lessa and E. Vogt. New York: Harper and Row.

Drury, Nevill. 1978. *Don Juan, Mescalito, and Modern Magic: the Mythology of Inner Space.* London: Routledge and Kegan Paul.

Jilek, Wolfgang G. 1982. *Indian Healing: Shamanic Ceremonialism in the Pacific Northwest Today.* British Columbia: Hammond House Publishing Ltd.

Levi-Strauss, Claude. 1979a. "The Effectiveness of Symbols." In *Reader in Comparative Religion.* Ed. W. Lessa and E. Vogt. New York: Harper and Row.

Levi-Strauss, Claude. 1979b. "The Structural Study of Myth." In *Reader in Comparative Religion.* Ed. W. Lessa and E. Vogt. New York: Harper and Row.

Medicine Eagle, Brooke. 1985. "Shaman." In *Shaman's Drum.* Summer 1985.

Nachtigall, Horst. 1976. "The Culture-Historical Origin of Shamanism." In *The Realm of the Extra-Human: Agents and Audiences.* Ed. A. Bharati. Paris: Mouton Publishers.

Noll, Richard. 1985. "Mental Imagery Cultivation as a Cultural Phenomenon: the Role of Visions in Shamanism." In *Current Anthropology.* V. 26:4. pp. 443-463.

Potapov, C. P. 1976. "Certain Aspects of Study of Siberian Shamanism." In *Realm of the Extra-Human: Agents and Audiences.* Ed. A. Bharati. Paris: Mouton Publishers.

Sharon, Douglas, 1978. *Wizard of the Four Winds: A Shaman's Story.* New York: The Free Press.

Shweder, Richard. 1979. "Aspects of Cognition in Zinacanteco Shamans: Experimental Results." In *Reader in Comparative Religion.* Ed. W. Lessa and E. Vogt. New York: Harper and Row.

Taussig, Michael T. 1980. *The Devil and Commodity Fetishism in South America.* Chapel Hill: University of North Carolina Press.

Trungpa, Chogyam. 1981. *Journey Without Goal: the Tantric Wisdom of the Buddha.* London: Prajna Press.

Turner, Victor W. 1974. *Dramas, Fields and Metaphors.* New York: Cornell University Press.

Turner, Victor W. 1979. "Betwixt and Between: the Liminal Period in Rites de Passage." In *Reader in Comparative Religion.* Ed. W. Lessa and E. Vogt. New York: Harper and Row.

Unamuno, Miguel de. 1956. *Abel Sanchez and Other Stories.* Chicago: University of Chicago Press.

Wissler, Clark. 1911. *The Social Life of the Blackfoot Indians.* New York: American Museum of Natural History, Anthropological Papers, 7. Part 1.

5

Shamanism: An Archaic and/or Recent System of Beliefs

MIHÁLY HOPPÁL

1. Recent Developments in the Study of Shamanism

The last two decades have seen extensive conceptual and analytical debate about shamanism. This paper will trace the specific circumstances which cause us to use the concept of shamanism in a very wide sense, and will also outline the reasons for which it became such a prominent term in anthropological research. Shamanism, as a field of interest in ethnology, has a long history; however, there is no agreement among scholars as to the main features of shamanism among different peoples of the world.

The purpose of this paper is twofold: to give an overview of recent studies about shamanism, especially of those unknown to Western scholars, and to redefine the notion of shamanism using the concept of *belief system*. This redefinition is necessary because the social sciences tend to constitute rather than describe the reality under investigation. The symbolic usage of terms such as *mana, taboo, totem* and *shamanism* (53) could be considered an initiatory (shamanic) sickness of our scholarship.

To begin with an account of recent publications on shamanism in Siberia and Eurasia, one should first mention theoretical works by the German scholars Johansen and Motzki 1977 (43, 57), monographs by Backman and Hultkrantz on Lapp Shamanism (10), and a comprehensive study by Anna-Lena Siikala on "The Rite Technique of the Siberian Shaman" (65), who argues that *role-taking* should be regarded as the basis of the shaman's communication with spirits. The structure of seance defines the form of this communication.

In 1978 a collection of studies entitled *Shamanism in Siberia,* edited by Diószegi and Hoppál, was published by the Hungarian Academy of Sciences (see Oinas' review, *UAJb* 54.163, 1982). The essays were written by Hungarian and Soviet scholars, with the exception of three papers by Krader, Joki and Hultkrantz. This book enriched Siberian research with new data and ideas, giving, for example, detailed analyses of shamanism among the Buryat and the Baraba Turks (50, 18). After the untimely death of Diószegi in 1972, the fieldwork he had begun in Siberia during the sixties (16) was continued by scholars who survived him. In 1981 a symposium on Eurasian shamanism was organized by Hoppál, in cooperation with V. N. Basilov of the Ethnographic Institute of the Soviet Academy of Sciences. Specialists who attended agreed that new data are available, and that field materials from Siberia, the *'locus classicus'* of shamanism, provide a basis for comparisons with the results of recent field work outside Siberia. The proceedings of this symposium will be published (37), and some of the results will be quoted in this paper.

A colloquium organized by Roberte Hamayon on shamanism was held in Paris in 1981, and a year later a symposium on "Shamanism among Lowland South American Indians: A Problem of Definition" organized by Joanna Overing Kaplan took place in Manchester, England. Thus, a boom in shamanic research exists not only in Western Europe but also in the Soviet Union. It should not be necessary to mention the achievements of Russian scholarship; it is regrettable that the findings of this scientific research have been largely neglected by Western colleagues. One of the reasons for this neglect is the language barrier, the other reason is ideological: Western scholars are embarrassed by the anti-religious terminology used in Soviet publications. Within the Soviet Union, however, detailed studies have been published on shamanism, mainly at a theoretical level, which treat it as a *religious* phenomenon of the *past*. It seemed for a time that shamanism had disappeared, at least according to the slogans of the so-called "newspaper folklore." Scholarly publications which might correct this view were printed in a very limited number of copies in the USSR.

At the beginning of the 20th century the collectors of shamanic texts who described first-hand encounters with Siberian shamans were not trained ethnologists, at least in the beginning. They were political exiles, such as L. Sternberg, W. Bogoraz, W. Jochelson, and N. A. Vitashevsky, who during long periods in Siberia became experts in local tradition (65.80-82). Then, during the fifties, Siberian shamans went into self-imposed seclusion, sometimes because of persecution, and continued their activities in hidden ways. Professional anthropologists working for one of the ethnographic institutes of the Soviet Academy of Sciences met acting shamans during their repeated long-term fieldwork, but the texts they collected and the names of the shamans were kept secret in the central archives. The seventies were a turning point in this respect, as a number of new publications appeared in which shamanism was analyzed as an early form of religion or of social consciousness, both terms being code names for shamanism. Thus, shamanism was no longer a superstitious old faith (staraya vera) alien to the communist ideology.

Especially valuable works were published on the history and terminology of Buryat shamanism and a monograph on the early forms of religion among the Turk peoples of Siberia (56, 54, 2) also appeared. These collections of essays include excellent descriptions and materials concerning contemporary forms of Siberian shamanism. Acting shamans were met by anthropologists during the sixties and even the seventies among the Nenets, Selkups, Nganasans, Kets, Nivkhs and other aboriginal peoples of Siberia (74). Investigations into more modern forms of shamanism are of great methodological importance because only new, sophisticated and well-prepared methods of inquiry will help us to clarify old doubts and misunderstandings about shamanism.

1.2 Field Studies—Shamanism in Eurasia Today

Despite the fact that ethnological literature spoke of shamanism as if it were obliterated, it has turned out from Soviet and other publications of the past years that scholars have met acting shamans all over Eastern Eurasia. Photos, tape recordings, and even films were made about them. There is, for example, a two-hour long film at the Moscow Ethnographic Institute, unfortunately unedited, taken among the Nganasans (a Samoyed ethnic group). The entire text collected from the shaman in the film, terminology and myths have not yet been edited, although a portion is to be published in the near future (a personal communication by Yuri Simchenko).

G. N. Grachova, a well-known scholar of the folklore of Finno-Ugric peoples, attempts to reconstruct a belief system on the basis of shaman song texts she collected among the Nganasans. She maintains that these songs may be instrumental in the acquisition of a familiarity with the world view of participants in the shamanic seance. Between 1969 and 1976, Grachova recorded several tapes on the Western part of the Taimir peninsula. The word-by-word translations of these texts and the accompanying field materials provide a degree of completeness which until then had not been attained, at least as far as the earlier, rather fragmentary notes are concerned (25). This abundance of detail, the thorough description of the cultural context and the knowledge of the language constitute the particular significance of recent Soviet collections.

E. A. Alekseenko collected a great deal of material on the Kets, a small Paleo-Siberian people neighboring the Ob-Ugrians. In her published studies on Kets shamanism, Alekseenko compares the different types of Siberian shamanism, noting which features are common to all peoples, and which ones vary from people to people. Her analysis is based on her collections made among these people and on highly detailed samples and data, mainly from 1970 to 1972. Alekseenko deems it important to compare the interrelationship of cultural elements within their systems, and not merely the elements themselves, taken at random.

Continuing with contemporary Soviet researchers, Z. P. Sokolova is an expert on the Voguls and Ostyaks. Sokolova took part in nine expeditions between 1967 and 1972. In her article she quotes eyewitnesses who saw acting shamans as late as the 1950s curing the ill, helping women in labor, and sacrificing reindeer and horses at sacred places. Notes from the middle of the 18th century even mention human sacrifices. Sokolova found special tools of shamans still in use among Voguls, and made photos of their attire and grave idols. At the end of her study she summarized the three characteristic types of Vogul shamans: 1. those working with a drum; 2. those calling the spirits by musical instruments; and 3. those telling fortune. "Major" and "minor" shamans were also distinguished among them (67).

In studies by Soviet authors the "ethnographic present" means in reality the 1960s and 1970s, that is, today's world. V. N. Basilov, in a series of articles on Central Asian shamanism (6, 7), notes that many of the older informants are still alive, or, if dead, have passed on their knowledge to others who continue to adhere to the old beliefs. Basilov also reviewed research on shamanism presently underway in the Soviet Union (9). The new data make it necessary to prepare a comprehensive monograph in the near future along the lines of Eliade's book.

S. I. Vajnstein has furnished invaluable data for future analysis, among them his recent studies of Tuvan shamanism (73). He outlines their belief system and presents the cult of *eren,* a benevolent spirit helping men and shamans. His encounters with the shamans of this small nation of Central Asia from the 1950s on—at which time his father was living in exile near the Mongolian border helping him to collect a vast amount of data. In 1963, for instance, he was able to personally follow a shaman in action curing a sick person, with the exorcism of the sickness-causing evil spirits at the center of the ceremony. He describes in detail the process of ecstasy and the fight with evil spirits, with enormous drumbeats indicating that the shaman shot "steel arrows" at the spirits of sickness (72). It is worthwhile to note that in the 1930s, there were still some areas in Tuva where shamans outnumbered lamas (74.130).

During her fieldwork in the late 1960s, the East German scientist Erika Taube met several female shamans, in addition to the more customary males (70). West German scholar Walter Heissig, an expert on Mongolian religion, reported that Buddhism in present-day Mongolia had completely lost its influence, while shamanism, despite all persecutions, continues as a form of popular religion. Incantations of pure, mixed, and completely Lamaized forms can be recorded by field research in all parts of Mongolia even today. In one East Mongolian region, where in the 1940s up to thirty shamans of both sexes could still be counted, shamanism was still in full swing in 1951 (33.45). Various forms of shamanic activities have been discovered in the recent past, not only in Siberia and Mongolia, but also in Tibet (12) and Nepal (38, 61). In Nepal Andras Höfer carried out extensive fieldwork from 1969 to 1974, collecting ritual texts with the help of religious specialists. There are five types of spiritual leaders there: the *lama,* the *bombo* or shaman, the exorcist of evil spirits called the *lambu,* the *village chief,* who has the most thorough knowledge of ritual texts addressed to the various Hindu divinities. Only the lama and the bombo undergo some form of lengthy training or initiation. These functions are generally passed down from father to son, although to become a shaman in Tibet, as in other parts of Eurasia, is an affair of a personal "calling" (vocation). Today the primary function of the shaman is healing by means of his own trance technique with the assistance of his drum. His knowledge encompasses the healing of both men and animals. In the course of development of these rituals, the roles of the lama and the shaman have become distinct from each other, and have come to complement each other. It is worthy of note that in June of 1977, Höfer found six initiated *lamas* as well as six practicing *bombos* or shamans (healers) and two *lambus* (exorcists of evil spirits) in a Tamang village of 546 inhabitants. Belief in the power of the rituals performed by these men and in that of the magic activities (offerings and healing) remains unbroken (39.35).

Returning to the Far Eastern regions of Siberia which the aboriginal Chukchees and Nivkhs inhabit, local shamans had played the central role in everyday life until the 1930s, when they were eliminated under the pretext of "class struggle" (74.216). C. M. Taksami, himself a Nivkh, met an old woman among the Nivkhs on Sakhalin Island at the beginning of the 1960s, who had quite often practised shamanism in her youth (68.169). Taksami recently submitted an interesting survey entitled *Survivals of Early Forms of Religion in Siberia* (69). His main field of research, however, has been the folklore of ethnic minorities in the Far East. The work done by him deserves attention all the more for the fact that his recent field research shows that the ancient customs and beliefs are still living among the original inhabitants of the remote Sakhalin Island. These people sacrifice animals to the spirit of the mountains and raise sacrificial heaps along the roads,

as a result of their belief in guardian spirits. They respect the
spirits of forests, waters and game—a peculiar environmental
protection in a modern sense. It is understandable that up to now
magic acts linked with hunting have been central to the beliefs
of these peoples. This belief system is still functioning and, as
Taksami has stated, it is not true that shamanism has entirely disappeared. At the same time, however, it would be very difficult
today to find a shaman in the classic sense of the word.

Finally, Korea is situated in the Far Eastern part of Eurasia,
and its culture and history have not yet been taken into account
by European students of shamanism, even though it is still a matter of living religious practice there. Korean scholars have published several volumes, one of them presenting illustrations and
documentary photos only, on Korean shamanism (46, 47, 48).
The data used and analyzed in Taegon Kim's work were collected by himself (Kim) during fieldwork throughout South
Korea from 1960 to 1982. Other analyses have also been published recently in addition to Kim's article (48, 14). These
authors report that the practice of shamanism is a living reality
there, and ceremonies are performed according to tradition. It is
thought-provoking that in South Korea, which has followed the
Japanese economic miracle, this old form of religion has been
preserved; it has not only survived but is even flourishing.

In the 1960s a new generation of experts appeared both in the
East and in the West in shaman studies. In contrast with the arm-
chair scholars characteristic of the first half of the century, fabri-
cating theories about bygone shamanism from their desks, the
younger generation summarized their field experiences instead.

Here it should be emphasized that these studies prove unequiv-
ocally—even if we disregard South America and other continents
for the moment—that shamanism is a living cultural phenomenon. Further on we will consider shamanism on this basis, stress-
ing some aspects which have been neglected up to now.

2. Aspects and Prospects

2.1. *The Shaman: Patient or Healer*

Positivist philology did not really believe in shamanism. It ac-
counted for it by calling it a phenomenon which had been preserved in a number of descriptions, but which remained distant

and strange, like a message brought from another planet. Furthermore, a belief was spread according to which shamanism was merely of archeological interest to philology, valuable only in terms of religious and cultural history, belonging to vanished phenomena of the past. But recent research has shown a growing conviction among scholars that there is indeed some therapeutic value in shamanism. This belief became prevalent, not only because anthropologists have tried the psychoactive drugs themselves, but also because they have begun to believe in the social function of the shaman's role. In their eyes the shaman is not a trickster but rather a psycho-therapeutic healer who knows the ways of healing and has suffered to acquire that knowledge.

At the beginning of the century, students of shamanism such as Y. G. Bogoraz, A. Ohlmarks, N. Y. Vitashevsky and M. A. Czaplicka held that the psychopathological effect of the harsh natural environment in the North played an important role in the formation of shamanism. The psycho-pathological phenomenology of Siberian shamanism has always been a major consideration (16); however, recent investigations and the reevaluation of earlier data have proved that most shamans emerge from among the *healthiest members* of the community.

Although Mircea Eliade argued convincingly against the view that shamans are often neurotic, unstable or epileptic (21.30), such negative views can, interestingly enough, still be held by scholars today:

> Briefly stated, my position is that the shaman is mentally deranged...there is no reason and no excuse for not considering the shaman to be a severe neurotic or even psychotic (15.14).

As early as 1959, László Vajda remarked that "whatever the connections between psychic disorders and shamanism, emotionally disturbed individuals can bring their strong drives and motivations into shamanic practice and present its transformation into a ritual routine" (71). As a matter of fact there is no reason to write about the pathological roots of shamanism, as this cannot be used as a point of reference in light of recently collected data. Shamans are much healthier than the rest of the population (55.26), due to the psychic and physical strains of the deep trance. "Lapp shamans only shamanized until the age of fifty when their teeth fell out. Strangely enough, this was exactly the phrase used for a Samoyed shaman on his retiring'' (40.49). Shamans must be perfectly *healthy* individuals who have the ability to achieve a high degree of concentration at times, keep an excellent physical condition and display keen intelligence (21.27-31).

A Hungarian psychiatrist, A. Kelemen, stated that curative activity includes not only biological but also expressly socio-psychological elements in the context of a given culture. Forms of behavior observed in shamans, which ethnological literature tends to qualify as neurosis, were examined by Kelemen, a practicing physicist, from a pathological point of view, and his conclusion was that the phenomena of shamanism which might be considered psycho-pathological are related either to the symptoms of schizophrenia, or to those of epilepsy or to those of encephalitis. The initiatory experiences of a would-be shaman strictly follow the models prescribed by the culture according to the world concept of the community. The theory of hysteria is similarly misleading, since the shaman carrying out the healing rite must maintain a high level of composure and concentration, guiding the psychic experience of the group (45).

In fact, the expectations of the group are decisive in choosing the person who will be shaman, and studies up to now have rather ignored this socio-psychological aspect (34, 65). Recent psychological tests have also shown that the features of a shaman's personality primarily include creativity and the ability of synthesis, both without pathological traits.

The shaman must first cure himself of the initiatory sickness, and only afterwards can cure the other members of the community. Recent studies in South Asia have shown that, out of more than a hundred Thai and Malayan shamans and mediums, none was mentally ill. Quite the contrary, they had strong personalities and had consciously accepted their highly demanding role as healer of the community (31).

The shaman is rather a psychotherapist than a psychopath. This had already been discussed by M. E. Opler in his article as early as in 1936, "Some Points of Comparison and Contrast between the. Treatment of Functional Disorders by Apache Shamans and Modern Psychiatrict Practice'' (59). Levi-Strauss later compared the healing methods of shamanism to those of psychoanalysis in a similar manner, noting that:

> The shaman plays the same dual role as psychoanalyst.... Actually the shamanic cure seems to be the exact counterpart to the psycho-analytic cure, but with an inversion of all elements...the psycho-analyst listens, whereas the shaman speaks (52.194-195).

A recent development, though not without antecedents, has been the evaluation of the healing function of shamans from this new angle. When reevaluating earlier ethnographic data, a strong contrast has been revealed between contemporary Western medicine and shamanic healing. Rogers, for example, states that:

> Thousands of individuals in lesser developed countries and others in more advanced nations experience stresses resulting from dual and antagonistic systems of treating illness in traditional and modern medicine. Medical anthropology and transcultural psychology are needed in order to arrive at intelligent, humane understanding about the use and efficiency of the shaman's healing methods (63.173).

Ethnographic analysis has shown that in so-called non-literate societies a shaman works as both an expert in medicinal herbs as well as a psycho-therapist in the modern sense of the word. With his healing methods, rich in symbols, he relieves the patient's affliction and returns him to a productive role within the community—a characteristic method of the shaman's healing is symbolically to take the illness upon himself, removing the illness by sucking the "evil spirit" out of the patient.

Modern clinical tests have also confirmed some hypotheses built on ethnographic descriptions. It has been revealed that the recovery of North American Indians under modern psychiatric treatment, after clinical treatment had failed, was greatly promoted by the intervention of the "Indian doctor." The sick person was initiated in the course of a ghost dance ceremony, and the shock effect of the experience and concurrent awareness of belonging to a community mobilized the healing power of the traditional indigenous culture (42.158). It has also been revealed that movements reviving Amerindian ceremonies, which began to flourish in the 1970s, possess an incredible healing power in the life of Indians who have lost their culture, living in big cities and facing identity disorders. Indians who are likely to become neurotic (alcoholics, drug addicts or suicides), for reasons outlined above, are being resocialized by these community ceremonies.

The healing power of shamans has been recorded for South American Indians in addition to North American. Gerhard Baer discussed the former quite comprehensively in his Manchester lecture. He concluded that, in South American Indian communities, the most important social function of a shaman is the role of mediator, serving as a three-way intermediary between the group he is guiding, the inhabitants of the spirit world, and Nature. The essence of mediation is to establish and maintain an equilibrium, first of all, to cure the sick and relieve tensions within the group—which can only be done if the three spheres are balanced. Another important lesson is that the religious system (the belief system and value system) or, more generally, the ideological sphere mediated by the shaman, legitimizes the social structure and the structure of power (3.11).

Since similar phenomena are experienced in the modern world and not merely among tribes in the jungle, it should be stressed that the life of so-called "primitive" societies can be viewed as a model, indeed as a living—and not an artificially created—model, the study of which would be instructive. Among other things, the healing model employed by the shaman, through rite with the characteristics of mytho-religious consciousness, is never simply the *right* which triumphs over the *wrong,* but rather it is the *stronger* knowledge which triumphs over the *weaker.* This power can only be obtained by long preparation, fasting, sexual abstinence, purity and concentration in such a way that the shaman keeps order over his immediate environment, maintaining rather a "psycho-social" than "psycho-mental" equilibrium over it by remaining in a state of constant mental and physical alertness.

Recent interest in hallucinogenic agents has been a new and interesting aspect in the research on shamanism starting in the 1960s and 1970s (28). It is no accident that interest in mind-expanding drugs rose at this time, since these decades coincide with the emergence of the "drug cult" in the West. It was then that anthropologists started to examine hallucinogenic agents used by pre-literate societies, as well as their function in different cultures (20). Although the use of hallucinogenic plants and mushrooms was known to be a part of shamanism, European and particularly Soviet research somehow ignored this aspect. We are in complete agreement with Michael Harner who stated that:

> Undoubtedly one of the major reasons that anthropologists for so long underestimated the importance of hallucinogenic substances in shamanism and religious experience was that very few had partaken themselves of the native psychotropic materials (28).

By now there are a number of firsthand field reports on different cultures analyzing the cultural variables of a drug-induced altered state of consciousness (19).

In Eliade's work ecstasy was only a technique. Siikala was the first to compare shamanic ecstasy with altered states of consciousness. There is a chapter in her book which deals with the questions of culturally patterned altered states of consciousness (65.31-52). In order to analyze the mechanism of ecstasy in shamanism, it may be helpful to turn to the results of hypnosis research, since hypnosis is an altered state of consciousness which can be induced under efficiently controlled experimental conditions. Traditionally, however, hypnosis is conceptualized as a sleep-like state—it is induced by procedures aiming at decreasing one's activity level: relaxation instructions, suggestions, of sleep and eye closure. This traditional hypnosis excludes the usual forms of ecstasy characterizing the shamanic trance.

Éva Bányai (Department of Comparative Psychology, University of Budapest) developed a completely new active-alert induction procedure by which a hypnotic-like altered state of consciousness could also be achieved under experimental conditions. In this method the subject rides a bicycle ergometer under load, with the eyes open. While exercising in this manner, verbal suggestions are given to enhance his alertness, attentiveness and a feeling of freshness (4). The effect of the active-alert induction procedure was subjected to complex analysis, taking into consideration the subjective experiences, behavioral manifestations and psychological changes. The active-alert induction was administered in four experimental series to a total of 94 subjects. The analysis of subjective experiences revealed that—in contrast with traditional hypnotic induction—the applied induction technique was effective in inducing a hyper-alert ecstatic state, or, as the subjects expressed it, a peak experience. The subjects felt a very active participation in their task. Beside these differences, active-alert hypnosis was also characterized by a relinquishment of the planning function, a lack of reality testing and a notion that attention can be highly focused.

As a result of active-alert induction the hyper-alertness of the subjects was also manifested in behavioral signs. The speed of pedaling increased, posture became more tense and movements were accelerated and often exaggerated in extent. Similar to traditional hypnosis, after active-alert induction the responsiveness to every type of test suggestion (motor facilitation and inhibition, positive and negative hallucinations, hypnotic dream, hyperamnesia, analgesia, post-hypnotic suggestion and amnesia) increased in comparison to the wake condition. The manner of administering the test suggestions was essentially the same in the active-alert induction as in traditional hypnosis: dissociations, clear, vivid, dream-like visual imagery, memory improvement without effort, rationalization of post-hypnotic suggestions were present after both inductions (5).

The above analytical results were presented by Bányai at a Symposium on "Shamanism in Eurasia" (1981) and accepted as a relevant contribution toward the understanding of the psychophysiological basis of ecstasy.

As the subjective and behavioral modifications induced by active-alert induction demonstrate, active-alert hypnosis may become an appropriate experimental model of the ecstatic trance states of shamanism. These studies have been reviewed here in order to provide new insights and models of shamanic approaches to the human psyche, through the shamans' way of healing, which is one of their main social functions.

2.2. Shaman as Symbolic Mediator

Although Eliade discusses shaman as psychopomp (21), enumerating a series of examples of the symbolism in the shaman's costume and drum, the allegoric aspects of shamanism have been treated in more detail only in the most recent studies.

In his paper "The Shaman as Representative of his Grouping," Ivan Kortt dealt with the motif of 'dismemberment' and with the symbolism of the skeleton represented symbolically on the shaman's attire. In initiation rituals the dismemberment of the shaman-to-be seems to be a symbol of temporary death followed by rebirth. This means simply that initiation is closely connected with death, and the bones of the skeleton symbolize the whole clan or lineage. According to Kortt's analysis, the shaman serves as the representative of his clan in the other world. In Siberian shamanic rituals there is an important hidden meaning connected with symbolic rebirth, particularly in ecstatic initiation, which takes place in the other world (i.e., the spirit world), where the shaman candidate acts as a mediator between the two worlds (49).

Similar conclusions were drawn by Juha Pentikäinen in his paper presented at the symposium on Eurasian shamanism, in which he analyzed the Sāmi (Lapp) world-view. There is—as the Lapps believe—an upper world of skies and heavenly gods, a middle stratum occupied by human beings, and another world, or the upside-down world, the land of the dead. These realms, although discrete, with well-defined occupants and a distinct locus, often interact or manifest themselves in the human realm. These interactions produce observable, experienced phenomena encountered by individuals in the course of their lives. The Sāmi shaman, *noaide,* in his many roles, is the main leader of this interaction, the mediator between the forces and elements of the three worlds of the universe (60).

In Siberian myths, especially in those of the Buryats, shamanism and human deaths are intimately associated in their very origins. The shaman as a mediator is placed at those extremely critical points where the human and suprahuman spheres do indeed overlap. The shaman's activity covers the liminal spheres of the world which are dangerous for ordinary human beings and for shamans as well. His or her mediating activity relies on beliefs in symbolically taking all the difficulties (pain, sickness, responsibility of decision-making, etc.) upon himself or herself. All these observations and data truly stress the utmost significance of the symbolic aspects of the mediation process. Most recent publications agree that this mediation is a central part of shamanistic ideology. Here shamanism as an "ideology" is understood not as a religion, but rather as a special system of beliefs centered around symbolic mediation as discussed above. A. L. Siikala paid little attention to the symbolic aspect of shamanism, but rightly stated that:

> The shaman's function as mediator between the normal and the supranormal worlds is based on systems of belief according to which difficulties threatening the even pace of life are caused by representatives of the spirit world, and they can be eliminated with the help of benevolent spirits (65.319).

In Siikala's opinion the main task of the shaman is to create a direct and reciprocal state of communication aimed at the spirit world, and the very structure of the shamanic seance reflects this communication.

The same opinion is held with regard to the shamans of North and South American Indians, inasmuch as they are viewed as those who "served as mediators between the sacred and profane worlds" (11.110). Or, as B. Myerhoff puts it: "The Shaman is above all a connecting figure, bridging several worlds for his people, travelling between this world, the underworld and the heavens" (58.99). As a mediator, the shaman is the restorer of balance. In other words, he maintains a shamanic equilibrium of power relations within his community and the outside worlds. Those who have access to the channels of communication have more power within their community.

The shaman as a mediator is a specialist in ritual communication and in maintaining the fragile state of social/psychological equilibrium by symbolic mediation between worlds of ordinary and non-ordinary realities. He has special symbols which give him power, and all in all shaman ceremonies symbolize the process of eliminating ordinary reality in order to gain access to another state of consciousness, or, to put it even more briefly: symbols make the shaman.

2.3 Shaman as Poet/Singer

In this section I call attention to another important, but somehow neglected, aspect of shamanism. The so-called poetic aspects of shamans' songs have recently been analyzed in three interesting papers (Hajdú 1978, Joki 1978, Simoncsics 1978). Nobody would deny that a strong affinity exists between shamanic performance and the ritualized narration of myth (legend or a heroic epic) by singers of traditional oral narratives. Here the poetic aspect of shamanic narratives is understood at least at two levels: first stylistic, and second functional.

As R. Mastromattei characterized shamanic texts by their ecstatic quality, claiming that "a text becomes shamanic primarily *qua* recited in an ecstatic context" (Mastromattei 1971.7). Since there are only very few studies on the poetics of shaman songs, this would be an urgent task for future research—not only the collection of shamanic texts, but also a detailed analysis of phonetic and semantic levels would seem to be important, given active-alert hypnosis as a model of ecstasy. Similarly, glossolalia can be seen as the audible (phonetic) expression of the neuropsychological trance process (23).

The oral ecstatic performance and collective singing were important features of the pre-ecstatic phase of the Lapp seance (60). In symbolic healings performed by the shaman, magic incantations were used throughout Eurasia (cf. *cantatio* 'singing', Latin *cantio* = song). The shaman mediated between illness and health with the help of songs. Here symbolic, poetic and healing functions are intertwined. In 1968, for example, a therapeutic seance in Northern Afghanistan was performed by a *baxsi* or shaman with the aid of *qobuz* or horsehair fiddle and singing (13.160).

There are data suggesting that the shaman and the singer of oral tradition (i.e., the poet of non-literate societies) were the same person. A. T. Hatto chose "Shamanism and Epic Poetry in Northern Asia" for his Foundation Day lecture topic, in which he noted that heroic epics were sung by shamans among the Voguls and Ostyaks. Narration was normally in the first person, and the "voice" was that of the hero. There is an "inner style" of shamanic epic narration among the Ob-Ugrians, and the roles of shaman and bard once overlapped among the Samoyed as well (30.7-9). Among the Buryats shamans were the principal guardians of the rich heroic oral literature (21.30).

Reference should be made here to V. V. Ivanov's proposal for a new etymology of the word "shaman." There is a Sanskrit word *saman*, "song." This implies that the shaman is literally the person who sings the song, with long genealogies, to cure, to conjure, to heal. He is not simply an "ascetic," but also a wise man and poet. One of the main roles of oral-traditional poetry in culture is to create a bridge between past and present. This again is a form of symbolic mediation with the aim of maintaining group identity by means of oral tradition. The ailing identity consciousness of a given society (ethnic minority) is nurtured by the poet-shamans through repeated ecstatic or quasi-ecstatic oral performances. In modern contemporary poetry, examples could be found to label some modern poets as a continuation or extension of shamanic traditions—employing songs as a psycho-social healing method even today (76, 22).

From this point of view a recent renaissance of shamanism could be seen as a new and contemporary form of folklore, one could use the term *folklorism* here which, in contrast to folklore, is a politically or economically manipulated form of contemporary folklore. As a matter of fact, shamans have assumed new roles in the cultural integration of their peoples. With respect to the relationship between native religion and ethnic identity, the former plays an exceptionally important role in the preservation of the traditional system of values and beliefs, or, in a broader sense of the word, in the preservation of a culturally distinctive way of life. Shamans or other religious leaders (native ritualists, medicine men, folk healers, singers or poets) have played a prominent role, for instance, in the recent renaissance of North American Indian ceremonialism (42, 62).

Here again we return to a neglected aspect of shamanism, viz., the role of the shaman in the preservation of cultural identity. This role could be defined as a mediation between the cultural heritage of the past and the present situation.

The performance of shaman songs by a Nganasan shaman (D. Kosterkin) before the participants of the 7th ICAES in Moscow in 1974 (25.89) could be seen as folklorism. A South Korean *kut*-ceremony performed in a folk-festival or a North American sun dance ceremony could fall into the same category, but it is necessary to bear in mind that, in spite of their differences, there is a common feature in all of these: these pseudo-shamanic events serve just as much to maintain the cultural continuity of their groups. Contemporary shamans, in their capacity as healer or poet/singer, have accepted the role of symbolic mediation as a means of the cultural policy of identity-preservation. This may well be a contemporary form of folklore, or even a new function of it, taking shape in front of our very eyes. At this precise point we return to the beginning of the present essay, emphasizing the contemporary character of shamanism.

3. Towards a New Definition

In the literature dealing with the question of shamanism, there is a constant dissatisfaction with the definition of the term "shamanism" itself, since it is applied to entirely different cultural complexes occurring within different ecological contexts, not to mention their different inner structures.

The earlier definitions of shamanism are based on the assumption that ecstasy is the main feature of the shamanic rite (21). In any case, however, it was a very widely accepted practice to treat shamanism in general as a religious phenomenon (75.61) or as a form of religion ("certain definite grade of the cult of the spirits") (16.8) or even as an early form of religion on the evolutionary ladder. This last view is held by Soviet scholars.

Most recently, according to another definition, "spirit possession" and shamanism regularly co-exist, and the most analytically fruitful use of the term "shaman" is, as I. M. Lewis argues, to designate a charismatic religious *role* involving the mastery or control of spirits. This role is best described in terms of a recruitment pattern involving separate but interrelated phases: the initiatory trauma; a process of treatment; and finally the achievement of control over the spirits. In the last phase the patient has been transformed into an initiated healer-shaman (53). This usage detaches the concept "shaman" from any specific "shamanic" cosmology, liberating it for general cross-cultural use in the analysis of religious functionaries and roles.

Other definitions attempt to understand and define shamanism from social perspectives, as an institution which serves to construct a meaningful semantic universe by the process of symbolic mediation. Shamans as mediators create order and reestablish balance within their groups such that their role is socially embedded in their cultures (35).

This social integration of shamanism throws some light on the sphere of everyday beliefs. Here I list some examples to illustrate these everyday aspects of shamanism not taken into consideration by previous research. The everyday aspects are to be found in descriptions: sleep, the initiatory or, more exactly, the preceding or closing act of shamanic ecstasy (20); yawning, the gesture of taking in helping spirits through the mouth (40.49); dream, a state of acquiring knowledge; or fasting, one of the possible and widespread techniques of preparation for trance in different cultures. A number of data are available in this respect, not only in descriptions of Siberian shamanism, but also in accounts taken among the Lapps, Mongolians, Koreans, and Hungarians. Fasting is also mentioned with regard to North American Indians, e.g., the Kwakiutl shaman, before the healing ceremony, purifies himself by vomiting, taking a hot bath and long fasting, so that fasting was experienced mentally as well as physically. Purification meant a physical and mental, or even psychical, preparation for trance, which improves the efficiency of psychoactive agents (64.102).

> When a young man decides to undergo apprenticeship, he first spends a month or more in isolation, purifying his body of the substances that would otherwise obstruct his learning and cause bad visions (51.68).

Fasting, yawning, sleep, trance, possession, motifs of shamanic flight, and drums or bows as means of prophecy are the elements of the everyday system of beliefs, but at the same time they belong to the shamanic complex as well. Thus A. Hultkrantz tends to give a correct definition of shamanism as the complex of beliefs, rites and traditions clustered around the shaman and his activities. All these traits constitute a well-organized net of interrelationships, a religious configuration *within the religion*. In some hunting and pastoral religions of Siberia; this configuration is so profiled and domineering that observers from the outside have mistaken shamanism for a religion (10.10). In a definition, the concept of belief system is of central theoretical importance as a recently accepted term, standing for a set of rules guiding everyday behavior (36).

Shamanism is a complex system of beliefs which includes the knowledge of and belief in the names of helping spirits in the shamanic pantheon, the memory of certain texts (sermons, shaman-songs, legends, myths, etc.), the rules for activities (rituals, sacrifices, the technique of ecstasy, etc.), and the objects, tools and paraphernalia used by shamans (drum, stick, bow, mirror, costumes, etc.). All these components are closely connected by beliefs given in the shamanic complex.

Of these elements, some always appear jointly with specified others, and, of course, the set of elements which makes up the shamanic belief system is always different in different cultures (65.322). On the basis of beliefs, the members of a given community believe that shamans are able to get in touch with spirits for different purposes (healing, prophesying) or to take a journey to the underworld in the state of trance, with the help of a rhythmical background music (a drum or other instrument), or hallucinogenic agents, in order to contact deceased.

I suggest conceiving shamanism as a belief system, because this term is more neutral than its alternative definition as a form of religion. The heretofore neglected aspects of this phenomenon which this paper has presented are more secular in character than they are religious.

In our post-religious world it is perhaps more proper to speak about beliefs, attitudes, convictions, or ideological practices (Glaubensvorstellungen) than religion. In this sense shamanism is a belief system which involves the acceptance of certain social roles (a healer, poet, or ideologue, or all of these together). These are no longer in the sacred sphere of culture today, but on the border of the sacred and the profane; not in that of religion, but rather on the threshold between religious and everyday beliefs. This is one of the main lessons to be drawn from the most recent research, and this may be an explanation for shamanism adapting itself to our own everyday life—as the examples listed above demonstrate. It appears in extremely varied forms, but renews, formulates and expresses—with varying degrees of success—an overtly altruistic ideology which, in our egoistic and materialistic times, contains a decisively positive program for life.

References

1. Alekseenko, E. A.: "Samanstvo u ketov." In: *Problemy obscest-vennego soznanie aborigenov Sibiri* 90-128. Leningrad: Nauka 1981.
2. Alekseev, N. A.: *Rannie formy religii turkoiazycnykh narodov Sibiri.* Novosibirsk: Nauka 1980.
3. Baer, G.: "Social Aspects of the South American Shaman." Paper for the 44th Congress of Americanists, Manchester 1982.
4. Banyai, E. I. and E. R. Hillgard: "A Comparison of Active-alert Hypnotic Induction with Traditional Relaxation Induction." In: *Journal of Abnormal Psychology* 85 (1976).218-224.
5. Banyai, E.I.: "On the Technique of Hypnosis and Ecstasy: an Experimental Psychophysiological Approach." In *Shamanism in Eurasia* (edited by M. Hoppal). Gottingen: Herodot 1984.
6. Basilov, V. N.: "Shamanism in Central Asia." In: *The Realm of Extra-human. Agents and Audiences* (edited by A. Bharati), 149-157. The Hague-Paris: Mouton 1976.
7. Basilov, V. N.: "Vestiges of Transvestism in Central Asia." In: *Shamanism in Siberia* (edited by V. Dioszegi and M. Hoppal), 281-289. Budapest: Akademiai Kiado 1978.
8. Basilov, V. N.: "Some Results of the Study of the Vestiges of Shamanism in Central Asia." Paper for the 1st Intercongress of ICAES, Amsterdam 1981.
9. Basilov, V. N.: "The Study of Shamanism in Soviet Ethnography." In: *Shamanism in Eurasia* (edited by M. Hoppal). Gottingen: Herodot 1984.
10. Backman, L. and A. Hultkrantz: *Studies in Lapp Shamanism.* Stockholm: Almqvist-Wiksell 1978.
11. Bean, L. J.: "California Indian Shamanism and Folk Curing." In: *American Folk Medicine* (edited by W. D. Hand), 109-123. Berkeley: University of California Press 1976.
12. Berglie, P. A.: "Lo sciamanesimo tibetano." *Conosenza Religiosa* 3/4, 354-361, 1982.
13. Centlivres, M.; P. Centlivres; M. Slobin: "A Muslim Shaman of Afghan Turkestan." *Ethnography* X, 2, 160-173, 1971.
14. Cho Hung-youn: "Zum Problem des sogenannten Yoltugori des Ch'onsin'gut im koreanischen Shamanismus." *Mitteilung aus dem Museum fur Volkerskunde* (Hamburg) 1, 77-107, 1980. Chicago: University of Chicago Press 1980.
15. Devereux, G.: *Basic Problems of Ethnopsychiatry.* Chicago: University of Chicago Press.
16. Dioszegi, V.: *Tracing Shamans in Siberia: The Story of An Ethnographical Research Expedition.* Oosterhout: Anthropological publications 1968.

17. Dioszegi, V. and M. Hoppal (eds.): *Shamanism in Siberia*. Budapest: Akademiai Kiado 1978.
18. Dioszegi, V.: "Pre-Islamic Shamanism of the Baraba Turks and Some Ethnogenetic Conclusions." In: *Shamanism in Siberia* (edited by V. Dioszegi and M. Hoppal), 83-168. Budapest: Akademiai Kiado 1978.
19. Dobkin de Rios, M.: "Man, Culture and Hallucinogens: An Overview." In: *Cannabis and culture* (edited by V. Rubon), The Hague: Mouton 1973.
20. Dobkin de Rios, M.: "The Wilderness of Mind: Sacred Plants." In: *Cross-Cultural Perspectives*. Beverly Hills & London: Sage Publications 1976.
21. Eliade, M.: *Shamanism: An Archaic Technique of Ecstasy*. New York: Pantheon 1964.
22. Giordano, F.: "Translation of the Sacred: the Poet and the Shaman." In: *North American Indian Studies* (edited by P. Hovens), 109-121. Gottingen: Herodot 1981.
23. Goodman, F. D.: *Speaking in Tongues: A Cross-Cultural Study of Glossolalia*. Chicago: University of Chicago Press 1972.
24. Goodman, F.D.; J. H. Henney; and E. Pressel: *Trance, Healing and Hallucination: Three Field Studies in Religious Experience*. Malabar, Florida: Krieger Publishing Company 1982.
25. Gracova, G. N.: "Samani u Nganasan." In: *Problemy istorii obscestvennogo soznanija aborigenov Sibiri* (edited by I. S. Vdovin), 69-89. Leningrad: Nauka 1981.
26. Grambo, R.: "Sleep as a Means of Ecstasy and Divination." *Acta Ethnographica Academie Scientiarium Hungaricae* 22, 3-4, 417-441, 1973.
27. Hajdu, P.: "The Nenets Shaman Song and Its Text." In: *Shamanism in Siberia* (edited by V. Dioszegi and M. Hoppal), 355-372. Budapest: Akademiai Kiado 1978.
28. Harner, M. (ed.): *Hallucinogens and Shamanism*. London-Oxford-New York: Oxford University Press 1973.
29. Harner, M.: *The Way of the Shamans: A Guide to Power and Healing*. San Francisco: Harper and Row 1980.
30. Hatto, A. T.: *Shamanism and Epic Poetry in Northern Asia*. London: University of London 1970.
31. Heinze, R. I.: "Shamans or Mediums—Towards a Definition of Different States of Consciousness." *Phoenix Journal of Transpersonal Anthropology* VI, 1-3, 25-44, 1982.
32. Heissig, W.: "Zur Frage der Homogenitat des ostmongolischen Schamanismus." In: *Collectanea Mongolica* (edited by W. Heissig), 81-100. Wiesbaden.
33. Heissig, W.: *The Religions of Mongolia*. London-Henley: Routledge and Kegan Paul 1980.

34. Honko, L.: "Role Taking of the Shaman." *Temenos* 4, 26-55, 1969.
35. Hoppal, M.: "Folk Beliefs and Shamanism of the Uralic Peoples." In: *Ancient Cultures of the Uralian Peoples* (edited by P. Hajdu), 215-242. Budapest: Corvina 1975.
36. Hoppal, M.: "On Belief Systems." In: *Text Processing* (edited by W. Burghardt and K. Holker), 236-252. Berlin-New York: De Gruyter 1979.
37. Hoppal, M. (ed): *Shamanism in Eurasia*. Gottingen: Herodot 1984.
38. Hofer, A.: "Is the *bombo* an Ecstatic? Some Ritual Techniques of Tamang Shamanism." In: *Contributions to the Anthropology of Nepal* (edited by C. von Furer-Haimendorf), 168-182. Warminster: Aris and Phillips 1974.
39. Hofer, A.: *Tamang Ritual Texts, I. Preliminary Studies in the Folk Religion of an Ethnic Minority in Nepal*. Wiesbaden: Steiner 1981.
40. Hultkrantz, A.: "Lapp Shamanism from a Comparative Point of view." *Fenno-Ugrica Suecanna. Journal of Finno-Ugric Research in Sweden (Uppsala)* 2, 45-58, 1979.
41. Ivanov, V. V.: *Ocerki po istorii semiotiki v SSSR*. Moskva: Nauka 1976.
42. Jilek, W. G.: *Indian Healing: Shamanic Ceremonialism in the Pacific Northwest Today*. Hancock House Publ. 1982.
43. Johansen, U.: "Aspekte des Schamanismusforschung." *Anthropos* 3/4, 1977.
44. Joki, A. J.: "Notes on Selkup Shamanism." In: *Shamanism in Siberia* (edited by V. Dioszegi and M. Hoppal), 373-386. Budapest: Akademiai Kiado 1978.
45. Kelemen, A.: "Schamanistische Uberbleibsel in den Volksglaubens und Volksheilkunde Ungarns." *Curare* (Wiesbaden) 3, 217-224, 1980.
46. Kim Taegon: *A Study of Shamanism in Korea. Korean Shamanism*. Series IV (No. 8). Seoul 1981.
47. Kim Taegon: *Illustrated Book of Shamanism in Korea. Korean Shamanism*, Series III (No. 7). Seoul: Kyung Hee University, Institute of Folklore Studies 1982.
48. Kim Taegon: "An Arche-Pattern Analysis of the Functions and Meaning of Shaman Rituals." Paper for symposium on *Theater and Ritual* (MS).
49. Kortt, I.: "Lo sciamano rappresentante della societa nell' aldila." *Conosenza Religiosa* 3/4, 362-377, 1982.
50. Kraeder, L.: "Shamanism: Theory and History in Buryat Society." In: *Shamanism in Siberia* (edited by V. Dioszegi and M. Hoppal), 181-237. Budapest: Akademiai Kiado 1978.

51. Langdon, J. E.: "*Yage* Among the Siona: Cultural Pattern of Visions." In: *Spirits, Shamans, and Stars* (edited by D. L. Browman and R. A. Schwart), 63-80. The Hague: Mouton 1979.
52. Levi-Strauss, Claude: *Structural Anthropology*. Garden City, N.Y.: Doubleday Anchor Books 1967.
53. Lewis, I.M.: "What is a Shaman?" *Folk* 23.25-36, 1981.
54. Manzigeev, I. A.: *Buryatskie samanisticeskie i do samanisticeskie termini*. Moskva: Nauka 1978.
55. Mastromattei, R.: "Oral Tradition and Shamanic Recitals." In: *Oralita: Cultura, Letteratura, Discorso* (edited by B. Gentili and G. Paioni). Urbino: Ateneo 1981.
56. Mikhailov, T. M.: *Iz istorii buryatskogo samanizma*. Novosibirsk: *Nauka 1980*.
57. *Motzki, H.: Shamanismus als Problem religionswissenschaftlicher Terminologie*. Koln: Brill 1977.
58. Myerhoff, B. G.: "Shamanic Equilibrium: Balance and Mediation in Known and Unknown Worlds." In: *American Folk Medicine* (edited by W. D. Hand), 99-107. Berkeley: University of California Press 1976.
59. Opler, M. E.: "Some Points of Comparison and Contrast between the Treatment of Functional Disorders by Apache Shamans and Modern Psychiatric Practice." *American Journal of Psychiatry* 92, 6, 1371-1387, 1936.
60. Pentikainen, J.: "The Sami Shaman—A Mediator between the Three Worlds of the Universe." In: *Shamanism in Eurasia* (edited by M. Hoppal). Gottingen: Herodot 1984.
61. Peters. L. G.: *Ecstasy and Healing in Nepal: An Ethnographic Study of Tamang Shamanism*. Los Angeles: Undena Publications 1981.
62. Posern-Zielinska, M.: "Native Religions and Ethnic Identity of the American Indians." In: *North American Indian Studies* (edited by P. Hovens), 183-199. Gottingen: Herodot 1981.
63. Rogers, S. L.: *The Shaman: His Symbols and His Healing Power*. Springfield, Ill.: Charles Thomas Publ. 1982.
64. Shepker, H. J.: "Forms of Ecstasy in the Traditional Culture of the Haida Indians." In: *North American Indian Studies* (edited by P. Hovens), 99-108. Gottingen: Herodot 1981.
65. Siikala, A. L.: *The Rite Technique of Siberian Shaman*. FF Communication No. 220. Helsinki 1978.
66. Simoncsis, P.: "The Structure of a Nenets Magic Chant." In: *Shamanism in Siberia (edited by V. Dioszegi and M. Hoppal)*, 387-402. *Budapest: Akademiai Kiado 1978*.
67. *Sokolova, P. P.: "Problems of Research in the Ob-Ugrian*

Shamanism." In: *Shamanism in Eurasia* (edited by M. Hoppal). Gottingen: Herodot 1984.

68. Taksami, C. M.: "Samanstvo u Nivkhov." In: *Problemy istorii obscestvennogo soznanija aborigenov Sibiri* (edited by I. S. Vdovin), 165-177. Leningrad: Nauka 1981.

69. Taksami, C. M.: "Survivals of Early Forms of Religion in Siberia." In: *Shamanism in Eurasia* (edited by M. Hoppal). Gottingen: Herodot 1984.

70. Taube, E.: "Notizen zum Schamanismus bei den Tuwinern des Cengelsum (Westmongolei)." *Jahrbuch des Museums fur Volkerkunde zu Leipzig* 23, 43-69, 1981.

71. Vajda, L.: "Zur phaseologischen Stellung des Shamanismus." *Ural-Altaische Jahrbucher* 31, 456-485, 1959.

72. Vajnstejn, S. I.: "Vstreca s velikim samanonom." *Priroda* (Moskva) No. 8, 79-83, 1975.

73. Vajnstejn, S. I.: "Shamanism in Tuva." In: *Shamanism in Eurasia* (edited by M. Hoppal). Gottingen: Herodot 1984.

74. Vdovin, I. S. (ed.): *Problemy isotrii obscestvennogo soznania aborigenov Sibiri.* Leningrad: Nauka 1981.

75. Voigt, V.: *Shamanism in Siberia* (edited by V. Dioszegi and M. Hoppal), 59-80, Budapest: Akademiai Kiado 1978.

76. Zolla, E.: *The Writer and the Shaman.* New York: Harcourt and Brace 1973.

77. Zolla, E.: "The Teaching of Carlos Castaneda." In: *North American Indian Studies* (edited by P. Hovens), 247-253. Gottingen: Herodot 1981.

78. Zolla, E.: "Lo sciamanesimo coreano." *Conosenza Religiosa* 3/4, 392-407, 1982.

II

The Shamanic State of Consciousness

The altered state of consciousness typical of shamans is in a category by itself. Shamans rely on insight at a level beyond the discursive intellect and seem to draw on a data bank not available to ordinary waking consciousness, as Achterberg points out. She stresses the component of imagination and vivid imagery, and holds that the objects and tools used in healing are empowered by imagination. This is not imagination in the sense of idle fantasy but can be effective in diagnosing and in healing.

Achterberg suggests that the SSC corresponds to the mystic state in which one is in harmony with the "great unified order of things," and thus shamans can "move with the fabric of the universe" and communicate with all nature, including animals and spirits. Health to shamanic societies means being in harmony with the whole of things, and healing results from establishing this harmony. Inducing an altered state in the patient through imagery can be part of the process.

Krippner points out that dreaming is an integral part of shamanism. Shamans tend to dream of spirits and in some cultures even receive power through dreams. Krippner finds characteristics of the "fantasy-prone" personality in shamans—seeing visions, hearing "voices," etc. Rogo states that some cultures produce shamans with ESP by making it a requirement for that status. He sees the same paranormal abilities in shamans that have been studied in other groups and feels the need for more investigation of this aspect of the SSC.

Swan presents a vivid account of a shaman at work. Observers see marked changes in Rolling Thunder while he performs a healing ceremony, as he successively takes on the guise of a wise father, an eagle, a badger. The patient too goes into an altered state, and all those present are affected. Rolling Thunder considers that he himself does not heal but is an agent for the Great Spirit, that healing comes from the world of spirit.

6

The Shaman: Master Healer in the Imaginary Realm

JEANNE ACHTERBERG

> I don't know what you learned from books, but the most
> important thing I learned from my grandfathers was that
> there is a part of the mind that we don't really know
> about and that it is that part that is most important in
> whether we become sick or remain well.
>
> Thomas Largewhiskers,
> 100-year-old Navaho Medicine Man

The shamans' work is conducted in the realm of the imagination, and their expertise in using that terrain for the benefit of the community has been recognized since the dawn of civilization. Their voyages allow them to experience the Creator, seek wisdom, and heal the ailments of the body. I will focus upon the healing aspect here, describing the phenomenon in the allegory of the scientist.

My research over the past twelve years has largely been on the role of the imagination in disease, so it seemed logical to study the ancient practice of shamanism. Furthermore, it appears that we who stand in the glitter of a technological age have overlooked the critical elements of the healing arts which are so integral to shamanic medicine. The current widespread interest in the shamanic practices, often manifested as an uncritical reverence for anything loosely affiliated with native culture, surely must reflect a longing for a more humanistic, spiritual inclusion in medicine. One might say that the Medicine Wheel of Western civilization has looked to the North far too long now, having much knowledge, but little feeling.

Yet, if any of the shamanic lore related to imaginary healing is to be incorporated into modern health care, it must satisfy the criteria of scientific observation and measurement. These tests will not decrease any power of the shamans' work, nor will shamanism be "explained away" by scientific principle. Science, like art, merely provides a metaphor for reality at some level. And, whether one likes it or not, it is the scientific metaphor that dictates medical practices in this country.

At the same time, we should not forget that the shamans are likely to regard the scientific interpretation of their work as either grossly in error or just plain foolish. Since their own explanations tend to be based on the supernatural, they are currently (perhaps eternally) beyond the pale of the scientific yardstick. So, in respectful cognizance of the stance of the shaman and the scientist, I will present information from these divergent points of view.

Preverbal and Transpersonal Healing

The primary theme that has emerged from the study of the imagination as healer relates to two basic ways the image is believed to positively impact health, both of which are represented in shamanic work. First is what I have called *preverbal* imagery. Here, the imagination acts upon one's own physical being. Images communicate with tissues and organs, even cells, to effect a change. The communication can be deliberate or not. It is preverbal in the sense that it probably evolved much earlier than language and uses different neural pathways for the transmission of information. The second type of healing imagery is *transpersonal*, embodying the assumption that information can be transmitted from the consciousness of one person to the physical substrate of others.

The scientific method is currently far more applicable to the study of the preverbal type of imagery. It can be described using facts derived from physiology, anatomy, chemistry, and the behavioral sciences. The proposition can, and has been, tested using the scientific method. (These investigations are discussed at length in *Imagery in Healing: Shamanism and Modern Medicine.*) Transpersonal imagery requires the existence of channels of information flow that have not been identified by the tools of science. The validation of transpersonal imagery must therefore be sought in the more qualitative types of observational data gathered by the anthropologists, theologians, medical historians, and others, as well as through intuitive, philosophical speculation. The greatest support for this theory comes from the tenacity with which humans have clung to a belief in transpersonal healing, and has been reinforced in the belief system for at least 20,000 years. The traditional concept of shamanism would place it within the classification of transpersonal healing, and it is upon that issue that the shamans have established their repute. However, preverbal imagery plays a strong role as well. The shamans' ritual work has a direct therapeutic effect on the patient by creating vivid images, and by inducing altered states of consciousness conducive to self-healing.

The Meaning of Health and Disease in the Shamanic System

In the shamanic traditions, avoiding death is not necessarily the purpose for the practice of their medicine. Our Western mistrust of these systems often comes from the observation that shamanic healing may not have resulted in an extension of life. Healing, for the shaman, is a spiritual affair. Disease has origins in and gains its meaning from the spirit world. To lose one's soul is the gravest occurrence of all, since it would eliminate any meaning from life, now and forever. Much shamanic healing is to nurture and preserve the soul, and to protect it from eternal wandering.

Illness, as conceived even in the modern sense, is regarded as something entering the body from without; something that needs to be removed or destroyed or protected against. In the shamanic system, the primary problem is not the external element, but the loss of personal power which permitted the intrusion in the first place, whether it be an arrow or an evil spirit. Actually, this is rather advanced thinking, since recent discoveries in medical science support a description of the disease process in similar terms. To briefly summarize the issue, the so-called primary external causes of major illness—viruses, bacteria, and other invisible elements in the environment—are a threat to health only when a person's natural protective mantle develops a weakness.

In the tribal societies where shamanism has flourished, the

practice of healing overlaps and is integrated with all of secular and sacred life, with prayer, farming, marriage, war, and taboo. Richard Grossinger (1980) notes that the shaman cannot work exclusively in the context of disease; history provides no basis or technology for the isolation of disease apart from the rest of the human condition. The dangers of isolating one part of living from another are recognized, and there is little interest in merely lengthening life, but rather in restoring balance. He also observes, in defense of the holistic, shamanistic medicine, that when we treat disease as a concrete entity capable of technologic remediation, we lose the notion of an integrated system. The outward signs of disease are pathological changes, "but it is also the place where all other crises and necessities of the organism come together. It is the most intimate writing of the turbulence and changes of life on the single bodies and collective body of the biosphere. Nothing else, except maybe dream or vision, forces the organism to reconcile itself instantaneously with the devastating pagan powers of which it is made." (p. 13) Illness, he says, tugs one toward the reality of both biological and social existence. Disease can lead to vision and personal growth, and in light of this, "the world of sterile chemicals and operating tables is a cruel reversal and a wasteful joke." (p. 23)

The shaman is well-skilled at differential diagnosis of spirit disorders. Sometimes the soul may be diagnosed as having been frightened, other times depressed, and worst of all, it may have exited altogether. Both physical and mental symptoms are characteristic of the different states, and are regarded as quite serious. Without intervention, the patient may well die without resolving the problem that caused the disease in the first place, and thus be doomed to an eternal life of being out of synchrony with the universe.

Any current thrust toward romanticizing shamanic medicine or folk medicine in general should be tempered with the knowledge that often the remedies prescribed were clearly wrong and harmful from the standpoint of physical well-being. Louise Jilek-Aall (1979), a physician and anthropologist, observed many procedures in Africa which defied the course of nature. Birthing procedures, for example, dictated by custom, resulted in high infant mortality and a high incidence of epilepsy—a disorder known to be related to birth trauma.

Other conditions of early tribal life such as major debilitative illnesses from impure food and water resources, rampant parasitic infestation, and a limited life expectancy were regarded as normal conditions of living. Our advanced technology in sanitary conditions and nutrition has significantly reduced those problems in industrialized countries. In cultures which still have shamanic activities, the imported health facilities seem to be regarded as the first line stance against injury, infection, and endemic disease.

Unfortunately, "civilization" has created new health problems in the stead of those that it has ameliorated. For example, in contemporary Western medicine, life's natural passages are viewed as deficiency diseases which require medical attention. Newborn babies, about-to-be-mothers, menopausal women, and people who are simply experiencing old age are hospitalized and medicated as if pathology were present. Even marriage and death require the legal stamp of medical approval. Growth rituals in our society have been turned over to the health care system; thus, the natural fruition and maturation of the human condition are regarded as sicknesses, and in need of intervention.

The shamans are pivotal figures in the rites of passage for their respective cultures in quite another way. Their wisdom is consulted in events which are believed critical to living, such as naming the infants, in the Vision Quest or puberty rites which signify the beginnings of adult responsibility, and in the ceremonial occasions of birth and marriage. This stands to reason in a shamanic culture, where the shaman, as well as being a healer, serves as a philosopher/priest privy to the special knowledge.

The function of any society's health system is ultimately tied to the philosophical convictions that the members hold regarding the purpose for life itself. For the shamanic cultures, the purpose is spiritual development. Health is harmony with the world view. Health is an intuitive perception of the universe and all its inhabitants as being of one fabric. Health is maintaining communication among the animals and plants and minerals and the stars. It is knowing death and life and seeing no difference. It is

blending and melding, seeking solitude and seeking companion-
ship to understand one's many selves. Unlike the more modern
notions, in shamanic society, health is not the absence of feeling;
no more so is it the absence of pain.

The Shamanic State of Consciousness

The shamanic state of consciousness (SSC) is the very essence
of shamanism, and critical to the premise that the shaman is the
past and present master of the imagination as healer. Medical
historian Gordon Risse (1972) claims that in the state of consciousness used in shamanic healing, mental resources are
employed which modern persons either no longer have access to
or are not interested in using in view of their reliance upon
coherent and rational conscious thought. For difficult problems,
the shaman turns to inner experiences instead of rationality for
solutions. Using sensory memories, as well as abstractions and
symbolisms, "he reviews his subconscious flow of pictures
without the use of the critical powers activated by consciousness
as well as the grid of causality, time, and space." (p. 22) The
shaman, in effect, is plugging into a data bank that can't be
known in the normal, waking state of consciousness. A description of the SSC which allows external verification, reproducibil-
ity, and is reliable across observers, will be the closest that this
generation of scientific technology will come to understanding
how the workings of the shaman's imagination could possibly act
upon another person for diagnosis and cure as claimed.

Negligence in understanding the distinction between the SSC
and usual waking states of consciousness, and all that the definitions of those states imply, has led to erroneous conclusions
about shamanistic healing. The belief that shamans dealt
primarily with psychiatric cases (thus using the imagination to
heal only imaginary ailments), or that the shamans' skills were
based upon trickery and hallucinations (i.e., the shamans were
psychopathological themselves) is a failure on the part of the
observer to understand the ramifications of differing states of
consciousness.

People who are accustomed to thinking in terms of more than
one reality, such as metaphysicists, some quantum physicists,
and mystics, have no problem in understanding the implications

of the shamanic state of consciousness. When thoughts are conceived of as things, or things as thoughts (or, more precisely, as the inevitable, eternal interchange between mass and energy), then the shamanic system, as embodied in the special state of being, can be viewed as something beyond an exclusive conglomerate of superstitious behavior, dishonest quacks, and gullible, desperate patients. (It shoulld go without saying, though, that crass fraud exists in healing systems, including shamanism.)

The implications of the existence of a real but nonordinary reality should be extrapolated to the rituals and symbols used in healing ceremonies. "Ritual" and "symbol" are concepts contemporary Western cultures hold dear as metaphorical, or as pretend acts and items. In the SSC these become—they actually are—what the shaman says they represent. When a shaman dons the skin of his power animal and dances around the campfire, it is the power animal dancing in the SSC, not the man and a skin in some theatrical rendition. When the shaman sucks a bloody object out of an ailing patient's chest, or presses into the patient's gut and retrieves a spider and claims to have extracted a disease, the Western scientist tends to evaluate the magician-like performance in ordinary reality's terms. Did the cure make the patient physically well? Was the "thing" gotten from the patient medically related to the disease?

Such questions are irrelevant to the shamanic sense of health. Getting well may have little or nothing to do with the body; and since there is not such a thing as a symbol, only the thing itself, the chicken gizzard or the blood-stained down are exactly what the shaman says they are—and that is whatever was revealed during the SSC. The symbols are the shaman's way of distilling the journey and presenting information in a way the community might appreciate. They are not lies, but rather a system used to communicate a little-understood reality.

The SSC represents a discrete altered state of consciousness, following Charles Tart's (1975) categorizations. The reality encountered is different from what Tart calls the consensus reality (Castaneda's ordinary reality and Harner's ordinary state of consciousness) but not necessarily to be equated with other kinds of altered states of consciousness such as those noted in REM or dream sleep, hypnosis, meditation, while in a coma, or after taking psychedelic drugs. Peters and Price-Williams (1980) analyzed shamanic practices in 42 cultures and also concluded that shamanic ecstasy was a specific type of altered state. The notion that there exists only a consensus reality, and every other perception is pathological, has significantly impeded the taxonomy of altered states. I submit that the SSC is indeed different from those states cited above, but may correspond to the realm of consciousness described by the mystics, and expounded upon by such fine writers on the topic as Evelyn Underhill (1912) and William James (1961), e.g., a state of insight into the depths of truth, unplumbed by the discursive intellect, and used to establish a conscious relation with the Absolute.

The SSC corresponds significantly to Lawrence LeShan's (1975) description of "clairvoyant reality," which he uses to describe states of being experienced by both mystics and psychic healers. He contrasts clairvoyant reality with sensory reality, where information comes in through the senses, time is discrete and moves only in one direction, and space serves as a barrier for information exchange. The clairvoyant reality he describes as timeless, where objects may exist but only as part of the unified whole, and neither time nor space can prevent information exchange. His definition, then, is akin to the idea of a non-ordinary reality as stated by Castaneda, as well as the SSC.

Psychic healing, as LeShan describes it, is well within the rubric of the type of healing with the imagination that I have previously categorized as transpersonal healing. It could be argued that mystics and psychic healers are also shamans, since they enter an altered state of consciousness at will to help other persons, use spirit guides, etc. However, the definition of shamanism implies that a social role is being served which is integral to and recognizable by the community (Price-Williams, 1980). Psychics and mystics normally do not meet the latter implication. Of a certainty, what LeShan and others refer to as psychic phenomena are aspects of shamanism: clairvoyance, precognition, telepathy, mediumship, special diagnostic and healing abilities. Regardless of terminology, the territory appears to be the same.

The SSC in a Research Perspective

Out of the body "journeys" have been reported following significant periods of sensory deprivation, sensory overload, or monotonous or repetitive stimulation—all three of which are part of the usual ritual for attaining the SSC. One of the most logical experimental paradigms for investigating the SSC, therefore, is a situation of controlled sensory deprivation, or restricted environmental stimulation technique (or REST).

The usual experimental milieu involves either a flotation tank or a room with reduced stimulation. The findings from the extensive work in this area, as recently reported in a most thorough and scholarly work by Peter Suedfield (1980), indicate that the response to reduced or restricted stimulation is culture specific, and that it manifests in certain ways and changes over time as anxiety, motivation, and the experiential complex is altered. Most people surely don't participate in REST to attain the SSC, and experiments are rarely conducted to study the effect of REST on self-discovery or on transcendental states. Generalizations from REST to the SSC must be made with this caution in mind.

In the flotation tank, particularly, the logical bonds between self and nonself are quickly dissolved. The body is free-floating, nonconstricted by clothing; sensory and motor systems are not called into play, and there is no competition for the energy required by the imagination. The brain is allowed space and time to range freely through areas that are beyond sensory input and motor exposition. There is widespread agreement among researchers that under such conditions creativity and special problem solving abilities are enhanced, and vivid visual images are commonly reported as the source for new information. In some of the earliest work in the area of deprivation, Heron (1957) and Zubek, Welch, and Saunders (1963) reported on unusual shifts into slower alpha activity following 96 hours and 14 days of perceptual deprivation, respectively, corresponding to Tart's findings on the OOB experience. Suedfield (1980), in reviewing the findings of EEG and REST, offers support for this effect on alpha activity, and cites evidence pointing to its persistence days after exposure to the REST situation. An increase in theta waves (the very slow brain waves associated with creativity) is noted, particularly in the temporal region of the brain, but not with the same consistency as the change in alpha waves. Therefore, it appears that a slowing of alpha might be of relevance in discriminating aspects of the SSC, but the significance of the relationship remains unclear.

Setting the Stage: Rituals and Symbols

Shamanic rituals and symbols provide one of the more fascinating sagas about how human beings attempt to relate to the supernatural in order to create a condition of health, in its broadest sense. My purpose, though, is not to offer a compendium of shamanic practice, since that has been done quite well already by Mircea Eliade (1964) and others. I shall only offer a summary statement and a few examples.

Four issues relevant to healing can be abstracted out of the voluminous writings on shamanistic ritual and practice. The first, and one that connot be overemphasized, was discussed in the previous section: the rituals and symbols of healing have a quite different yet very real meaning in the non-ordinary reality or shamanic state of consciousness. Second, many rituals and symbols are culturally determined, speaking to the needs of only a special population. Next, there are some similar symbols and rituals found in all parts of the world, indicating a kind of collective unconscious at work. And finally, while these tools of the trade cannot in any way be separated or omitted from the concept of shamanism, it is not the tools and rituals that heal, it is the power endowed in them by the imagination.

Since shamans do their healing work in something other than the wide-awake, beta brain-wave, linear-thought state of mind, they naturally first have to adopt satisfactory ways of exiting from that condition. The healee, too, may well be involved in the practices intended to induce an altered state of consciousness. This constitutes the serious beginning of the healing ritual, although the ritual setting itself may have taken days to prepare. Virtually anything that has ever been used to alter consciousness has probably been included in one or another shaman's rituals, with most of the techniques geared toward hypostimulation or hyperstimulation of various sensory systems. Some examples follow.

1. Intensive temperature conditions. The sweat lodge or sauna-like structure is a common method for inducing an altered state of consciousness. The heat experienced in these structures, with or without ritual, can induce a massive systemic effect which includes rapidly increased pulse rate, nausea, dizziness, and syncope (fainting); in short, the warning signs of the impending medical condition we call heat stroke. Cultures that use the heat in a healing sense do not seem concerned about negative effects, and often prescribe it as a cure for serious illness even in the young and the elderly. There is little question that the physiological response to such intense stimulation is partially a function of what one has learned to expect.

There is a biochemical component to high body temperatures during fevers which reflects the natural reaction to toxins, and is correlated to the immune system in action. The artificially induced high temperatures of the sauna may mimic or induce this activity (as does sustained aerobic exercise). Furthermore, the sweat or sauna may act as a sterilization procedure, killing bacteria, viruses, and other organisms that thrive at body temperature but are susceptible to heat. The growth of tumors may also be inhibited when core body temperature is significantly elevated. Heat directed at the tumors has been an experimental treatment for cancer in approximately fifty medical centers in this country. Apparently, the heat is not only effective in killing cancer cells, but also makes the surviving cancer cells more vulnerable to radiation and chemotherapy. In any case, drinking lots of water and then taking a sauna results in feelings of detoxification and clearing of the mind. The heat itself can help create an altered state of consciousness and promote the intense concentration necessary for healing.

The ability to self-generate internal heat is typically regarded as necessary for shamanistic healing. One of the putative derivations of the word *shaman* is the Vedic *sram*, "to heat oneself or practice austerities." (Blacker, 1975) According to an Eskimo shaman, "Every real shaman has to feel an illumination in his body, in the inside of his head or in his brain; something that gleams like fire, that gives him the power to see with closed eyes into the darkness, into the hidden things or into the future, or into the secrets of another man." (Lommel, 1967, p. 60) Agreement for this premise comes from Evans-Wentz' (1967) work on Tibetan yogins, who claim many of the same abilities as the shaman. The advanced yogins are said to be able to produce psychic heat that renders them impervious to the temperature extremes, even to long-term exposure to snow while wrapped only in sheets dipped in icy water.

In order to create their special state, the yogins use a process of imagery; one which involves visualizing a sun in various parts of their bodies and the world being permeated by fire. It is said that as a result of practicing these exercises over a long period of time, the yogin has the ability to learn of past, present, and future events.

The relationship between the hypermetabolic state produced by increased heat and acquiring unusual knowledge is beyond any scientific interpretation. But consider the incredible mental control over physiology that must be exercised in order for dramatic temperature shifts to be made. Temperature regulation is one of the most complex autonomic functions in the human body. The mere maintenance of homeostatic temperature requires a moment-by-moment interplay between air temperature, skin temperature, and a regulating center in the preoptic hypothalamus in the brain. Regulation is required even when sitting nude in a comfortable room since about 12% of body heat is quickly lost under these conditions.

In order to sustain body heat in unusual climes such as the icy Himalayas or to increase body heat significantly above normal levels, as is reported by the shamans, the body has available only three known mechanisms. These are: shivering or other muscular activity; excitation of chemicals to increase the levels of circulating norepinephrine and epinephrine (and subsequently cellular metabolism); and increased thyroxine output, which also increases the rate of cellular metabolism. (Guyton, 1982).

External temperature can be raised by diverting internal body heat to the periphery through an increased rate of blood flow in the skin. It is profusely documented throughout the biofeedback literature that this can be accomplished with various mental techniques such as imagery, relaxation, and temperature biofeedback. These procedures have been used effectively to treat a myriad of health conditions, including migraine, Raynaud's Syndrome and other circulatory disorders, arthritis, pain, and stress-related diseases. Increased peripheral temperatures (usually measured on the hands and feet) are an indicator of reduced sympathetic nervous system activity; hence, a reduced stress response. Of course, none of this may be of any relevance to the Tibetan yogin, nor to the Arctic shamans who also endure extreme cold, since diversion of blood to the periphery would quickly result in a fatal decrease in core temperature. The yogins and shamans have apparently found a means to continue an indefinite heat exchange, which means they have the ability to regenerate those chemicals involved for a long time. We can only conclude that a powerful ability to self-regulate the thermal response is apparent, and those who involve themselves in such affairs regard the internal heat as a pathway to knowledge.

2. *Physical or sensory deprivation.* Physical deprivation takes many forms, and the mystical experience it induces is by no means unique to the shamanic cultures. Typically the shamans fast before doing difficult work. The fast may include dispensing with food, or with salt, or even with water. Other deprivations include going without sleep for several nights, avoiding animal protein and milk products, and abstaining from sex. Most ceremonial work is done in darkness, or with the eyes covered to shut out ordinary reality. Visions are sought by staying isolated in deep caves, or in the monotonous landscape of the tundra or desert.

In sum, the shamans use a culturally sanctioned means of deprivation to find their way into the SSC. Their methods have the potential to cause significant physical and mental shifts by inducing electrolyte imbalances, hypoglycemia, dehydration, and loss of sensory input. The shamans seem willing to push their bodies to the physiological limits in order to awaken the mind. What the modern world regards as dangerous threats to health, even to life itself, are viewed by the shaman as routes to knowledge.

3. *The use of sacred plants.* Hallucinogenic substances are employed throughout shamanic healing traditions as the fastest way to encounter the supernatural; however, it is important to realize that the plants are not essential to shamanic work. The topic captured the imagination of anthropologists in the 1960s concurrent with a heightened awareness of drugs in this country. The voluminous reading available includes the following: the role of hallucinogens in some North and South American and European shamanic traditions has been reviewed in a book edited by Michael Harner (1973); Gordon Wasson (1968) has reviewed the use of the fly-agaric mushroom among the Siberians, East Indians, and Scandinavians; Weston LaBarre has written a classic

treatise on peyote (1938); and Peter Furst (1972) has edited a volume on the ritual use of hallucinogens.

Anthropologist Carlos Castaneda, too, has described in widely-read detail (1968) his use of psychotropic power plants as visionary aids while under the mentorship of Yaqui shaman Don Juan. There are mixed reactions in scientific circles regarding the authenticity and meaning of Castaneda's experiences, but there is some consensus that even if they were confabulated they are highly representative of cross-cultural encounters with the supernatural.

The greater number of Castaneda's experiences are not properly within the shamanic healing tradition, but should best be classified as sorcery, or power-seeking. However, his journeying to find the place "between the worlds" involves using techniques of the imagination identical to those of healing shamans. Don Juan guided Castaneda through episodes following the use of Datura (Jimson weed), Psilocybin mushrooms, and peyote. But the drugs were resorted to only after it became obvious that Castaneda's waking state of consciousness was too restricted to expand into the mystical, magical, non-ordinary reality. Castaneda stated that he would always question the validity of his experiences under the influence of the psychotropic plants, and he regarded the final stage of consciousness expansion—the pure wondering perception of viewing the world without interpretation—as not possible with the drugs. (From an interview with Sam Keen, published in Noel, 1976.)

On the other hand, since there is a relationship between the shamanic tradition and the use of sacred plants, we do need to consider their use, and certainly what relationship they might play in a shamanistic renaissance. First of all, as mentioned, they provide a rapid means of altering consciousness. Second, in preliterate societies, both death and dreams foretold of other states of being, and the answers to these—the greatest of mysteries—were most likely sought through experience rather than intellectual discourse. The noted psychotropic effects of the power plants, such as losing the boundaries of self, enhanced awareness of the continuity of all things, and a sense of awe and wonder, gave the shamans the insight and knowledge they craved of the world beyond the senses. Because of these properties, the plants are universally called "medicine" and referred to as being "sacred." Using them for recreational purposes would be unthinkable.

Unlike those of some mystical persuasions, the shamans do not seek enlightenment for its sake alone, but with the explicit purpose of aiding the community. Their path is circular, i.e., they move up and out into other realms but then return again with knowledge and power. Whenever the sacred plants are used in the healing arts, their effects must be subtle enough to permit the shaman to function in this way. Ritual work cannot be done in a comatose state of oblivion, or when control is relinquished to narcotic effects. The shamans ingest appropriate amounts of the plants to allow for postexperience recall, and for enough awareness to be cognizant of the multiple realities being encountered. One foot, so to speak, stays in ordinary reality.

We must evaluate the "sacred plant" aspect of healing cautiously. The modern world of medicine would give forth with a collective shudder at the thought of the healer taking powerful, dangerous chemicals, especially when the same states of mind can be achieved through nonchemical means. But is there not a parallel here between this and providing the patient with powerful, dangerous chemicals, when evidence is rapidly accumulating that the imagination itself can create every conceivable physical change? The chemical crutches, in both instances, are only evolutionary steps in learning to use the forces of consciousness to heal.

The drugs used in a spiritual tradition were medicine—the best medicine the world knew for thousands of years. But for a culture that has progressively alienated itself from the spirit world in all its institutions, a culture that has tried its hardest to separate mind from body, the drugs provide only a tantalizing taste of mysticism, which our current myth cannot explain and will not incorporate.

4. Auditory aids to altered states. Repeated, monotonous stimulation of any sense changes the focus of awareness. For the shaman, the usual choice of sound stimulus comes from drums, rattles, sticks, or other percussion instruments. Chants and songs, of course, are important to all cultures in healing ceremony.

Often, the chants are phonemes strung together. There is no ready interpretation or translation for them available in the language of ordinary reality, only in feeling states. They may serve the purpose of bypassing the logical, language part of our brains, and tickling the intuitive. (A devout Catholic friend made the observation that Mass lost much of its impact when it was no longer given in Latin. "When you didn't know what the words meant, you communicated more directly with God.")

The shaman's drum reigns as the most important means to enter other realities, and as one of the most universal characteristics of shamanism. The drum can be made of about anything that sets up a reasonably deep tone. According to Drury (1982), it is made of the wood of the world tree, and the skin is sometimes directly linked to the animal the shaman uses to encounter the place of spirit. The wonderfully resonant water drums may be made of old metal cooking pots filled partway with water and wrapped with an animal skin—a time-consuming process that must be repeated often during long ceremonials.

The sounds of the percussion instruments and the rattles are time-honored methods for consciousness altering, and are considered to have a numbing or analgesic effect. "On a contemplative level," says Drury, "the sound of the drum thus acts as a focusing device for the shaman. It creates an atmosphere of concentration and resolve, enabling him to sink deep into trance as he shifts his attention to the inner journey of the spirit." (Drury, 1982, p. 8)

Several physiological facts support the role of sound in this regard. First, the auditory tracts pass directly into the reticular activating system (RAS) of the brain stem. The RAS is a massive "nerve net" and functions to coordinate sensory input and motor tone, and to alert the cortex to incoming information. Sound, traveling on these pathways, is capable of activating the entire brain. (Guyton, 1982) Strong, repetitive neuronal firing in the auditory pathways and ultimately in the cerebral cortex, such as would be experienced from the drums, could theoretically compete successfully for cognitive awareness. Other sensory stimuli from ordinary reality, including pain, could thus be gated or filtered out. The mind would then be free to expand into other realms.

The pain model established by Melzack and Wall (1965) (i.e., gate theory) can be appropriately applied here. Their model is the most widely cited, universally accepted model of the pain mechanism. (With the recent advances in identifying pain modulating chemicals such as the endorphins, the gate theory is considered only part of the story, however.) Melzack and Wall have proposed that since the pain message travels on small, sluggish fibers, the perception of pain can be effectively blocked by other incoming stimuli traveling on more rapid conducting fibers. The model has been used to account for the pain-relieving effects of acupuncture, mild transcutaneous electrical stimulation, and massage. Powerful sounds, such as the drumming, which have the capacity to activate all brain centers, could well fulfill the requirement for faster, more competitive stimulation.

The direct effect of acoustic stimulation on the brain was reported in a classic study by Neher (1961; 1962). He recorded EEG's in normal subjects while they listened to low frequency, high amplitude sound from a drum. The purpose of the study was to determine whether the drumming could cause "auditory driving," so named because some stimuli are known to "drive" or provoke a pattern of firing frequencies in surrounding systems.

In Neher's work, auditory driving responses were elicited at 3, 4, 6, and 8 beats per second, and the subjects expressed subjective accounts of both visual and auditory imagery. He concluded that susceptibility to rhythmic stimulation is enhanced by stress and metabolic imbalances (hypoglycemia, fatigue, etc., all to be expected as part of the shamanic ritual). He also proposed that sound stimulation in the frequency range of 4-7 cycles per second would be most effective in ceremonial work, since this could enhance the theta rhythms which occur in the temporal auditory regions of the cortex. Theta rhythms, I might add, have also been shown to be related to creativity, unusual problem solving, vivid imagery, and states of reverie (Green & Green, 1977). Unfortunately, while Neher's premise is sound, his study was critically flawed because he did not control for movement artifact. The EEG cannot discriminate between eye blinks, head nods, and brain waves, and what Neher may have been recording was any or all of these, done in keeping time with the drum's rhythm.

Jilek (1982) offers still more information on theta driving capacity of drumming in work with the Salish Indians during their spirit dance ceremonial. In analyzing the records of drumming, he determined the rhythms encompassed a frequency range of from .8 to 5.0 cycles per second. One-third of the frequencies were above 3.0 cycles per second, or quite close to the theta wave frequency. He also notes that the rhythmic acoustic stimulation in the ceremonies involves many drums and is significantly more intensive than Neher used in his experiments.

Let us consider in greater detail now the mechanism through which auditory stimuli might serve to alter brain function. A neuron carrying information through the sensory complex of the nervous system can either fire or not fire, and messages in all systems are based upon the frequency of this firing. For example, suppose sensory information from some system was able to "drive" the entire motor cortex. Then the rate of neuronal firing in the motor cortex would be identical with whatever frequency was occurring in the driving sensory system. This could produce extremely bizarre and maladaptive effects if it happened readily, which it apparently does not except in severe epileptics. Most of the work on "driving" has been done with the visual system. A repetitive visual stimulus such as a strobe light has been shown to cause "photic driving" in widespread areas of the cortex, in studies conducted with animals, persons with epilepsy, and in normal subjects.

Evidence from meditation research (Benson, 1975; Benson, Beary & Carol, 1974) indicates the auditory stimulus need not be external but only imaged in order to effect a significant physiological change. Transcendental meditation, the relaxation response (espoused by Herbert Benson), and other adaptations of *raja yoga* involve imaging a word or sound (or mantra) over and over again. One might call this an imaged chant. (In all fairness to Benson and his colleagues, this is my interpretation and not theirs.) Physiological response and benefits have been reported to include decreases in heart rate, blood pressure and muscle tension, and increased alpha and theta activity in the EEG. The methods have been touted as an important method of controlling stress and establishing a "wakeful hypometabolic state" which can restore the body to a comfortable, healthful level of homeostatic balance.

5. *Spirit allies*. The last aspect of the imagination that we will deal with here is one of the outstanding characteristics of shamanhood: the spirit helpers. These are the spirit forms, usually of animals, who protect the shaman in dangerous work, and whom they claim as the source of their knowledge. These are the professors in that medical school of the great beyond. For the Japanese shaman, they may take the exalted form of a transformation of the Buddha. (Blacker, 1975) A Netsilik Eskimo, regarded as a major shaman of his time, had no fewer than seven spirits—a sea scorpion, a killer whale, a black dog with no ears, and ghosts of three dead people. (Balikci, 1967) In American Indian tribes, the spirits may be animals having special cultural significance—bears, eagles, wolves.

Deer are widely associated with shamanic work. In Siberia, real-life reindeer shared the fly-agaric journeys with the shaman. (Wasson, 1968) In Iran and China, deer horns are still valued as both magic and medicine (LaBarre, 1979), and powdered horn is widely sold as an aphrodisiac. The deer spirit is believed to leave the sacred peyote buttons as tracks to guide the shamans on their supernatural course, according to the myths of the Huichols. Even in prehistoric times, the deer had healing significance, based on man/deer shaman art forms that have been found on caves and artifacts.

Now we can analyze the use of spirit guides with the tools of modern science and derive perfectly sane and acceptable reasons for any truths that might evolve from spirit communication. If the spirits only symbolize the intuitive, communication would be akin to the left side of the brain asking the right side "What's happening?" The shamans would be those individuals who could best combine logic and intuition. However, in shamanism humans are naturally in communication with animals, spirits, and even rocks because they are one and the same in the great unified order of things. Shamans are those who can acutely sense and move with the fabric of the universe, and are led along their healing path by sources of wisdom manifest in what have come to be known as spirit guides. Again, the shamans' qualifications are undeniably based upon their demonstration of a vivid imagination, and their ability to stay in control of the situation—regardless of where their information comes from.

Conclusion

What conclusions can be drawn from looking at the widespread cultural manifestation of shamanism? In assessing this highly subjective material, one might best conclude that the pathway through the skylights of consciousness is the same regardless of how and where the voyage is begun in ordinary reality. The descriptions of the methods of diagnosis and healing are quite similar: entering the patient, becoming the patient, and reestablishing the sense of connectedness. And all of this is done in a state of consciousness quite different from the one used to drive a car, or to write a prescription. The cultural addenda to the basic principles of healing are largely occasioned by whatever local resources are present to serve as "medicine."

Medicine itself can be defined here in two ways: first, as the vehicle of transport for the shaman (and often the patient) to enter the requisite state of consciousness; and second, as the material symbols of the healing state—the medicine bundles, sacred art, intrusive objects removed from the patient, the power animal, the curing stones, and so forth. An accomplished shaman would theoretically require neither of these types of medicine, using instead only well-developed powers of the imagination. The symbols and rituals that hold power for a culture appear necessary to open the healing mechanism for the patient who is not as well-schooled spiritually as the shaman.

Finally, for shamans of all genre, the distinction between body, mind, and spirit is nil. Body is mind, and mind is spirit. Although the terminology I have used might seem to indicate that the shamans are dealing with the body, mind, and spirit as separate entities, in the literal sense they do not. Nor do the shamans technically move from physical places to spirit realms, because they are already one and the same. Self is stone, and the stone is the universe. According to Grossinger (1980), the shaman does not think "Here spirit enters into matter," but "assumes spirit is always in matter, is matter—not only during the disease but from the moment of embodiment and the onset of creation itself." (p. 97) Yet, at the same time it is not incorrect to recognize the individual qualities of body, mind, and spirit. In this system they are considered both part of each other and separate from each other, much as a tree is part of, and separate from, the earth and the sky. This type of discussion is significantly impeded by the limitations of English expression which evolved from a very different point of view about the true nature of things.

References

Achterberg, J. *Imagery in Healing: Shamanism and Modern Medicine.* Boston/London: Shambhala, 1985.

Balikci, A. "Shamanistic Behavior among the Netsilik Eskimos." In *Magic, Witchcraft and Curing*, edited by J. Middleton. New York: The Natural History Press, 1967.

Benson, H. *The Relaxation Response.* New York: Morrow, 1975.

Benson, H.; Beary, J. F.; and Carol, M. P. "The Relaxation Response," *Psychiatry* 37 (1974): 37-46.

Blacker, C. *The Catalpa Bow.* London: Allen & Unwin, 1975.

Castaneda, C. *The Teachings of Don Juan: A Yaqui Way of Knowledge.* Berkeley and Los Angeles: University of California Press, 1968.

Drury, N. *The Shaman and the Magician.* London, Boston, and Henley: Routledge & Kegan Paul, 1982.

Eliade, M. *Shamanism: Archaic Techniques of Ecstasy.* New York: Pantheon Books, Bollengen Foundation, 1964.

Evans-Wentz, W. Y. *Tibetan Yoga and Secret Doctrines.* London: Oxford University Press, 1967.

Furst, P. T. ed. *Flesh of the Gods: The Ritual Use of Hallucinogens.* New York: Doubleday/Natural History Press, 1972.

Green, E., and Green, A. *Beyond Biofeedback.* New York: Delta, 1977.

Grossinger, R. *Planet Medicine: From Stone Age Shamanism to Post-Industrial Healing.* Garden City, New York: Anchor Press/Doubleday, 1980.

Guyton, H. C. *Human Physiology and Mechanisms of Disease.* 3rd ed. Philadelphia, W. B. Saunders Co., 1982.

Harner, M. ed. *Hallucinogens and Shamanism.* New York: Oxford University Press, 1973.

Heron, W. "The Pathology of Boredom." *Scientific American* 196 (1957): 52-56.

James, W. *The Varieties of Religious Experience*, New York: Collier Books, 1961.

Jilek, W. G. *Indian Healing*. Blaine, Wash.: Hancock House, 1982.

Jilek-Aall, L. *Call Mama Doctor*. Seattle, Wash.: Hancock House, 1979,

LaBarre, W. *The Peyote Cult*. New Haven: Yale University Press, 1938.

LaBarre, W. "Shamanic Origins of Religion and Medicine." *Journal of Psychedelic Drugs* II, 1-2 (1979): 7-11.

LeShan, L *The Medium, the Mystic, and the Physicist*. New York: Ballantine Books, 1975.

Lommel, A. *Shamanism*. New York: McGraw Hill, 1967.

Melzack, R., and Wall, P. D. "Pain Mechanism: A New Theory." *Science* 150 (1965): 971-979.

Neher, A. "Auditory Driving Observed with Scalp Electrodes in Normal Subject." *EEG and Clinical Neurophysiology* 13 (1961): 449-451.

Neher, A. "A Physiological Explanation of Unusual Behavior in Ceremonies Involving Drums." *Human Biology* 34 (1962): 151-160.

Noel, D. C. *Seeing Castaneda: Reactions to the "Don Juan" Writings of Carlos Castaneda*. New York: G. P. Putnam's Sons, 1976.

Peters, L. G., and Price-Williams, D. "Towards an Experiential Analysis of Shamanism." *American Ethnologist* 7 (1980): 398-418.

Risse, G. B. "Shamanism: The Dawn of a Healing Profession." *Wisconsin Medical Journal* 71 (1972): 18-23.

Suedfield, P. *Restricted Environmental Stimulation*. New York: Wiley–Interscience, 1980.

Tart, C. *States of Consciousness*. New York: E. P. Dutton, 1975.

Underhill, E. *Mysticism*, 4th ed. London: Methuen and Co., 1912.

Wasson, R. G. *Divine Mushroom of Immortality*. Ethno-Mycological Studies, No. 1. New York: Harcourt, Brace, Jovanovich, 1968.

Zubek, J.; Welch, C.; and Saunders, M. "Electroencephalographic Changes During and After 14 Days of Perceptual Deprivation." *Science* 139 (1963): 490-492.

7

Dreams and Shamanism

STANLEY KRIPPNER

In recent years, there has been an increase in the attention paid to shamanism, both on an academic and on a popular level. One aspect of shamanism that has gained special consideration is the emphasis shamans place on dreams, both in their "call" to the shamanic profession and on the part of the clients they are called upon to assist.

Shamans are men and women who claim to be able to voluntarily alter their consciousness, engaging in unusual experiences that supposedly enable them to help and heal members of their tribe. In psychological terms, shamans purport to self-regulate their attention so as to obtain information that enables them to ameliorate the condition of members of their social group.

Cultural Myths

In the cultural myths of many societies, there are accounts of three zones: the Upper World, Middle Earth, and the Underworld. In the Golden Ages of these societies, it was said that people travelled between these worlds with ease. There was no rigid division between wakefulness and dreams; if someone could imagine or dream an event, that action actually could take place. Some type of sin or arrogant act brought about a Fall; the bridge connecting these realms collapsed and travel between zones became the exclusive privilege of deities, spirits, and shamans.

Other cultural myths tell of an "original shaman," selected by the gods and capable of incredible powers. These shamans were supposed to have been capable of levitation, flying, and bodily transformation. These feats were rarely repeated by later shamans, again because some type of human behavior had evoked divine displeasure (Eliade, 1964).

Receiving the "Call"

Contemporary shamans enter their vocations in several ways—through heredity, through recovery from an illness mediated by spirits, during a vision quest, in an initiatory dream. In Okinawa, spirits notify the elect through visions and dreams; most of the recipients who are "called" attempt to ignore the spirits, but eventually surrender (Lebra, 1969). Most shamanic traditions take the position that refusal to follow the spirit notification will result in sickness, insanity, or even death.

Among the Inuit Eskimos, one is "called" by dreaming about spirits. The dreamer is then "possessed" by an animal spirit that compels him to withdraw from society and wander naked. Eventually the initiate gains control over the spirit and celebrates his victory by making a drum (Oswalt, 1967). Dreams of deceased relatives are held to mark one's "call" among the Wintu and Shasta tribes of California (Park, 1938). Among the Southern Valley Yokuts of California, shamanic power may come, unsought, in a dream or from a deliberate quest (Wallace, 1978). In California's Dieguenos and Luisanos tribes, future shamans can be selected as early as nine years of age on the basis of their dreams (Almstedt, 1977). Among several other American Indian tribes, initiatory dreams contain such birds and animals as bears, deer, eagles, and owls; the dream creature instructs the dreamer to take its power and begin shamanic training (Rogers, 1982, p. 21).

In 1980, I interviewed Margaret Umlazi, a Zulu *sangoma,* or shaman, when I visited southern Africa. Margaret told me that she was attending a missionary school when she began to have epileptic seizures. Medical treatment was ineffective, so Margaret visited a sangoma who listened carefully to her description of the seizures. The sangoma asked Margaret if she recalled any recent dreams. Margaret replied:

I was taken to a large pool of water by spiritual beings who
I could not see. A python came out of the water, wrapped itself
around me, and pulled me into the pool. My father brought a
goat to the water so that I could be delivered from the python.
I found myself coming out of the pool and heard a whistle
from the snake. As I looked back, I saw the python turning
into my dead grandfather. I felt the wind blowing on me as I
awakened.

The sangoma told Margaret that spirits had come to her in the
dream, notifying her that she must follow the shamanic path.
Zulu tradition holds that spirits travel in the wind, that pythons
represent healing power, and that large bodies of water symbolize change and rebirth. In addition, goats typically are used
in celebration feasts once a shamanic apprentice has completed
a phase of his or her training. The fact that the python changed
into her grandfather indicated that her departed family members
favored her becoming a sangoma. Margaret embarked on her
long apprenticeship; once she finished it, she began to see clients
herself. Her epileptic seizures gradually subsided and did not
recur once her training was complete.

Shamanic Training

The training program for apprentice shamans varies from one
part of the world to another, but typically lasts for several years.
Usually, apprentices will learn their skills from master shamans.
The apprentices are taught nomenclature (e.g., the names and
functions of deities, spirits, and power animals), history (e.g.,
the geneaology of the tribe), technology (e.g., rituals, music,
dances), herbology (e.g., the difference between medicinal and
sacred plants), secret knowledge (e.g., location of "power
places," identification of "power objects"), tribal mythology,
and dream interpretation procedures.

The apprentice can also obtain knowledge from his or her
guiding and helping spirits. Ruth Benedict (1983) has observed
that a shaman's guardian spirit will often take the form of a bird
or an animal. This spirit protects the shamans as they enter
potentially dangerous altered states of consciousness, and even
accompanies them to the Upper World and the Underworld.
Shamans also employ a number of helping spirits, especially as
they engage in divination and healing.

Sometimes the training period is quite brief. In the Washo tribe of Nevada and California, the initiate would receive his power through a dream, then would be awakened by a whistle. He would follow the whistle, and it would change to a whisper that would dictate instructions. For example, it might tell him to bathe on four successive mornings and treat a sick person on four successive nights. If that person recovered from the illness, the initiate's status as a shaman would be confirmed (Rogers, 1982, p. 22).

Dreams and Illness

The Cashinahua Indian shamans of Peru "pursue dreams," believing that the more dreams they have each night, the greater the power they will accrue. Other individuals in the society may want to reduce their number of dreams because it is held that dreaming interferes with skill in hunting. Thus, the hunters may request an herbal preparation that will "calm the dream spirits" (Kensinger, 1974). Zambian shamans believe that they can derive their powers of diagnosis in dreams, giving accurate descriptions of the illness without examining the client (Frankenberg & Leeson, 1976). Among the Iroquois, it was believed that unfulfilled "natural desires" were expressed through dreams. These dreams were able to provide clues to the shaman as to what could be done to restore a client's health. Often, the client would be encouraged to act upon these desires in ways consistent with the tribe's social structure (Wallace, 1958).

Many tribes hold that dreams represent the soul's nocturnal voyage, and some believe that it is vulnerable to abduction by a witch, sorcerer, or malevolent spirit during night-time dreaming. In such cases, it is necessary for the shaman to search for the soul and retrieve it, often engaging in fierce spiritual battles along the way (Eliade, 1964). The Northwest Coast Indians of North America carve "soul catchers" out of bone for this purpose. Malay shamans make images of dough and roll them over the client's body to bring back the soul (Rogers, 1982, pp. 41, 109).

For the Maricopa Indians, unpleasant dreams are the most common source of illness, bringing on pains, colds, and diarrhea

(Spier, 1933). Dreams are also held to be a primary cause of illness among the Paviotso Indians. Children can become ill if their parents' dreams are unfavorable or if bad dreams are experienced by visitors. In either event, shamanic assistance is called for to halt the effect (Park, 1938).

Interpreting Dreams

In many societies, an important function of the shaman is dream interpretation. The Taulipang shamans of the Caribbean are considered to be experts in explaining their own dreams and dreams of others (Rogers, 1982, p. 11). Australian aborigine shamans move into "Dreamtime" with great facility to assist the hunting activities of their societies (Halifax, 1982, p. 61).

Rolling Thunder, an intertribal medicine man living in Nevada, frequently would interpret dreams for members of his community. I saw one young man bring him a dream about a white buffalo fighting with a black buffalo. Rolling Thunder listened to the dream carefully, then asked the dreamer what part of himself he thought each buffalo symbolized. Rolling Thunder is reported to have appeared in the dreams of other people from time to time. In 1986, I received the following report from a student:

> I wrote a letter to Rolling Thunder several years ago. In the letter I asked him about a bird with which I was enamored. This bird, the ivory-billed woodpecker, was last seen two decades ago and was considered extinct by some ornithologists.
>
> I heard from Rolling Thunder's people that my letter was a good one and they were referring it to him personally. Some weeks later, I had a dream and spoke to Rolling Thunder. It seemed like he spoke in Spanish and said that some of the birds still lived in Cuba or Mexico. The dream was very vivid. I told Rolling Thunder that I wanted to talk longer with him, but he said that he was tired, travelled a lot, and had even more travelling to do. As he left me, I felt a sense of excitement that I have rarely experienced.
>
> A few weeks ago several ivory-billed woodpeckers were seen in Cuba! I was really excited when the news confirmed the answer Rolling Thunder had given me in the dream (Perry, 1986).

The Shamanic Personality

These types of reports have convinced some scholars that shamans must suffer from some type of neurosis or psychosis. However, Bruce Boyer (1962) conducted in-depth interviews with Apache shamans and administered the Rorschach Inkblots to them. He also administered the test to Apache tribal males and Apaches who claimed to be shamans but who had no affirmation from their communities for this role.

In evaluating the shamans' responses, Boyer found some evidence for hysteria but none for schizophrenia. He observed some preoccupation with body reactions, sex, and excitability among shamans, but these can be important aspects of shamanism (Eliade, 1964). When an ambiguous, unclear inkblot was described, shamans and non-shamans gave similar descriptions with a few exceptions. Shamans demonstrated a keener awareness of pecularities, more humor, and more philosophical responses. The pseudo-shamans, on the other hand, showed more signs of mental illness than did members of the other two groups.

Boyer concluded that "shamans are healthier than their societal co-members...This finding argues against (the) stand that the shaman is severely neurotic or psychotic, at least insofar as the Apaches are concerned" (p. 179). Richard Noll (1983) also concluded that the "schizophrenic metaphor" of shamanism is untenable. He compared their experiences in altered states of consciousness with symptoms of mental illness. (His report is based on material found in the third edition of the American Psychiatric Association's *Diagnostic and Statistical Manual.*)

I suspect that shamans may fall into the category of "fantasy-prone personality" identified by S. C. Wilson and T. X. Barber (1983), who found that about four percent of the general American population is fantasy prone in that they "see" visions, "hear" voices, and "touch" imaginary companions. Dreams play an important role in the lives of fantasy-prone individuals; they claim to receive guidance in their dreams and even talk to dead relatives or spirits while dreaming.

The characteristics of Wilson and Barber's fantasy-prone individuals are also the characteristics of shamans, including their finding that "subjects with a propensity for... fantasy are as well adjusted as...the average person. It appears that the life experiences and skill developments that underlie the ability for...fantasy are more or less independent of the kinds of life experiences that lead to psychopathology" (p. 379).

Shamanic Wisdom

Michael Harner (1981b) warns against taking a reductionistic approach to the dreams and visions of shamans. Fantasy productions are nearly limitless in the scenarios possible. Yet the belief systems and techniques of shamans are "similar in different parts of the world" (p. 28). It appears, therefore, that shamans have tapped into an important human capacity that was especially useful in the evolution of societies and that is still of value for shamanic groups today.

Shamans have achieved a degree of concentration beyond the ability of the average person. They can sustain exhausting efforts during healing rites that sometimes last for several days. They manifest physical prowess and are able to self-regulate many bodily functions. They have mastered a complex body of knowledge through instruction and direct experience; they are able to apply this wisdom to individual situations in appropriate manners (Krippner & Hooper, 1984).

Dreams are an integral part of shamanism. Knud Rasmussen, the Arctic explorer, is said to have inquired of an Eskimo acquaintance if he was an *angakok* (or shaman). The man responded that he had never been ill nor had ever recalled dreams; therefore, he could not possibly be an angakok (Halifax, 1982, p. 72). This sentiment is echoed, in one way or another, by inhabitants of other tribal societies. It is apparent that shamans represent not only the oldest profession, but are the original professional practitioners endowed with the responsibility to understand dreams—their own and those of their clients.

References

Almstedt, R. F. (1977). Diegueno curing practices. *San Diego Museum Papers, 10,* 9-10.

Benedict, R. F. (1923). *The concept of the guardian spirit in North*

America (Memoir 29). Menasha, WI: American Anthropological Association.

Boyer, B. L. (1962). Remarks on the personality of shamans, with special reference to the Apache of the Mescalero Indian reservation. *Psychoanalytic Study of Society, 2,* 233-254.

Eliade, M. (1964). *Shamanism: Archaic techniques of ecstasy.* Princeton, NJ: Princeton University Press.

Frankenberg, R., & Leeson, J. (1976). Disease, illness, and sickness: Social aspects of the choice of healer in a Lusaka suburb. In J. B. Loudon (Ed.), *Social anthropology and medicine* (pp. 223-258). San Francisco: Academic Press.

Halifax, J. (1982). *Shaman: The wounded healer.* New York: Crossroad.

Harner, M. (1981a). *The way of the shaman: A guide to power and healing.* San Francisco: Harper & Row.

Harner, M. (1981b). The way of the shaman: *The Laughing Man* interviews anthropologist and shaman Michael Harner. *The Laughing Man, 3*(4), 24-29.

Kensinger, K. M. (1974). Cashinahua medicine and medicine men. In P. J. Leon (Ed.), *Native South Americans: Ethnology of the least known continent* (pp. 283-288). Boston: Little, Brown.

Krippner, S., & Hooper, J. (1984, April). Shamanism and dreams. *Dream Newtork Bulletin,* March/April, pp. 14-17.

Lebra, W. P. (1969). Shaman and client in Okinawa. *Mental Health Research in Asia and the Pacific, 12,* 216-222.

Noll, R. (1985). Mental imagery cultivation as a cultural phenomenon: The role of visions in shamanism. *Current Anthropology, 26,* 443-452.

Oswalt, W. H. (1967). *Alaskan Eskimos.* San Francisco: Chandler.

Park, W. Z. (1938). *Shamanism in Western North America: A study in cultural relationships.* Chicago: Northwestern University Press.

Perry, A. (1986, July 18). Personal communication.

Rogers, S. L. (1982). *The shaman: His symbols and his healing power.* Springfield, IL: Charles C. Thomas.

Spier, L. (1933). *Yuman tribes of the Gila River.* Chicago: University of Chicago Press.

Wallace, A. F. C. (1958). Dreams and the wishes of the soul: A type of psychoanalytic theory among the seventeenth century Iroquois. *American Anthropologist, 60,* 234-248.

Wilson, S. C., & Barber, T. X. (1983). The fantasy-prone personality: Implications for understanding imagery, hypnosis, and parapsychological phenomena. In A. A. Sheik (Ed.), *Imagery: Current theory, research, and application* (pp. 340-387). New York: John Wiley & Sons.

8
Shamanism, ESP, and the Paranormal

D. SCOTT ROGO

Richard Erdoes is a European-born writer who explored the world of the Sioux through his friendship with one of their medicine men. He talks of his own experiences during the *yuwipi* ceremony in his *Lame Deer, Seeker of Visions* (Erdoes, 1972). His entire family was present at a performance in North Dakota, which included some forty local Sioux residents. The setting was an old railroad car that had been converted into a house. The only light was provided by an old kerosene lamp, but it was extinguished when the ritual began. It commenced with ceremonial drumming, and soon afterward, tiny lights began appearing throughout the room. "They came floating up out of the darkness for a fraction of a second," writes Erdoes, "and they were gone almost before eye and brain had been able to register them." While making these observations, the writer could also sense that the shaman's rattles were flying through the air.

But the real climax to the performance came when Erdoes's own camera equipment went haywire. This happened right after the writer first felt the rattles taking flight:

> One of my electronic flash units chose this particular moment to go berserk. It began flashing of its own accord. At once there was a chorus of angry voices: "Shut off that damn light, no pictures!" I frantically tried to yank out all connections between battery and strobe, groping around in total darkness, and only made things worse. The strobe went off

133

into a long series of brilliant flashes at intervals of 1/1000th
of a second. I was in a cold sweat. If anybody believed that
I was taking advantage of the situation by taking sneak
photographs, I would no longer be trusted as a friend. I
decided that I had to interrupt the ceremony. I said in a very
loud voice: "This light has gone wild. I'm trying to disconnect
it. I have already put my jacket over it. I'm not trying to take
pictures."

There was an immediate response: "It's O.K. It doesn't
matter. We'll wait. This is a good meeting. The spirits are
here. They know you."

Someone pushed a blanket over to me. "There, cover it all
up." At the mention of a blanket the strobe finally gave in and
stopped flashing. The ceremony resumed. (Erdoes 1972,
280-1).

Reports such as this may not impress the skeptical. The fact
that these reports are purely anecdotal does not mean, however,
that they can be simply dismissed. Why aren't such field observations just as valid and important as any other type of observations reported by anthropologists?

There exists a rich anthropological literature on shamanism,
which is still practiced today among the Eskimos, Siberians,
Mongols, and all through South America and Africa. Mircea
Eliade's classic book *Shamanism—Archaic Techniques of
Ecstasy* (Eliade 1964) cites over 500 major works on the subject
written between the mid-19th century and the 1970s. There are
even more by now. Yet despite this large body of literature, few
anthropologists have studied the psychic side of shamanism.
Most ethnographers have addressed their research purely to the
sociological significance of the practice. Eliade himself suggested that the art of shamanism arose as a ritualized method of
attaining deeply meaningful altered states of consciousness.
I. M. Lewis, one of England's most renowned anthropologists,
has countered this view with his own theory that shamanism
evolved as a method of social control whereby one member of
a tribe acts as a voice box (through his "communications") for
the established norms and mores (Lewis 1971). Neither of these
eminent researchers has ever grappled directly with the issue of
whether shamanism developed as a practice because, in all
cultures and religions, certain people have sought and developed

powerful psychic abilities and have institutionalized their practices over the ages.

Psi and the Shamanic Tradition

The shaman's duties are centered around bringing through communications from the dead and the gods, counteracting spells and black magic, and sending his soul to the netherworlds on behalf of his tribe or clients. By tradition the shaman is supposedly endowed with several specific supernatural (or psi) powers. The same phenomena are mentioned over and over within widely separated cultures. These include the power to heal, to diagnose and "read" people clairvoyantly, to control the weather, to levitate, to become immune to fire, and to project the soul from the body.

Let us look at five "typical" shamanic cultures—cited in Mircea Eliade's celebrated study (1964)—which (by tradition) cultivate certain psychic powers in their shamans, who are said to practice the paranormal arts of that culture.

(1) The newly initiated Araucanian shaman of South America is taught to pray specifically for clairvoyant ability. This ability is to be used to "see" into a patient's body and to diagnose ills. This practice is a mainstay of the shaman/healer in this culture. The initiate allegedly receives psychic healing powers as a result of his prayers.

(2) Shamans among the Caribs of Venezuela and Central America traditionally possess the ability to know psychically the innermost secrets of their tribesmen, including knowledge about the fate of the dead. It is interesting to note that these abilities are very similar to the religious traditions of the Roman Catholic Church, whose mystics and saints were (and are) known to discern psychically the nature of unconfessed sins and the disposition of a deceased individual's soul. Such shamanistic practices may be cross-cultural and inherent in the development of mystical gifts and powers within a wide range of religious traditions.

(3) Several psychic feats are traditionally said to be part of Amerindian culture, including the ability to control the weather, to become immune to fire, to discern clairvoyantly who has perpetrated certain crimes, and to see into the future.

(4) In Malayan shamanism special initiates allegedly possess the power to see into the future and to discover the whereabouts of lost objects.

(5) Another fascinating psychic feat is regularly ascribed to the shamans of the Kamba in East Africa. As in so many other African cultures, the Kamba shamans practice voluntary spirit possession and trance. The Kamba have high expectations of their shamans. If a shaman "brings through" a spirit from another locale or tribe, he is expected to speak in the language or dialect of the spirit's tribe—even if he has never learned or studied it.

There is good evidence to believe that some shamans actually control such powers. A few Western anthropologists have been fortunate enough to witness some stunning displays of psychic capabilities in shamans.

Most shamans are not reluctant to talk about their supernatural powers. Joan Halifax, a medical anthropologist on faculty at the New School for Social Research in New York, discovered this fact in the 1970s when she was traveling the world interviewing these wonder-workers (Halifax 1979). She met Maria Sabina, a celebrated Mazatec shaman in Mexico, in 1977. The old woman was then 83 years old, and she enthralled her visitor with accounts of the many psychic experiences which had arisen from the development of her powers. These include a vision of her own son's death and its tragic inevitability. "I saw the entire life of my son Aurelio and his death and the face and the name of the man that was to kill him, and the dagger with which he was going to kill him," she explained. "It was useless for me to say to my son that he should look out because they would kill him, because there was nothing to say. They would kill him and that was that" (Halifax 1979, 134-5).

Nor is Halifax the only anthropologist who has heard such claims. Marlene Dobkin de Rios, an anthropologist from California, learned during her studies of shamanism in Peru that most of the local healers openly bragged about their psychic experiences (Dobkin de Rios 1972).

Eye-witness Reports of Shamanic Powers

Eye-witnessed accounts of primitive shamans and their powers appear in a fairly obscure report by Vladimir Bogoras, a Russian

ethnologist who made an intensive study of the Chukchee
Eskimos of Siberia and the St. Lawrence Islands at the turn of
the century (Bogoras 1904-1909). Shamanism has practically
died out among the Chukchee today, especially in Alaska, but a
few powerful shamans were still practicing their mediumship
when Bogoras was conducting his field work. He was fortunate
enough to witness several of their displays.

Bogoras encountered the strange world of shamanism during
a performance he attended on the St. Lawrence Islands. The
scene was the shaman's tent, and the wonder-worker sat directly
in front of Bogoras as the demonstration commenced. The
shaman proceeded to invoke the spirits while his followers laid
a walrus skin over his shoulders but did not attach it in any way.
The Russian visitor found his attention directed increasingly to
the skin, which seemed to take on a life of its own. The part
draped over the shaman's back began elevating and contorting
about, although it never actually left the shaman's shoulders.
Bogoras finally grabbed the skin to see how the trick was being
done, but found he could not pull it off the shaman's back—
despite the fact that it was obviously not permanently attached.
Bogoras himself was even thrown about the tent by the skin's
contortions. The shaman sat quietly throughout the whole
display.

Later during his investigations, Bogoras watched another
shaman perform a feat of psychic surgery. A young boy of fourteen was brought to his tent, and the healer magically produced
an incision in the lad's body. Bogoras actually examined the boy
and was able to confirm that an opening had somehow been made
in the skin. Later the shaman closed it up so that no trace of it
was left.

During his extensive investigations, Bogoras heard many
stories about the "spirit voices" that whistle and speak during
Chukchee "seances," and was eventually able to document this
rare phenomenon. The scene was a Chukchee tent in Siberia, and
the subject of the investigation was a shaman famous for his spirit
voices. Bogoras wanted to make a recording of the vocalizations,
though it never crossed his mind that the voices might actually
be real. The anthropologist had long believed that these spirit
voices were produced by clever ventriloquism and nothing more,
but nonetheless he wanted to record them for posterity.

Before the performance began, Bogoras placed a recording funnel some distance from the shaman, who sat stationary throughout the demonstration. There was little light in the tent, so that the ritual was conducted in almost total darkness. The shaman invoked the spirits, and it wasn't long before several spirit voices broke out in the tent. Bogoras was startled to realize that the voices sometimes emanated from various points in the tent and not merely from the shaman's immediate vicinity. This curious effect was also caught by the apparatus that recorded the entire demonstration. Writing about this experience some time later, Bogoras openly admitted that there existed "a very marked difference between the voice of the shaman himself, which sounded from afar, and the voices of the 'spirits,' which seemed to be talking directly into the funnel."

The Russian researcher was never able to break through his scientific training and bias to admit that he had witnessed the miraculous. In his final report, published in 1904 by the American Museum of Natural History, he explained that everything he witnessed was no doubt due to trickery, though he never offered any hint as to how the feats could have been fraudulently performed.

Bogoras' research and observations were later corroborated by an anthropologist from the United States. Riley Moore was a celebrated physical anthropologist who visited the Chukchee several years after Bogoras published his findings. He, too, sat in on several shamanic displays and later admitted to his colleagues that he had heard the same independent voices. He also heard odd poundings on the door of a structure in which one of the rituals was held. Moore was so intrigued by his observations that he interviewed several of the local Eskimos and collected accounts of the sometimes spectacular psychokinetic displays they had witnessed during similar seances. Unfortunately, Moore never published any of this material (cited in Murphy 1964).

The psychic phenomena of shamanism often seem to be cross-cultural—i.e., the same or similar paranormal displays tend to crop up in isolated cultural settings. The manifestations of the Chukchee are similar in this respect to some of the rituals and ceremonies practiced by Amerindian groups. The Ojibwa Indians (whose settlements range from the Great Lakes region to

Eastern Canada) sometimes conduct "shaking tent" rituals, so named for the curious way the tents sway and contort during the invocations. The best source of information on the ritual was published in 1942 by A. Irving Hallowell, who explored the world of the Saulteaux Ojibwa-speaking peoples in Manitoba. His monograph on *The Role of Conjuring in Saulteaux Society* includes both historical and eye-witness perspectives of the shaking tent.* He was unable personally to collect any firm evidence that the tent's movements were paranormal, although some suggestive evidence did come to his attention—both from informants and through earlier published field studies of the Indians. (For instance, one person who spoke with the researcher claimed that he watched a conjuring tent shake even after the shaman left it.) Hallowell did, however, witness the possible extrasensory powers of the shamans who perform these demonstrations. The following incident occurred in 1930 when the researcher was watching his first shaking tent ritual:

> There was a small flap left open in the canvas at the "front" of the tent. The audience sat opposite to this at a distance of some five or six feet. During the performance this flap was periodically thrown open and the conjurer could be seen dimly within. I asked what kind of a journey I would have, as I expected to leave in a couple of days. The conjurer said that I would arrive at my destination safely, but that I would have a little trouble on the water. (On the way back the canoe was flooded in lining [shooting] a rapid, and I almost lost my notes and photographs and some of my belongings.) (Hallowell 1971, 16) Other predictions made by the shaman were also corroborated.

Shamanism and Extrasensory Perception

Accounts of ESP in shamans parallel observations by parapsychologists on clairvoyance (or distant seeing) and on precognition (or knowledge of future events) in psychic subjects. Among observations of shamans' purported psychic ability, probably

---

* For a more popular survey which includes some impressive eye-witness testimony, see pages 123-137 of *American Indians Myths and Mysteries* by Vincent Gaddis (Radnor, PA: Chilton Books, 1977).

more have been made of the Eskimo than of any other group. The Canadian anthropologist Diamond Jenness researched the Copper Eskimos, who live on the coast of the Arctic Ocean in the Northwest territories of Canada. Their shamans divine the future and seek out clairvoyant information by way of dreams.

Jenness had at least one opportunity personally to authenticate the art. In a book on his research published in 1922, Jenness talks about his friendship with an Eskimo shaman named Ilatsiak, who often claimed that his spirit helper came to him in his dreams to deliver important messages and prophecies. The anthropologist reports how one day the shaman

> entered our house and reported that during the night his spirit had told him that something had gone wrong on our schooner; it was the thing, he said, that made the vessel move. We thought that he must mean the propeller, for we had put a new one on during the winter and had to keep the ice open around it. By a strange coincidence, however, we discovered during the day—what Ilatsiak could hardly have been aware of—that a boom we were using to roof our provision cache had snapped during the night owing to the weight of snow above it (Jenness 1922, 200-1).

David Read Barker, an anthropologist until recently affiliated with the University of Virginia, made an in-depth study of the literature on anthropology and the paranormal in the 1970s and uncovered not a few such accounts by searching through a large body of ethnological writings dating back many years. He presented his research at a meeting of parapsychologists held in Vancouver, Canada, in 1974, under the auspices of the Parapsychology Foundation. Most of the accounts he unearthed are brief and hard to analyze, but a few are more impressive. He found, for instance, that a French missionary in New Caledonia reported that he was eye-witness to a remarkable display of traveling clairvoyance by a native shaman in 1930. The seer was also the chief of the tribe the missionary was visiting, and the event took place during a public meeting.

"In the course of a great joyous feast," the missionary wrote in his memoirs, "he suddenly plunged himself into despair, announcing that he saw one of his illustrious relatives in Arama [a town several miles away] agonizing. A canoe was speedily sent to Arama, a three hour trip from there. The chief had just died'' (Barker 1980, 175).

An equally impressive story was collected by A. Irving Hallowell during his work among the Saulteaux of the Beress River in Manitoba, Canada. He reports that one of his local informants was present at the shamanic ritual whose purpose was to locate her son who had been missing for a week. The woman had brought tobacco and tea for the conjurer in payment for his services. After the performance had progressed for awhile, the voice of a young man manifested through the entranced shaman and explained that he was all right, and even stated where he was currently camping. The woman left the seance reassured.

Two days later the young man arrived home. He reported that during the night of the seance he had been asleep at the very location indicated through the shaman, yet he had no recollection of anything unusual occurring that night (Hallowell 1971, 68).

Some of the best firsthand and most contemporary accounts of shamanic wonders have come down to us from the late Adrian Boshier, an amateur anthropologist who witnessed several psychic displays during the many years he lived in the wilds of Africa. Boshier, who was born and raised in England, always felt a deep affinity for the dark continent, even before he actually traveled there. His family finally emigrated to Africa when he was little more than a teenager. Though totally inexperienced in the fine art of wilderness survival, he immediately decided to take up the life of a nomad. He lived without provisions in the bush for many years, and eventually became a respected authority on African customs, folklore, and archeology. Because he was epileptic and refused to take medication for his seizures, the local natives believed that he had a special talent for shamanism, and even apprenticed him to a sorcerer for extensive training. Boshier eventually adopted much of the world view taught by the natives, including their belief in the supernatural.

Much of this belief evolved from his own encounters with the local sorcerers. When he addressed a meeting of parapsychologists in London in 1973, he explained how he had visited one shaman who divined his past and future by throwing bones in front of her and "reading" their configurations. He reported that she was able to reveal many "personal details concerning my life, which were absolutely correct."

Later he had the opportunity to test thoroughly an African shaman. This incident took place when Boshier was working in conjunction with a museum in Swaziland, where he was conducting research on shamanism in cooperation with a celebrated local diviner named Ndaleni.

> "Ndaleni first came to the Museum some sixteen months ago in the company of another witchdoctor," he reported to the conference, "and immediately agreed to my testing her spirit. Leaving her in my office with the other witchdoctor and Miss Costello, I went to a neighboring building and took out the skin of a gemsbok [South African antelope]. This I hid beneath a canvas sail on the back of my Landrover. I then called her outside and told her I had hidden something which she must find. With the aid of the other witchdoctor, she knelt down and began to sing softly. Then, in trance state, she informed me that I had hidden something across on the other side of that building, over there. She told me that it had more than one color, that it came from an animal, that it was raised up off the ground. Suddenly she got up, ran around the building, out into the front where the Landrover stood and knelt down beside it. Again she began singing softly, and within five minutes of this she tore off one of her necklaces, and holding it in front of her like a divining rod, she walked around the Landrover, climbed into the back and took out the skin" (Boshier 1974, 27).

Incidents such as these indicate that at least some shamans possess genuine psychic abilities. But do all shamans make use of them? Is the average shaman psychic? This is a difficult question to answer, especially since shamans—like so many of the great mediums of the Victorian Age—are notorious for resorting to trickery in order to impress their clients. Yet it certainly seems likely that some cultures habitually produce shamans of great power, since these societies actually *test* their shamans for ESP during their apprenticeship and only invest as a shaman those who pass.

For example, among the Tungus of Siberia the initiate must appear before a more experienced shaman, who calls forth a particular spirit in the presence of the entire tribe. The initiate must relate the biography of the spirit and also name the other shamans through whom it has manifested. The Korekore tribes of Rhodesia take the test one step further. Their apprentice shamans are required to bring through a specific spirit known to the village, and must be able to recite correctly his life story and tell where his shrine is located. The shaman must then pick out the staff, concealed within a bundle of similar ones, which the spirit's last shaman had used.. The Manchu shamans of Mongolia are required to walk over burning coals before being accepted as genuine seers and healers (Eliade 1964).

These traditions, tests, and anecdotes all point in the same direction—that the shamans of so many world cultures are neither clever tricksters nor instruments of social control, but may indeed represent psychics of great power and advanced development. Perhaps parapsychologists here in the West should look more closely at these gifted practitioners, who seem to possess powers that oftentimes exceed even the best capabilities of our local psychics. The mystery of the shaman and his powers may, however, remain an unsolved riddle. Many anthropologists interested in shamanism have reported on the widespread belief held in many cultures that the glorious days of the truly great shamans are over. Many of Joan Halifax's informants explained that the shamans of today possess only a vestige of the powers once available to them. So perhaps we will never know whether the shamans of the primitive world are indeed great psychics or merely the current practitioners of a lost psychic art.

References

Barker, David. 1979. Psi phenomena in Tibetan culture. *Research in Parapsychology—1978*. Metuchen, NJ: Scarecrow Press.

Barker, David. 1980. Psi information and culture. In *Communication and Parapsychology*, edited by Betty Shapin and Lisette Coly. New York: Parapsychology Foundation.

Bogoras, Vladimir. 1904-1909. *The Chukchee*. New York: Memoirs of the American Museum of Natural History.

Boshier, Adrian. 1974. African apprenticeship. *Parapsychology Review*, 5 (#4), 1-3, 25-7.

Dobkin de Rios, Marlene. 1972. *Visionary Vine*. San Francisco, Chandler Publishing Co.

Eliade, Mircea. 1972 [1964]. *Shamanism*. Princeton, NJ: Princeton University Press.

Erdoes, Richard. 1972. *Lame Deer, Seeker of Visions*. New York: Simon & Schuster.

Halifax, Joan. 1979. *Shamanic Voices*. New York: Dutton.

Hallowell, A. Irving. 1971. *The Role of Conjuring in Saulteaux Society*. Reprint: New York, Octagon Books.

Jenness, Diamond. 1922. *The Life of the Copper Eskimo*. Ottawa: Report of the Canadian Arctic Expedition, *12*.

Lewis, I.M. 1971. *Ecstatic Religion*. New York: Penguin.

Murphy, Jane M. 1972. Psychotherapeutic aspects of shamanism on St. Lawrence Island, Alaska. In *Magic, Faith & Healing* edited by Ari Kiev. New York: Free Press.

Rose, Ronald. 1956. *Living Magic*. New York: Rand McNally.

9

Rolling Thunder at Work: A Shamanic Healing of Multiple Sclerosis

JIM SWAN

Some people are seven feet tall. Others can run a four minute mile and lift hundreds of pounds of weights. According to the Native American medicine man Rolling Thunder, spiritual healers come to their calling by birth. "It's a power which comes to you," Rolling Thunder once said, "which you have to honor, respect and use; otherwise it can make you sick."

"Once you accept your callin', you never stop learnin'," Rolling Thunder has often said. Having completed his formal training as a medicine person long ago, he continues to have periodic dreams, visions and encounters with plants and animals that

---

Rolling Thunder was born into the Cherokee nation in 1915. He served as apprentice to several medicine people and gradually passed through the seven sacred ceremonies that mark tribal recognition of the development of status as a medicine person. His career as spiritual healer has taken him to places like the Menninger Foundation and the A.R.E. Clinic in Virginia Beach, VA, where he has performed a number of seemingly miraculous healings before medical professionals.[1] In 1981 Rolling Thunder retired from the Southern Pacific Railroad after 35 years. For many years he literally lived two lives—that of a brakeman and, when he was off duty, that of a medicine man working with an ever-growing circle of people and tribes. In addition to performing healings, he has worked as a spiritual advisor with a number of celebrities, including Bob Dylan (who named the *Rolling Thunder Revue* in his honor), Joan Baez, the Grateful Dead rock band and Muhammad Ali.

become his teachers. Over the course of the ten years I have known Rolling Thunder, two dreams he has told me of seem especially informative about his nature.

In one extremely vivid dream he saw a huge golden door open before him. Slowly the shining golden portal swung open and through the door came Quetzalcoatl, the half-man, half-feathered-serpent mythic hero of the Aztecs. Quetzalcoatl danced through the door and merged into Rolling Thunder's body in a blaze of golden light. Rolling Thunder woke up crying, feeling almost as though he was on fire. For the next three days anyone he touched received a strong shock like touching an electric circuit.

Later he reported having a second vivid dream involving an encounter with the devil. This frightened him, he said, until he realized that this was his trickster side and that having known his heroic side, he could then come to know and express his "shadow" without losing his sense of spiritual grace.

In the spring and summer of 1982, I was one of a small group of people in the Seattle, Washington, area having the good fortune to see Rolling Thunder perform a traditional healing on a woman diagnosed as having multiple sclerosis (MS). The woman was a client of mine in psychotherapy, working through the depression associated with having MS. Because of my friendship with Rolling Thunder and working directly with the woman, I was able to observe closely the healing interaction between them during a four month period. The process and results were moving and important to me, so I will relate them as well as memory permits. But first I'll say a little about MS.

Despite the impressive artillery of techniques assembled by modern medicine, some illnesses remain a mystery. One of these is MS or multiple sclerosis. According to medical texts, MS has no known cause nor cure. It is a set of associated symptoms, first described by Charcot in 1872. MS is a progressively worsening disease of the central nervous system affecting some 500,000 people in the U.S. It typically appears between the ages of 20 and 40 as numbness or partial paralysis of one or more limbs, transient blindness and associated malfunctioning of the nervous system. From onset to death, the duration is typically 10 to 20 years, with progressive loss of body functioning. Death is

usually by suffocation, although many people become despon-
dent and commit suicide. Once in a great while MS will spontaneously disappear for no apparent reason.

First impressions are always important, and my first contact
with this MS patient touched me deeply. When she called on the
phone for an appointment, she said in a weak but cheerful voice
that she wanted to work through some depression. On the day of
her first visit, I left the office door open after the previous client
left and told the secretary to send the woman into my office as
soon as she arrived. A call came in that my next client was on
her way but might need some help, so I got up and walked into
the hallway. Some 30 feet away was a young, attractive woman
coming down the hall with a cane in one hand and the other
sliding along the wall for support. I started to come forward to
help, but she assured me, "I'll be all right. I can do it myself."
I stood back and watched as she negotiated the 30 feet in nearly
two minutes.

She was in her early 40s, divorced, with several children.
Three and one-half years previously she had begun to have some
numbness in her legs and would occasionally stumble or fall. A
physician diagnosed her as having multiple sclerosis and placed
her on a conventional schedule of physical therapy. The numbness and loss of strength in her legs grew worse, slowly
spreading to her arms and hands, she told me bravely. After
about a year and a half, she went to a special center for the treatment of MS. She was shocked. "They all seemed to be just
waiting around to die," she said, and walked out determined she
would not. Her search for alternatives had taken her to
chiropractic and then to a Chinese herbalist. When the symptoms
didn't go away, she began to feel depressed and then came to see
me.

For nearly a month I saw her twice weekly, sometimes for two
hours at a time. Research on the psychological mechanisms involved in healing quite clearly shows that having a desire to live
is an essential beginning point for recovery, and I wanted to keep
this flame of hope alive. We started with conventional talking,
but quickly moved into using gestalt, imagery, Feldenkrais exer-

cises and the general psycho-emotional program used by the Simontons in treating people with cancer and other serious illnesses.[2] We reasoned that if MS had no known cause, the use of these additional depth-probing techniques could only help.

While she gained new insights into herself and her depression began to go away, her physical symptoms did not improve. When these same techniques are used with people with cancer, asthma, and ulcers, with any luck the physical symptoms begin to go away; so I began to worry. One day she told me that she was part Cherokee Indian. This divulgence came synchronistically with a call from Rolling Thunder to schedule a talk and workshop for him in Seattle that August. There seemed to be a connection; so I asked if she had ever considered consulting a medicine man. When she said she would be willing to try, I told her about Rolling Thunder.

Having heard about Rolling Thunder, my client said she would like to ask for his help. I warned her not to count on anything, for Rolling Thunder will only "doctor" those people the Great Spirit says he should help. She said she understood. She bought some organic smoking tobacco, and promptly sent it off to Rolling Thunder in Carlin, Nevada.

Three days later, approximately the amount of time it takes for a first-class parcel to travel from Seattle to Carlin, she had an extremely vivid dream at night—the most vivid, she said, she had ever had. Standing at the foot of her bed, she said, were two figures. One was wearing a flowing black robe and "looked like Darth Vader." The other was a large, pink caterpillar. She awoke frightened and charged with so much energy that she couldn't sleep the rest of the night.

The next afternoon she fell asleep on the couch and had another vivid dream. This time she and Rolling Thunder were in a supermarket together. He laid out a "magic carpet" on the floor in the market. They both got on it and flew off around the world. Upon their return Rolling Thunder gave her a kiss. She awoke feeling both energized and embarrassed, she said, because she could still feel him kissing her. She then found that she could get up and move around the house for about an hour with more ease than she had known in years. This was the first sign of any positive change in her physical condition in three and one-half years.

During the next few months I continued to see her for counseling and worked with an herbalist and several other holistic therapists to see if we could reverse her symptoms. Her depression began to go away, but we had no luck with changing her physical condition.

Rolling Thunder arrived in town on a Sunday evening in August, one week before his lecture and workshop. The woman with MS had become strong enough to help organize his visit, and through mutual agreement, she and a friend became cooks for Rolling Thunder and his party of helpers. From the outset, Rolling Thunder made it clear that, regardless of what she did, he couldn't help her unless the Great Spirit gave him permission.

Rolling Thunder was staying at a retreat center near Snoqualmie Falls, Washington—said to be a place where numerous Indian treaties have been made and conflicts settled. On Tuesday evening, Rolling Thunder said he would like to talk with the woman. The party was staying in a two-story chalet made from an old barn. Rolling Thunder's room was on the second floor. He remained in his room, requesting the woman to come up and see him. Slowly she climbed the stairs on her hands and knees, refusing help from anyone. The message was quite clear from the outset that, if she wanted to get better, she would have to work at it.

The first meeting lasted nearly an hour, with Rolling Thunder asking a series of questions which collectively represented a very thorough case history, just as any physician would do. At the end of this time, he puffed on his corncob pipe for a few moments, made some suggestions about her diet and said that he would need to think about things.

On Thursday evening Rolling Thunder held his second session. Again the woman had to ascend the stairs by herself to the second floor of the house. A chiropractor, Dr. Christie Meshew, who is part Cherokee, had set up a massage table, and we helped the woman onto it. For nearly an hour Rolling Thunder performed a series of subtle physical manipulations of the woman's body, testing her range of flexibility as well as administering certain therapeutic treatments such as might be given by a physical therapist. In the process of this session, the woman seemed to drift off into a sound sleep, despite his movements of her limbs. When this happened he told Dr. Meshew and me to leave them alone. As we left the room, Rolling Thunder settled down into a big easy chair beside the woman.

Downstairs a group of us sat around talking. Although it was still early and we were drinking coffee, people seemed to slow down in their movements as a soft cloud of energy enveloped us. All but two of us fell asleep as if drugged. While no one was with Rolling Thunder upstairs, it appeared as though his physical manipulations had placed the woman in a trance which he then entered into himself. As we were all in the same house at the same time, the "spell" of his trance seemed to reach out and include the entire building, pulling most of us into its ambience. Half an hour later when Rolling Thunder came downstairs, there was a tear in his eye and his voice was husky as he said, "She's had a rough time," and then walked out the door into a grove of quiet red cedars.

Friday evening Rolling Thunder gave a lecture to some 400 people and shifted his attention to reporters from the media. Saturday morning he began a two-day workshop with 60 people and said nothing about the woman, except that he was waiting to hear from the Great Spirit. Sunday morning came, and Rolling Thunder announced to the group that at the conclusion of the workshop he would perform a healing ceremony for the woman and asked the people to stay around to help. Everyone immediately agreed that they would.

"Medicine people don't do things just for show," Rolling Thunder said as the formal workshop concluded, "but there's a right time and place for everything." With these words, he went back into the chalet to prepare himself, while outside two of his helpers, Cloud Lightning and Alan, set up a large pow-wow drum in a forest clearing. They asked us to form a circle, and they taught us a simple chant to sing. As our voices rose in harmony to the Shoshone welcoming song, "Hey, hey, hey, unduwah," Rolling Thunder emerged from the chalet.

Rolling Thunder stands about six feet tall and has the build and movements of a football quarterback, taking long gliding strides that express a sense of power in the way they quickly eat up distances. He sometimes wears brightly colored handmade shirts, and this day he was wearing a striking blue and golden one. During his time alone inside, however, he had made some additional changes which now made his presence awesome. As he strode out into the sunlight, on his head was a dark blue turban-like hat with several eagle feathers hanging down from it at odd angles. In front above his forehead was a silver seven-pointed star pin with a large turquoise stone set in the middle. On his cheeks were symbols painted in a white chalky substance. On several of us who were helping him he painted the same symbols; a circle on each cheek for the Grandfather Sun and the Grandmother Moon, and on the forehead a symbol which he described as the "Cherokee Tree of Life," consisting of a central axis trunk with several uplifting branches on either side.

He was wearing a black vest decorated with an elaborate floral beadwork pattern. Perhaps the most striking thing of all was a full badger skin hanging from his waist. The skin had been fashioned into a medicine bag, and from the mouth of the badger protruded several eagle feathers. Without saying a word, he was very clearly showing himself as a shaman and a man of power.

We all became quiet as he entered the circle. "Don't let me frighten you," he said with a laugh, and then proceeded to teach us a shuffling dance step which he called the "Cherokee Two-Step." Soon we were holding hands, stepping in rhythm to the beat of the drum and chanting. Rolling Thunder then stepped into the center of the circle and offered a prayer to the Great Spirit, the four directions, the earth mother and all the spiritual forces. He sent a puff of white smoke to each power he called as we stood in the silence broken only by the wind whispering through the branches and the distant call of a raven.

Finishing his prayer, we began to sing and dance again. Rolling Thunder proceeded to take off his badger skin medicine pouch and boots, as we circled around him. Again he looked skyward, this time raising his hands upward for several moments. As his eyes returned to us, it was immediately apparent that he had somehow changed. His expression had taken on a coldness, and his eyes had now become piercing—"like the gaze of an eagle" suddenly flashed through my mind as our eyes met for a moment. He began to dance in the circle, slowly at first, arms outstretched like wings. He moved about in circles like an eagle floating on a warm summer updraft. Gradually his pace quickened until it became frenzied, and he seemed to be plummeting down to earth. Then he abruptly stopped and let out a loud "whoop," startling everyone. As if the dance had been fully choreographed, we all instantly stopped moving and ceased chanting. Changing composure, Rolling Thunder jokingly said, "You didn't tell me you were all Indians." Laughter rippled around the circle. Nearly 45 minutes had gone by. Rolling Thunder asked us to move to a second circle around a fire that had been built in a nearby clearing ringed by some giant red cedars.

Cloud Lightning and Alan moved the drum to the second circle. Another helper, Mike Thor, moved around the circle with a smudge of sweet grass and cedar, directing the pungent smoke with an eagle feather, first to our hearts and then over the tops of our heads, purifying body, mind and spirit.

Rolling Thunder emerged from the chalet carrying a wool blanket and an old suitcase. He spread the blanket in the center of the circle and opened the suitcase. Taking out a wand of eagle feathers and a buffalo-tail wisk, as well as some crystals and other objects, he arranged them into a simple altar. Then a jug of water was brought to him. The water had been gathered from a sacred spring in an earlier ceremony.

At this point the woman was led out of the chalet. She was wrapped in a blanket, as she was wearing only underpants, and wore a feather in her hair. She moved very slowly, with the aid of a cane and two other women, who helped her lie down on the blanket and covered her.

Rolling Thunder picked up his buffalo-tail wisk and began walking around the woman, making sweeping gestures through the air and over her body, as if he were clearing the aura of the woman. He made several circles around her, put down the wisk, and then picked up his eagle feather wand. Again he circled her, brushing the area above and around her with graceful strokes. He then stood back. Raising the wand to each of the four directions, then directing it back downward toward her body, he seemed to call on the powers of the four directions to help.

Satisfied with this purification, he put down the eagle feathers and stood in prayer, raising his right hand upward to the world above. He then brought his left hand up to his mouth and spat into it. Suddenly he let out an ear-piercing "whoop!" and slapped both hands together. He stood for a minute staring at his hands as we continued to chant to the beat of the drum. Then he knelt beside the woman. He gently lifted the blanket and slid his hands under it, placing them on her back. In a few moments he withdrew, rose to his feet, and repeated the procedure of first raising his right hand skyward, then spitting in his left, and letting out a loud "whoop" as he clapped his hands together. This time as he stood looking into his hands, I seemed to see a purple glow form around his head and hands, like the kind of radiant light portrayed around holy people in religious paintings. Again he knelt down and slipped his hands under the blanket, laying them on her naked back.

Rolling Thunder soon stood and looked down at the woman. His composure seemed to change, and he dropped down beside her on all fours. He began to whine, growl and sniff her, like an animal on the prowl. It suddenly came to me that he'd become a badger, like his medicine bag; his movements closely mimicked those of a badger searching for a mouse. Crawling beside her, he was sniffing her excitedly. Then suddenly he began to whine, and the whine became a growl. He picked up the blanket, thrust his head underneath it, and began to suck on her lower back, making growling sounds. In a few moments he pulled back, picked up a clear glass mug and vomited up some greenish material that looked like pus. He washed his mouth with spring water and returned to her, again sniffing, whining, growling and then sucking on her back. He repeated this procedure several times until he coughed up only the clear water.

In ceremony and ritual work, sometimes, in the midst of the period of license, unusual things happen which Mircea Eliade calls "krakophonies."[3] At this moment, a giant black and orange wood wasp of the Ichneumon variety flew into the circle, seeming to head directly for Rolling Thunder. This species has a three-to-four inch body, as well as a long trailing ovipositor adding another three or four inches in length. The wasp made two or three circles around Rolling Thunder and then flew back off into the forest, as people in its line of flight jumped out of the way.

Now tired, Rolling Thunder rose to his feet and circled the woman, waving his buffalo-tail wisk over and around her body. He motioned for two women to come forward and help her up. They brought out a chair and helped her into it. Her face was radiant, and she smiled with new life, more than I had ever seen. We were silent as all eyes looked at her. "I am alive!" she shouted, rising to her feet. The women handed her the cane and began to help her walk back to the chalet. She was moving much more easily, and after a few steps she tossed away her cane—to our cheers. All around the circle people were crying and hugging each other.

"This woman has been healed today," Rolling Thunder pronounced. "I don't mean cured. If she leads a good life, walking the good red road, and takes care how she eats, then she'll begin to feel better. She'll need to be doctored maybe two more times, by me or someone like me. But if she does this, she'll live a long, full life and walk again. This is the Great Spirit's way. I only act as an agent for the Great Spirit here; the healing comes from the spirit world. I'm just the helper you might say. Ho!" He then collected his things and retreated to the chalet to rest.

While I was standing and talking with people, six people independently came up to me and said they had seen a purple glow of energy around Rolling Thunder's head and hands while he was working. If I alone had seen it, I could dismiss it as creatively inspired mental imagery. Six people independently reporting seeing the same thing either means our minds were all on the same frequency of creative thinking, or something very unusual and profound happened before our eyes.

Later inside the chalet, the woman changed back into her clothes and we talked. She said that while she was lying on the ground, she fell into a deep trance, seeming to leave her body and finding that she could look down on herself. She said she watched herself change into an Indian princess, who then got up and "went on the warpath." With these words, she got to her feet and began to walk. For the next few minutes she moved about the house without her cane or touching any walls for support, moving like this for the first time in several years. Several hours later she needed to use the cane again; but clearly she was moving about more easily, and her whole composure had taken on a new strength. One week later over the phone, she told me that she has her "ups and downs" but still moves better and feels much stronger. Her voice has a much more powerful quality to it. Shortly thereafter she moved, and in a few months I also moved. I do not know what has happened since then, but I have heard that she has been able to begin building a new life for herself with a much greater sense of power and purpose.

The next day I had coffee with a physician who had been present. "You realize that what happened in that ceremony can't happen," he said, his hand shaking a little. "I mean it did happen, at least something happened, but according to modern medical theory such things don't have any value except perhaps to encourage change through suggestion." The medical literature has many well-documented cases of apparent healings due to faith. Perhaps we can say that Rolling Thunder's charisma and manner were somehow able to inspire this woman to get well in a way which couldn't be otherwise accessed. If this is true, the fact that he was successful in changing her physical symptoms when all else had failed seems to suggest that his understanding of psychology demonstrates an expertise from which we could benefit greatly.

There are several things, however, which aren't so easily explained. The vivid dreams which she had in the beginning seem to speak of a transpersonal power which defies modern science, if she was telling the truth about Darth Vader and the giant pink caterpillar. The time Rolling Thunder seemed to induce a hypnotic trance through physical manipulation and then entered into the trance itself with her, pulling most of the rest of us in as well, is a classic form of shamanic healing and diagnosis which is well documented among shamanic peoples all around the world. Then we come to the "purple glow." Did we all imagine the same thing, or was there a special healing energy present which Rolling Thunder was working with? I've been around Rolling Thunder long enough to believe the latter to be the case.

Carl Jung suggested the human mind might be compared with a giant apartment building with many floors, each containing many potentialities. Most modern people, he observed, live only on one or two floors, forgetting about the rest. In the training of a shaman, through rituals, ordeals, ingesting psychoactive substances, prayer, meditation and fasting, under the guidance of teachers in this world and the next, the many floors of the mind are explored. What may appear as madness to the outsider, for a shaman is simply making the rounds in the multidimensional mind.

Watching Rolling Thunder working with a woman with an "incurable" disease, I saw him transform many times. He was a warm and wise father. He joked and played. He startled and frightened us. And he changed to take on the forms of nature, seemed to manifest energies, induced trances, sucked poisons out of the body, and affected dreams.

With so many wondrous floors and rooms in the building we call the human mind, it seems we may now want to turn to the shamans to help us recover what we have forgotten about the human soul before it is too late.

Shortly after submitting the preceding article on Rolling Thunder's healing ceremony, I received a letter from a friend who knew the address of this woman, whom he had treated in 1982. Contacting her, I found she was alive and much better. She reported that she was "not on her feet yet," but swam three times a week and rode horseback twice a week. She said, "I don't have the stress of getting well anymore," and that the "Indian part" of her was taking over. She found her interest strongly drawn into "nature, animals, rocks and the Great Spirit." After several years of darkness, she reported her life was "on the upswing," and that she no longer felt the constant, immediate stress of needing to get well to survive. She had not been doctored again by Rolling Thunder but had the help of some other alternative healers.

References

1. Krippner and Villoldo. *The Realms of Healing*. Millbrae, CA: Celestial Arts, 1976. Also, Green, E. and Green, A., *Beyond Biofeedback*. New York, New York: Delacorte, 1977; and Boyd, D., *Rolling Thunder*. New York, New York: Random House, 1974.
2. See *Getting Well Again* by Carl and Stephanie Matthews Simonton, Los Angeles, Calif.: J. P. Tarcher, Inc., 1978, for details on the psychological dimensions of cancer and related illnesses.
3. Eliade, Mircea. *The Sacred and the Profane*. New York: Harper and Row, 1957.

III

Shamanic Traditions

Certain features of shamanism such as altered states and journeys to alternate realities are universal and cut across cultural lines. However, they are expressed differently in different cultures. The articles in this section give the flavor of shamanism as it is practiced in different societies.

The Tamang shamans in Nepal are identified by a possessing spirit, usually an ancestor, and they must find a living guru in order to be initiated. Peters relates the Tamang belief in three souls, the lower soul, the heart soul, and the soul of light, which the shaman learns to master, thereby gaining supernatural powers. The initiation process has four stages in which the neophyte gains successively more control over the possessed state, learns to utilize his power increasingly through ritual, and transforms crude visions into clear ones. Social support of the villagers is an important part of initiation and of the shaman's vocation. Peters points out connections between Tamang shamanic practices and beliefs and Hindu-Buddhist yoga, especially between the Tamang concept of three souls and the yoga concept of chakras and kundalini.

Jewish prophets such as Elijah and Elisha can be considered shamans, according to Rabbi Gershom. The Old Testament reports the occurrence of altered states along with such feats as healing, raising the dead, subduing evil spirits, and prophesying. Some prophets might be considered Vision Questers who receive visions from otherworldly messengers, and dreams were a common source of guidance in bib-

lical times. Modern-day neo-Hassidics combine this ancient source of wisdom with contemporary insights such as those of transpersonal psychology.

Polynesian kahunas are shamans who enter an altered state to communicate with and influence forces in nature and interact with "gods" or spirits. King emphasizes that they understand the accumulation of inner power or mana and know how to manipulate it, and they take into account the mana of the spirits they contact. Hawaiian kahunas follow the Way of the Adventurer rather than that of the Warrior; they focus on enjoyment, love, and creating peace rather than on strength and protection in a dangerous world. Kahunas treat all realities as subjective and have diverse frameworks of reality which can be used for different occasions. They are expert at altering the reality of another person, which can result in healing or solutions to problems.

Pipeholders among the Plains Indians undergo long periods of training and austerities and must live strictly pure lives. They, like shamans, contact spirits in order to help others and effect outer changes. Perhaps not all pipeholders can be classified as shamans, but there is considerable overlap between the two categories. Freesoul explains that American Indians believe that connection with the spirit world is open to all, not only to a designated few, and they go on Vision Quests to contact spirits and gain intuitive knowledge.

10

The Tamang Shamanism of Nepal

LARRY G. PETERS

The Tamang is the largest ethnic group in Nepal, with about 520,000 people. They speak a Tibeto-Burmese language and reside primarily in the Himalayan mountains surrounding the Kathmandu Valley and in the valley itself (see Bista 1967:xi, 32, 52; W. Frank 1974:94).[1] In Tamang religion, there are two principal religious specialists: lamas and shamans *(bombo)*. Both are part-time practitioners fulfilling different social roles. Lamas officiate at the funeral ceremonies and calendrical rituals; shamans, whose "calling" and altered states of consciousness[2] are the subject of this paper, perform rituals in the treatment of mental and physical illness (Peters 1978).

The process of becoming a Tamang shaman is a long and arduous one. Training is both ecstatic and didactic. It involves mastering a trance state which, at first, overwhelms the individual; and there are numerous *mantra* and myths to be memorized. In order to become a shaman, years of effort are required; and when apprenticeship is completed, the financial rewards are not substantial. Bhirendra, my 44-year-old key informant, is a part-time shaman and a part-time farmer, mason, and laborer. When he was 13 he was called to the shamanic vocation by an experience that caused him to become "mad," compelling him to seek solitude in a forest and cemetery. There he was beset with visions in which evil spirits attacked him and nearly killed him before he was miraculously saved. This experience had a tremen-

161

dous effect on his life, motivating him to become a shaman; that is, he undertook a seven-year apprenticeship in which he learned deliberately to induce and control the mental state that initially made him ill.

The Tamang shaman's apprenticeship results in a mastery of altered states of consciousness involving voluntary entry into and exit from these states. Shirokogoroff (1935:268, 271), in his classic study of Tungus shamanism, described the shaman's most basic attribute as the "mastery of spirits" (also see Firth 1964:338). He observed that the shaman, in his trance, controls the spirits by using his body as a "placing" into which spirits are induced and exorcised. In other words, a dominant feature of the shaman's trance is "possession."[3] Such is also the case for the Tamang. Furthermore, they, like the Tungus, distinguish between individuals who are involuntarily possessed (interpreted as an illness) and the shaman who "possesses spirits." The same distinctions between these two types of trance are also noted by Oesterreich (1966:131ff), who refers to them as "spontaneous" and "voluntary," respectively. Bourguignon (1968:6-7) calls them "negative" and "positive"; Lewis (1971:55), "unsolicited" and "solicited." This movement from negative to positive possession is a major goal of the Tamang shaman's initiatory process.

While some investigators emphasize possession as a necessary feature of shamanism (Shirokogoroff 1935:371; Loeb 1929: 62-63), others contend that the true shaman experiences only visionary magical flight[4] (Eliade 1964:493, 499). Lewis (1971:49) includes both phenomena in his definition, noting that while either can be dominant, they may also coexist with various degrees of emphasis (see Reinhard 1976:16). In a cross-cultural survey of 42 cultures in which shamanism is reported. Peters and Price-Williams (1980:418) found 18 with spirit possession only, 10 with magical flight only, 11 with both, and 3 in which neither concept was used to explain the trance state. This confirms the hypothesis that shamanism is inclusive of trance phenomena given more than one interpretation.

Tamang *bombo* maintain that they magically fly, ascending and descending to heavens and underworlds where they encounter gods "face to face." It is believed that the vision at the time of the calling is an unripe or crude vision *(ta rang ga)*, while those voluntarily induced by initiated shamans are called clear visions *(ta top che)*. There are specific Tamang initiation ceremonies designed to transform crude visions into clear ones. As in possession trance, "control" distinguishes the shaman's magical flight from soul loss, which is thought by the Tamang to be a form of illness.

Numerous writers on shamanism have emphasized that the shaman is a sick man who has been healed (Ackerknecht 1943:46; Eliade 1964:27ff). Shirokogoroff (1935:271) writes, "The shaman may begin his life career with a psychosis but he cannot carry on his function if he cannot master himself."

Shamanic Transmission and Psychopathology

Tamang shamans are called to their profession through a crisis-type experience typical of many Asian shamans. As opposed to the deliberate "vision quest" that is a dominant feature in many forms of North American shamanism (Lowie 1954:157), the Tamang shaman has a spontaneous vocation in which he is inflicted by spirits that possess him and drive him into solitude, demanding he become a shaman. This unsolicited altered state of consciousness that afflicts future Tamang shamans is called crazy possession *(Ihakhoiba mayba)*. In this mental state, the neophyte shakes convulsively, indicating that he is possessed but not knowing why or by what. At times he may shout incoherently or weep. As mentioned earlier, he may have visions, but they are unstructured and chaotic. The future shaman's family becomes concerned because he forgets to eat and becomes lethargic when not beset with anxiety. Eventually, he may run naked into the forest and live with the animals for several days.

While the calling is involuntary and spontaneous, it is also similar to what Krader (1967:114) terms "quasi-hereditary" in that transmission of shamanic powers occurs within a lineage but not to a predetermined individual. The Tamang believe that dead shamans normally choose the male patrilineal kinsman they prefer.

The spirit that possessed Bhirendra, when he was called, was his dead grandfather, who chose him over his brothers and other male kin. According to the Tamang, the power (Ne. *shakti*) of the dead *bombo* searches for a "religious person," one who can carry on his duties. The possessing spirit eventually becomes the young shaman's main tutelary spirit (Ne. *mukhiya guru*).

The spontaneous calling is also comparable to what Czaplicka (1914:178), in a discussion of Siberian shamanism, describes as a "hereditary disease" in which the office of shaman remains within a family yet makes the new possessor suffer greatly. The following narrative is Bhirendra's description of his initiatory calling.

When I was 13, I became possessed. I later learned that the spirit was my dead grandfather, but at the time I did not know what was happening. I began to shake violently and was unable to sit still even for a minute, even when I was not trembling. My grandfather made me mad through possession, and I ran off into the forest, naked, for three days. My grandfather and the other spirits all wore pointed hats and were only three feet tall. They taught me magical formula [Ne. *mantra*] and gave me *shakti*. They fed me earthworms and I had to eat them or die. Still, each time I reached for the worms, one of the spirits' wives (who are monstrous looking) whipped my hands. She carried a gold sword and each time she whipped me she yelled, "Let's cut off his head!" But my grandfather said no because he wanted to teach me. He told me the correct way to take the food was with the back of my hands. When I did this, I was not whipped.

Finally, all the people in the village came looking for me. When they caught up with me, I stopped shivering and woke up. I was taken home and given food. My family was very concerned; I had no appetite and that night began shaking again. This time, I took my father's [also a shaman] magical dagger and went to where the three rivers cross [a cemetery]. The villagers did not follow me, for the gods had opened up a path. Even if someone had followed me, they would not have seen the path I was taking. They would walk into trees and thorns, and fall off cliffs. In the cemetery, I saw many evil spirits, some with long crooked fangs, others with no heads and with eyes in the middle of their chest, still others carrying decaying corpses. They attacked me and, before I knew it, they were all over me devouring my body. I was scared to death and, in a last hope, cried for the gods to save me, pleading that I was only a young boy. I drew out my father's magical dagger to defend myself, but it fell to the ground and struck a rock. This created a spark of light and everything changed. Suddenly it was daytime and the demons were gone. I was alive!

When Bhirendra returned home, he related his vision to his parents. Although his father was a *bombo*, it was decided that his maternal uncle, a very powerful shaman, would become the boy's guru. He taught Bhirendra numerous ritual methods and *mantra* and how to enter trances voluntarily. But Bhirendra's grandfather became his "internal guru," visiting him in his dreams to give him special instructions and *mantra;* that is, his dead grandfather's spirit, which had initially possessed him and made him mad, became Bhirendra's chief tutelary spirit. Whenever Bhirendra errs in his ritual undertakings, forgetting a *mantra* or performing something incorrectly, his grandfather comes to him in his sleep and slaps his hands.

Experiences similar to that reported by Bhirendra have been reported by shamans the world over. The psychopathology of these critical experiences is often noted. For example, Sternberg (1968[1925]:474) mentions that the election of the shaman is manifested by the outbreak of a serious illness, usually at the onset of sexual maturity. Czaplicka (1914:172) writes that, among the Tungus of the Trans-Baikal region, "to be called to become a shaman is generally equivalent to being afflicted with hysteria." In fact, there seems to be general agreement that the shaman, during the critical calling, suffers from some form of psychopathology, although there are various opinions as to what this illness is. As indicated, Eliade (1964: 27) and Ackerknecht (1943:46), as well as the Tamang, maintain that the shaman's initial experience (the calling) is equivalent to an affliction from which recovery is expected. However, there is much opposing argument in the literature over whether recovery actually does occur (Devereux 1956:28-29; Kroeber 1952; Lot-Falck 1970). Silverman (1967:22-23) compares such experiences to acute schizophrenia. In this form, the schizophrenia is merely one life episode, happening abruptly and leading to a nonparanoid resolution. This is opposed to the other "reactive" form, one leading to a paranoid solution in which the inner experience is not comprehended and the individual prematurely redirects his attention to the external world because of his terror of the inner world.

The acute shamanic experience, by contrast, is supposed to bring about a positive readjustment of the individual. Thus, from a psychiatric perspective, Silverman (1967:23) agrees with Eliade and Ackerknecht that "the shaman is a healed madman."

The process of becoming cured can be compared to Wallace's (1961:182-184) concept of "mazeway resynthesis," that is, a reorganization of one's way of structuring the world due to intolerable anxiety and crisis. Therefore, although the experience is critical, its outcome (psychological change and attainment of a career) seems highly therapeutic. Prince (1976:127) suggests that the type of psychotic experience undergone by the shaman parallels the therapeutic experience in that it breaks down rigid ego structures and reconstitutes them.

Bateson (1961:x-xiv) believes that the acute psychotic episode is sometimes part of a psychological process that leads to a resolution of a pathological stituation. He compares the episode to an initiation ceremony, with its death and rebirth being equivalent to the passage through psychosis. From this viewpoint, the acute schizophrenic episode, once begun, is guided in its course by an "endogenous process" that leads from psychosis to a completion involving a return to the normal world with new insights. Similarly, Prince (1980:180) writes, "The function of psychosis is to break down the ego and its maladaptive defenses (explained as death or world destruction) and to reintegrate as an adaptive ego (experienced as a rebirth)."

Freud was probably the first to apply this type of thinking to psychotic syndromes. In his analysis of Schreber's *Memoirs of My Nervous Illness,* Freud (1958a[1911]:71) suggests that paranoid distrubances should be looked upon as a dissolution of an overly rigid ego and an attempt at reconstruction which, in the case of the psychotic, is "never wholly successful." He writes, "The delusion formation, which we take to be a pathological product, is in reality an attempt at recovery, a process of reconstruction" (1958a:71).

Now, why is it that some individuals are successful in resolving such crises and others are not? Why do some people develop delusionary and paranoid systems? One factor suggested is the extent of sociocultural acceptance of the crisis experience. Wallace (1961:182ff.) indicates that culture enters into the process by imposing evaluations upon experience. Thus, culture can be either a hindrance or a support to mazeway resynthesis, depending on whether it views the experience as undesirable and negative, thereby invoking shame, anxiety, and feelings of alienation, or as positive and appropriate, providing a culturally sanctioned channel for nonordinary experience (cf. Laing 1967:100ff.). In other words, the status, role, and prestige accorded the shaman greatly enhance his chances of successful readaptation as opposed to a similar experience in another culture where such supports are unavailable.

Although shamans as a group cannot be considered either normal or abnormal (Kennedy 1974:1150; Peters and Price-Williams 1980:407), it is important to view the "shaman's calling" per se from a psychological perspective because of the widespread occurrence of this type of experiential phenomenon. Bhirendra's experience seems typical and has many of the qualities reported in numerous mystical or religious experiences. For example, the vision of the saving light is one element (Eliade 1965), as is the initiatory structure of suffering the "dark night of the soul" that precedes divine grace (Underhill 1955: 169-170). Bhirendra's religious experience occurred within the cultural context of shamanism; through it he found meaning in his life and, as a result of the training embarked upon after the experience, became a shaman.

The Tamang *bombo* does not live in an idiosyncratic universe, nor does he suffer from an "impairment of reality testing," cognitive distortion, or maladaptive behavior. The world of spirits, the dreams and visions of the shaman may seem abnormal from our cultural perspective, but from the perspective of the Tamang, it is all part of reality which consensus populates with numerous spirits believed to possess individuals, cause illness, and exist in other demonstrable ways. Seen from a relativistic point of view, shamanism is not a pathological delusion, but is comparable to what Spiro (1967:106) calls a "culturally constituted defense." The shaman's training is a set of psychotherapeutic techniques designed to channel and guide the chaotic feelings created during the calling into a culturally constituted pattern.

The Initiatory Levels

After the calling, all Tamang shamans must find a guru in order to be initiated, a process involving the learning of a body of myths and the mastery of ritual methods and techniques, including trance states. In my relationship with Bhirendra and his five disciples, I observed that the guru functions as a psychotherapist in that he explains to his trainees the meaning of their dreams, hallucinations and paroxysms and places them within the context of an initiatory system. The shaking becomes identified as the possession of an ancestor, and the visions and dreams are related to mythology and other aspects of the belief system. It has frequently been noted that the shaman functions as a psychiatrist in relation to his patients (Lederer 1973:Levi-Strauss 1963; Moerman 1979). This is equally true in his relationship to his disciples.

Shamanic training involves the deliberate production of trance states. The guru conducts numerous purification rituals in which the neophyte plays the drum in order to bring about possession or visonary states.[5] At each of the major healing rituals, the disciples sing the myths with the guru and call on the gods to possess them. The idea behind the training exercises is that the more one becomes entranced, the more control is gained over the trance state. Control, however, is something which one attains gradually.

There are four stages in the Tamang initiation process. Each stage, or initiatory grade, represents a higher attainment by the neophyte. The calling is the initial stage. Here, possession is unsolicited. As mentioned, the initiate's condition during this stage is described as "crazy possession."

The second stage (lha khreba[6]) begins with the training of the disciple by the human guru who prepares him for the performance of guru puja (Ne.), in which the possessing spirit (the tutelary guru) speaks out and identifies itself through the disciple. Bhirendra explained that during the ceremony the human guru first plays the drum and becomes possessed by the neophyte's tutelary spirit. Each time he becomes possessed, the guru attempts to transfer the spirit to the initiate by either passing the beating drum to him or by using two drums, if available. The neophyte may shake mildly with each attempted transfer until the spirit "hits" or takes possession of him, at which point he shakes violently. But the purpose of the ritual is not fulfilled until the possessing entity speaks through the disciple, identifying itself.

Guru puja is done formally to identify the possessing agent that called the neophyte, and this identification is made while the initiate is in a possession trance. The spirit then assumes the function of *mukhiya guru* (internal guru) and visits the candidate in his dreams to introduce him to all the spirits over whom the dead shaman gained mastery in his lifetime. This progresses simultaneously with the *bombo's* didactic training.

So, in the second stage one develops more control over the possessed state. The disciple begins to learn how to call on his tutelary guru to possess him voluntarily. The neophyte is still not fully in control and at times mumbles inconsistencies. This stage is described as being "ridden by the guru" or "having the guru upon one's shoulders." Although possession is induced and ended with the help of the human guru, the possessed state is not suitably controlled to be used in ritualistic situations.

In the third stage of initiation, after the performance of numerous purification rituals and *guru puja,* an even more controlled form of possession *(iha khresi)* becomes attainable. Here the *bombo* initiate gains control over the gods and is therefore able to utilize his powers in the performance of ritual duties. In this stage, the tutelary guru speaks coherently through the shaman. There are no more ramblings, laughing, or one-word utterances. The *bombo* can now make diagnoses and perform other types of divination. With the aid of the gods and spirits over which he has gained control, and through knowledge of ritual methods and myths learned from the guru, he can perform healing rituals. The initiate is now a shaman. In fact, many *bombo* never progress beyond this level. This is the stage of control which, as noted before, is so important in distinguishing pathological from controlled possession. The *bombo* expresses this distinction by saying that he is now "riding the guru," indicating that the relationship has changed: the shaman is now master of the spirit and thus of the affliction initially caused him.

It is interesting to note that initiatory progress through the grades corresponds to Tamang beliefs about the three souls of men, which are thought to be located in the solar plexus, the heart, and the top of the head. The *bombo's* shaking is said to be brought about through the lower soul *(sem chang),* which embodies the power of anger utilized by the *bombo* in sorcery.

When an individual dies, this soul may stay on earth and cause trouble as an evil spirit. When a neophyte first becomes possessed, it is the lower soul that is activated and is the first soul he must come to master. This is done through the heart soul *(yidam bhla)*, the soul of compassion and of speech, which is activated when the *mukhiya guru* speaks through the initiate while possessing him.

The third soul *(che wa)* is described as a light located between the eyes. It is the light of consciousness and also the light that shines from the eyes. When it is controlled, the shaman is said to have attained the highest power one can get through initiations *(ti sal borba*[7] *[ti sal,* "loss of consciousness"; *borba,* "to go off"]). At this stage, the *che wa* soul of the *bombo* can embark on magical flight. The shaman is able to soul-journey to the heavens and underworlds. At this level, crude visions are superseded by clear visions.

This final initiatory goal is achieved in two stages, marked by two ceremonies: *pho wang lung* and *gufa*[8] (Ne.). *Pho* is a concept with many related meanings. Bhirendra often identified it with the *che wa* soul; other times, with the tuft of hair worn by shamans at the crown of the head in the same spot in which the *mukhiya guru* is thought to reside. *Pho* is sometimes said to be the *mukhiya guru's shakti*. In order for the *che wa* soul to leave the body, the "heavenly doors" located atop the head at the fontanelle must be opened. At the time of death, the *bombo's* characteristic tuft of hair is pulled forward to the "heavenly doors" so that the *che wa* soul can leave the *bombo's* body and travel with the tutelary spirit to heaven, where the *bombo's* deeds and misdeeds are evaluated in order to determine future rebirth. This ritual act is known as "removing the *pho.*" The same ritual manipulation is repeated during *pho wang lung* and it has the same meaning—allowing the *bombo* to soul-journey, protected and accompanied by his *mukhiya guru.* Thus, there is an equation of the separation of the soul at death and during initiation. After *pho wang lung,* the initiate is said to have "attained *pho*" and thereby to have clear visions.

Gufa is the *bombo's* final initiation. Essentially, it is a climb to the highest heaven.[9] Although *gufa* means "cave" in Nepali, the *gufa* is not really a cave; rather, it is a hollow shelter made of rice straw, perched atop four tall stilts and normally used to store grain. For *gufa*, Bhirendra explained that it is erected in a cemetery and decorated with hundreds of white soul flowers *(narling mendo [bignoniaceae oroxylum indicum])*. Leading up to the *gufa* is a nine-rung ladder, serving as the *axis mundi;*[10] that is, it leads to the heavens, with each of the nine rungs representing a level of heaven. *Gufa* initiation takes place above the ninth level and lasts seven days, during which the initiate *bombo,* dressed in a ritual white frock and peacock-feather headdress, continually plays the drum. The little food and water he consumes is brought to him by his guru, who does not speak to him after the first day. On the first day, the guru stays in the *gufa* with the neophyte. They practice repeating the *mantra* the initiate will need to call on the gods and fight off the evil spirits he will confront. They play the drum all day and all night, and they sing and call on the gods to possess them. The process is repeated by the neophyte alone for the next six days. During this time the initiate has visions of ghosts and spirits, which he masters.

On the seventh day, before leaving the *gufa,* Bhirendra had the following vision in which he journeyed to the highest heaven and saw the supreme deity of the shamans, Ghesar Gyalpo.

> I walked into a beautiful garden with flowers of many different colors. There was also a pond and golden glimmery trees. Next to the pond was a very tall building which reached up into the sky. It had a golden staircase of nine steps leading to the top. I climbed the nine steps and saw Ghesar Gyalpo at the top, sitting on his white throne which was covered with soul flowers. He was dressed in white and his face was all white. He had long hair and a white crown. He gave me milk to drink and told me that I would attain much *shakti* to be used for the good of my people.

Bhirendra relates that he left the *gufa* and returned to his village. On his way back, he encountered many villagers who had come out to meet him along with his guru, and they carried him back to the village cheering. This kind of social support, as noted earlier, is an important psychological factor for the fulfillment of the shaman's vocation. Tamang culture provided an idiom for the expression of Bhirendra's calling; it rendered it an event by casting it into the world of meaning and thereby constituting a basis for action.

Tantric Yoga and Tamang Shamanism

There are historical connections between shamanism and Hindu-Buddhist yoga practices. In fact, the Siberian Tungus term *saman* (shaman[11]) derives from the South, and its original meaning is "ascetic" or "one who practices austerities." The religious practices associated with such holy men are thought to have stimulated and influenced the development of the more ancient Northern Asiatic shamanism (Eliade 1965:498; Mironov and Shirokogoroff 1924:130, n. 52; Shirokogoroff 1935:282). This influence and stimulation is conspicuous among the Tamang, who have assimilated many of the concepts of Hindu and Buddhist Tantra while retaining their essential animistic and shamanic belief system. That is, they have reinterpreted and given other values to certain Tantric yoga practices that are now intimately connected to their shamanic religion.

The most obvious of these influences is in the parallel betwen the Tamang concept of the three souls and the Tantric yoga concept of *chakra* (Skt.), the centers of energy located at various points between the base of the spine and the top of the head. Yogic stages of initiation are marked by the yogi's ability to move this energy, described as a coiled serpent (Skt. *kundalini*) in Hindu practice and as air-wind/vital force (Tib. *lung*) by the Buddhists, up a channel located in the spinal column to the top of the head or "crown center" (see Evans-Wentz 1958:32, 189ff.; Govinda 1960:140ff.; Woodroffe 1974:103ff.). Similarly, in the Tamang system, the lower levels of initiation correspond to the activation of lower souls located at lower levels in the body. The highest level of initiation involves the *che wa* soul, located in the forehead between the eyebrows, which leaves the body through the top of the head and travels to the uppermost level of the universe where the highest god resides.

In Hindu Tantric yoga, the seventh *chakra*, or crown center, does not belong to the plane of the body; it is the plane of transcendence beyond time, space, and material existence. This is why Woodroffe (1974:1ff., 25ff.) mentions "six centers" and "bodiless consciousness." The realization of enlightenment is the attainment of this seventh *chakra* when the *kundalini*, having ascended through the lower *chakras*, penetrates the uppermost chakra, producing enstasis (Skt. *samadhi;* see Eliade 1958a:37, 243-246; Govinda 1960:143; Woodroffe 1974:428ff.). The experience of arousing the *kundalini* to the crown center is described by yogis as something very similar to an "out-of-the-body" experience (Krishna 1971:11).

To a large extent, yoga has "somaticized" the symbolism and rites of shamanism. The *axis mundi* so typical of shamanism, the ladder reaching through the numerous levels of heaven, corresponds in Tantric yoga to the spinal column and the *chakras* that are likewise traversed in order to attain the final initiatory experience. The Tamang shaman's activation of the three souls, as undertaken at different levels of initiation, culminates in the ritual ascent to heaven during *gufa* and parallels the ascent of the *kundalini* in Tantric yoga.

Both Tantric yoga and shamanism also involve the "embodiment" of gods. The shaman becomes possessed by spirits which he masters; the master yogi "identifies" with gods representative of universal forces to the extent of becoming one with them and thereby coming to utilize these forces (Beyer 1973:66-69; Stabelein 1976:368). Furthermore, the initiatory experiences of shamans have many parallels in the experiences undergone by yogis in the process of awakening and raising the *kundalini*. For example, Krishna (1971:63-67) describes himself as being terror stricken, fearing his own death, "shivering as if stricken with ague," before being saved by a "glowing radiance." All of this is strikingly similar to what is described in shamanic "ecstasy."

Fischer (1972:190) distinguishes between enstasis (the goal of certain types of Eastern meditation and yoga) and ecstasy on the basis of the former being a hypoactive and nonhallucinatory state and the latter being hyperactive and hallucinatory. However, as indicated, it is possible for shamans to have meditative-type trances (Elkin 1977:56) and for yogis to have ecstatic experiences. Also, spirit possession, which is a hyperactive state, usually does not involve visual hallucinations (Bourguignon 1973:12). In Nepal, the Tamang shaman may begin his trance with frenzied dance and drumming, ending in a passive, hypoaroused trance in which he reports visions. Furthermore *samadhi* may be achieved through visionary or nonvisonary states. In the *Yoga-sutras*, Patanjali distinguished between "*samadhi* with support" and "*samadhi* without support"; that is, one way to achieve *samadhi* is to remain fixed on a thought or an internal object (Eliade 1969:90ff., 109ff.), and this may entail a visionary state. In both Hindu and Buddhist Tantra the controlled production and subsequent dissolution of "visualizations" are crucial to yogic initiatory progress (Bharati 1975:215; Govinda 1960:104ff.; Tucci 1961:68ff). Thus, at the higher initiatory levels, imagery becomes mastered in both Tantric yoga and shamanism.

The shaman's visions are produced differently from the yogi's in that they are not developed from concentration on icons (Skt. *mandala*) or other symbols upon which one fixes full attention. Yet, for both practitioners the images become part of an unfolding process: dreamlike creations that must be mastered. Like the shaman initiate, "the meditator cannot escape from the mysterious impulses of his own subconscious...which takes shape in these images...instincts which had been repressed (Tucci 1961:74-75).

The shaman is not, however, a seeker of enlightenment, nor does he seek detachment from the world as does the yogi. The shaman's trance is distinct from *samadhi* in that it does not have the same goal. In the *Yogasara-Sangraha* of Vijnanabiksu, *samadhi* is defined as an invulnerable state in which perception of the external world is absent (see Eliade 1958a:78-80). The shaman's trance is outwardly oriented. It is not autonomous, but is directed toward the community and therefore serves as a medium of communication between the supernatural or nonordinary reality and the community of men (Lowie 1954:161-164). Peters and Price-Williams (1980:418) found that the entranced shaman remains in communicative rapport with both audience and patient in 81 percent of the 42 cultures surveyed. The Tamang shaman, while spirit-possessed or on an imaginary flight, remains in rapport with the audience, describing what he sees or diagnosing the illness in the voice of the spirit and answering questions put to him by spectators.

Thus, both Tantra and Tamang shamanism employ techniques designed to produce altered states of consciousness as part of a discipline designed to alter a person's mode of being. Still, their psychological and social goals are quite distinct.

Notes

1. Fieldwork was conducted in 1976 and 1977 in villages three miles from Kathmandu city. Foreign terms are in Tamang, unless otherwise indicated (Ne. = Nepali; Tib. = Tibetan; Skt. = Sanskrit). The use of Tamang and Nepali is not arbitrary, but reflects occurrence in interviews with shamans. Personal names used here are pseudonyms.
2. Krippner (1972:1) defines an altered state of consciousness as a "mental state which can be subjectively recognized by an individual (or by an objective observer of the individual) as representing a *difference* in psychological functioning from the individual's 'normal' alert waking state" (cf. Ludwig 1969:9). More recently, Zinberg (1977:1) suggests using the term "alternate" rather than "altered," which has a pejorative connotation suggesting that such states represent deviation from the way consciousness ought to be. The word "altered" is employed here because it is in current usage. However, I agree with Zinberg (1977:1) that "different states of consciousness prevail at different times for different reasons...*Alternate states of consciousness* is a plural, all-inclusive term, unlike *usual state of consciousness,* which is merely one specific state of ASC."
3. Crapanzano (1977:7) defines possession as "any altered state of consciousness indigenously interpreted in terms of the influence of an alien spirit."
4 .After Eliade (1964), the term "magical flight" is used to connote an altered state of consciousness intepreted as a soul journey to heaven, other worlds, underground, or horizontally (to places in this world). An important variant of soul journey is the sending of a familiar or tutelary spirit on the journey. Both types are psychologically similar in that they involve the "seeing of visions."
5. There are numerous techniques for producing trances, ranging from fasting and other forms of deprivation to dancing (Bourguignon 1972), taking of hallucinogenic drugs (Furst 1976), and the use of percussion instruments (Needham 1967) such as the drum utilized

by the Tamang which, when beaten at certain rapid rates, may facilitate trance states (Neher 1961, 1962; see Prince 1968; Sturtevant 1968). There are also "meditative" type trances such as those employed by aboriginal shamans who sit or lie in "quiet contemplative states" when communicating with the supernatural (Elkin 1977:56).

6. *Iha khreba* is the term most generally but indiscriminately used for all forms of possession. When the shamans were queried in detail, the terms became specific to initiatory levels and types of possession, *iha khreba* being one form.

7. Tamang terms *Ihari nyiba* (cf. Hofer 1974:177, 182) and *Iha den cham nyiba* (both meaning "to go along with the gods") are interchangeable with *ti sal borba.*

8. *Gufa* is occasionally referred to in Tamang as *cham* or cave ritual.

9. Ritual climbs symbolizing ascent to heaven, according to Watters (1975), are part of the initiation ceremonies of the Kham Magars, another Tibetan group in Nepal (cf. Hitchcock 1968).

10. Eliade (1964:259ff.) mentions that in most cultures where shamanism is practiced, there is a concept of a central axis (sometimes conceived to be a ladder, bridge, and often a tree) connecting the various levels of the universe, and that traversing these levels is possible because they are linked together by this axis.

11. Casanowicz (1924:419) writes that the Siberian Tungusic meaning of the term ("one who is excited, moved, raised") is descriptive of the shaman's shaking.

References

Ackerknect, E. 1943. Psychopathology, Primitive-Medicine, and Primitive Culture. Bulletin of the History of Medicine 14:30-67.

Bateson, G. 1961. Introduction. *In* Perceval's Narrative. Gregory Bateson, ed. pp. v-xxii. New York: William Morrow & Company.

Beyer, S. 1973. The Cult of Tara. Berkeley: University of California Press.

Bharati, A. 1975. The Tantric Tradition. New York: Samuel Weiser.

Bista, D. B. 1967. People of Nepal. Kathmandu, Nepal: Ratna Pustak Bhandar.

Bourguignon, E. 1965. The Self, the Behavioral Environment and the Theory of Spirit Possession, *In* Context and Meaning in Cultural Anthropology. M. E. Spiro, ed. pp. 39-60. New York: The Free Press.

1968. World Distribution and Patterns of Possession States. *In* Trance and Possession States. R. Prince, ed. pp. 3-34. Montreal: R. M. Bucke Memorial Society.

1972. Trance Dance. *In* The Highest State of Consciousness. John White, ed. pp. 331-343. Garden City, NY: Doubleday & Company.

1973. Introduction: A Framework for the Comparative Study of Altered States of Consciousness. *In* Religion, Altered States of Consciousness, and Social Change. E. Bourguignon, ed. pp. 3-38. Columbus: Ohio State University Press.

Casanowicz, I. M. 1924. Shamanism of the Natives of Siberia. Washington, DC: Annual Report of the Smithsonian Institution.

Crapanzano, V. 1977. Introduction *In* Case Studies in Spirit Possession. V. Crapanzano and V. Garrison, eds. pp. 1-40. New York: John Wiley & Sons.

Czaplicka, M. A. 1914. Aboriginal Siberia. Oxford: Clarendon Press.

Devereux, G. 1956. Normal and Abnormal: The Key Problem of Psychiatric Anthropology. *In* Some Uses of Anthropology: Theoretical and Applied. J. B. Casagrande and T. Gladwin, eds. pp. 23-48. Washington, DC: Anthropological Society of Washington.

Eliade, M. 1958a. Yoga: Immortality and Freedom. W. R. Trask, transl. Princeton: Bollingen Foundation.

1964. Shamanism: Archaic Techniques of Ecstasy. W. R. Trask, transl. Princeton: Bollingen Foundation.

1965. Experiences of the Mystic Light. *In* The Two and the One. J. M. Cohen, transl. New York: Harper & Row.

1969. Patanjali and Yoga. C. L. Markmann, transl. New York: Schocken Books.

Elkin, A. P. 1977. Aboriginal Men of High Degree. New York: St. Martin's Press.

Evans-Wentz, W. Y., ed. 1958. Tibetan Yoga and Secret Doctrines. London: Oxford University Press.

Firth, R. 1964. Shamanism. *In* A Dictionary of the Social Sciences. J. Gould and W. Kolb, eds. pp. 638-639. New York: Free Press of Glencoe.

Fischer. R. 1972. On Creative, Psychotic and Ecstatic States. *In* The Highest State of Consciousness. J. White, ed. pp. 175-194. Garden City, NY: Doubleday & Company.

Frank, W. 1974. Attempt at an Ethno-Demography of Middle Nepal. *In* Contributions to the Anthropology of Nepal. C. von Furer-Haimendorf, ed. pp. 85-97. Warminster, UK: Aris & Phillips.

Freud, S. 1953 [1916-17] Introductory Lectures on Psycho-Analysis (Part 3). The Standard Edition of the Completed Psychological

Works of Sigmund Freud, Vol. 16. J. Strachey, transl. London: Hogarth Press.

1958a[1911]. Psycho-Analytic Notes on an Autobiographical Account of a Case of Paranoia. *In* The Standard Edition of the Complete Psychological Works of Sigmund Freud, Vol. 12. J. Strachey, transl. pp. 3-84. London: Hogarth Press.

Furst, P. T. 1976. Hallucinogens and Culture. San Francisco: Chandler & Sharp.

Govinda, A. 1961. Foundations of Tibetan Mysticism. New York: Samuel Weiser.

Hitchcock, J. T. 1968. Nepalese Shamanism and the Classic Inner Asian Tradition. History of Religions 7(2):149-158.

Hofer, A. 1974. Is the *Bombo* an Ecstatic? Some Ritual Techniques of Tamang Shamanism. *In* Contributions to the Anthropology of Nepal. C. von Furer-Haimendorf, ed. pp. 168-182. Warminster, UK: Aris & Phillips.

Kennedy, J. G. 1974. Cultural Psychiatry. *In* Handbook of Social and Cultural Anthropology. J. J. Honigmann, ed. pp. 1119-1198. Chicago: Rand McNally College Publishing.

Krader, L. 1967. Buryat Religion and Society. *In* Gods and Rituals. J. Middleton, ed. pp. 103-132. Garden City, NY: The Natural History Press.

Krippner, S. 1972. Altered States of Consciousness. *In* The Highest State of Consciousness. J. White, ed. pp. 1-5. Garden City, NY: Doubleday & Company.

Krishna, G. 1971. Kundalini: The Evolutionary Energy in Man. Berkeley: Shambhala Press.

Kroeber, A. L. 1952. The Nature of Culture. Chicago: University of Chicago Press.

Laing, R. D. 1967. The Politics of Experience. Harmondsworth, UK: Penguin Books.

Lederer, W. 1973. Primitive Psychotherapy. *In* Religious Systems and Psychotherapy. R. H. Cox, ed. pp. 236-253. Springfield, IL: Charles C. Thomas.

Levi-Strauss, C. 1963. The Effectiveness of Symbols. *In* Structural Anthropology. C. Levi-Strauss, ed. pp. 181-201. New York: Basic Books.

Lewis, I. M. 1971. Ecstatic Religion: An Anthropological Study of Spirit Possession and Shamanism, Harmondsworth, UK: Penguin Books.

Loeb, E. M. 1929. Shaman and Seer. American Anthropologist 31:60-84.

Lot-Falck, E. 1970. Psychopathes et Chamans Yakoutes. *In* Echanges et Communications. Melanges Offerts a Claude Levi-Strauss pour son 60th Anniversaire. J. Pouillon and P. Marando, eds. pp. 115-129. The Hague: Mouton.

Lowie, R.H. 1954. Indians of the Plains. American Museum of Natural History Anthropological Handbooks, Vol. 1, New York: McGraw-Hill.

Ludwig, A. M. 1969. Altered States of Consciousness. *In* Altered States of Consciousness. C. T. Tart, ed. pp. 9-22. New York: John Wiley & Sons.

Mironov, N. D., and S. M. Shirokogoroff. 1924. *Sramana* Shaman: Etymology of the Word "Shaman," Journal of the Royal Asiatic Society, North-China Branch (Shanghai) 55:105-130.

Moerman, D. E. 1979. Anthropology of Symbolic Healing. Current Anthropology 20(1):59-80.

Needham, R. 1967. Percussion and Transition. Man (NS)2:606-614.

Neher, A. 1961. Auditory Driving Observed with Scalp Electrodes in Normal Subjects, electroencephalography and Clinical Neurophysiology 13:449-451.

1962. A Physiological Explanation of Unusual Behavior in Ceremonies Involving Dreams. Human Biology 34:151-160.

Oesterreich, T. K. 1966. Possession: Demoniacal and Other. Secaucus, NJ: Citadel Press.

Peters. L. G. 1978. Psychotherapy in Tamang Shamanism. Ethos 6(2):63-91.

Peters, L. G. and D. Price-Williams. 1980. Towards an Experiential Analysis of Shamanism. American Ethnologist 7:397-418.

Prince, R. 1968. Can the EEG Be Used in the Study of Possession States? *In* Trance and Possession States. R. Prince, ed. pp. 121-137. Montreal: R. M. Bucke Memorial Society.

1976. Psychotherapy as the Manipulation of Endogenous Healing Mechanisms: A Transcultural Survey. Transcultural Psychiatric Research Review 13:115-133.

1980. Religious Experience and Psychosis. Journal of Altered States of Consciousness 5(2):167-181.

Reinhard, J. 1976. Shamanism and Spirit Possession: The Definition Problem. *In* Spirit Possession in the Nepal Himalayas. J. T. Hitchcock and R. L. Jones, eds. pp. 12-23. New Delhi: Vikas Publishing House.

Shirokogoroff, S. 1935. Psychomental Complex of the Tungus. London: Routledge & Kegan Paul.

Silverman, J. 1967. Shamans and Acute Schizophrenia. American Anthropologist 69:21-31.

Stabelein, W. 1976. Mahakala the Neo-Shaman: Master of the Ritual.

In Spirit Possession in the Nepal Himalayas. J. T. Hitchcock and R. L. Jones, eds. pp. 361-375. New Delhi: Vikas Publishing House.

Sternberg, L. 1968[1925]. Divine Election in Primitive Religion. *In* Congres International des Americanistes, Compte-Rendu de la XXIth Session, Part 2 (Goteborg 1924). pp. 472-512, Nendeln, Liechtenstein: Kraus-Thomson Organization.

Sturtevant, W. C. 1968. Categories, Percussion and Physiology. Man (NS) 3:133-134.

Tucci, G. 1961. The Theory and Practice of the Mandala, With Special Reference to the Modern Psychology of the Subconscious. A. H. Brodrick, transl. New York: Samuel Weiser.

Underhill, E. 1955. Mysticism: A Study in the Nature and Development of Man's Spiritual Consciousness, New York: Noonday Press.

Wallace, A. F. C. 1961. Culture and Personality. New York: Random House.

Watters, D. 1975. Siberian Shamanistic Traditions among the Kham Magar of Nepal. Contributions to Nepalese Studies: Journal of the Institute of Nepal and Asian Studies, Tribhuvan University, Kirtipur Nepal 2(1):123-168.

Woodroffe, J. (alias A. Avalon). 1974. The Serpent Power. New York: Dover Publications.

Zinberg, N. E. 1977. The Study of Consciousness States: Problems and Progress. *In* Alternate States of Consciousness. N. E. Zinberg, ed. pp. 1-36. New York: The Free Press.

11

Shamanism in the Jewish Tradition

RABBI YONASSAN GERSHOM

A number of years ago, I asked my teacher, Reb Zalman Schachter-Shalomi, the following question: "If I had been born an Indian, I would have become a medicine man. What should I do as a Jew?"

Reb Zalman replied: "Get in touch with the teachings of the early prophets. Elijah and Elisha—they were our shamans."

Shamanic prophets? But weren't the prophets mainly moral preachers? Yes, they did preach, but even a brief look at the Bible reveals that there were at least two kinds of prophets: some, like Jeremiah and Isaiah, stood on a soapbox in the marketplace, reciting long litanies and sermons. Others, like Elijah and Elisha, used few words, but are remembered for miracles performed in the name of YH'VH: healings, raising people from the dead, causing an axehead to float, sweetening bitter water, and increasing the volume of food. (See II Kings, chapters 2, 4, & 5) Still others, like the prophet Ezekiel, combined the two roles, both preaching and receiving messages from spirit beings through visions, dreams, and out-of-body experiences.

These are certainly the types of activities we associate with shamans. As I delved deeper into Jewish history and folklore, I discovered other individuals and schools of thought that might be called shamanic, many of which are not in the Bible. (Non-Jewish readers should note that the so-called "Old Testament" contains only a small fraction of the teachings preserved by the

Jewish people.) In this article, I would like to share some of my findings, and encourage others to explore this vast wealth of material.

To begin, we must re-define our perception of Jews. Western theologians are fond of talking about "Judeo-Christian" tradition, as if the Jews and the Christians were the same people with the same worldview. In fact, no traditional Jew thinks of him/herself as "Judeo-Christian." Rather, we Jews are a tribal people, who have common ancestors (Abraham and Sarah), a common language (Hebrew), a common land base (Israel), a common religion (Judaism), and common festivals where we share traditional songs, stories, and foods. We were originally nomads, divided into twelve clans such as the Deer of Naftali, the Snake of Dan, or the Lion of Judah. And while persecution and exile have often forced us to live in crowded urban ghettos, we have retained much of our tribal consciousness, reflected in our liturgy and rituals.

Once we begin to view Jews as tribal people, many of the Bible stories become clearer. I now see Abraham as a visionquester who goes alone to build an altar, sacrifice a sheep, and wait for the voice of the Creator to speak (Genesis 17). Moses hears YH'VH speak from a burning bush on top of a mountain, where he receives a staff of power and a great vision to lead his people out of slavery. And what about the dreams in which Jacob is told to place peeled sticks where his sheep and goats drink, in order to increase his share in the herd? (Genesis 30:25-31:13) This certainly appears to be an act of sympathetic magic: to make goats come out striped, show their mothers striped sticks! And for Jacob, it works.

Jacob's wrestling with an angel *(malach)* and receiving a blessing is part of a shamanic journey. Alone on the desert, on his way to meet his hostile brother Esau, Jacob was troubled. Would there be war or peace? Then comes the *malach*, a word which can mean either a spirit being (angel) or a physical messenger. Jacob wrestles with the *malach* and is wounded in the leg, but wins the battle and is blessed with a new name, as is the shaman. No longer would he be called *Yaakov*, "the Heel"; now he has become *Yisroel*, "the Godwrestler." (Genesis 32:23-33) If, as some Jewish stories suggest, the mysterious messenger was

Esau's guardian angel come to kill Jacob, then the episode is even more shamanic, because the power to subdue evil spirits is associated with medicine people the world over. Be that as it may, the change within Jacob has its effect on Esau, and the two brothers embrace in peace (Genesis 33).

The most common Hebrew word for prophet, *nah-vee*, is related to the words *nah-vah*, "to flow or gush forth," and *nah-vuv*, meaning "hollow." To be a prophet is to be a channel of *shay-fah*, divine blessing, often described as being "poured out like water" upon the people. The prophet Samuel is also called a *ro-eh*, meaning "one who sees." This is apparently an older term, because the Bible finds it necessary to explain that "formerly in Israel, when a man went to inquire of God, he would say, 'Come, let us go to the seer,' for the prophet of today was formerly called a seer" (I Samuel 9:9).

Samuel's "seeing" abilities include foretelling the future and locating lost objects. When Saul, the future king of Israel, first seeks him out to help locate some missing donkeys, he finds himself greeted with a royal welcome. The Creator had already informed the Seer that Saul was coming, and that he would become king! Samuel then correctly informs Saul that the donkeys have been found, and goes on to describe the exact sequence of events that Saul will encounter on his way home. One of these incidents includes meeting a band of prophets who are chanting in ecstasy, accompanied by musicians playing on lyres, tamborines, flutes, and harps. Saul is caught up by "the spirit of the Lord (YH'VH)" and he, too, begins to prophesy (I Samuel chapter 10). It would appear from this description that "prophesying," in Samuel's day, involved entering some kind of altered state, possibly induced by the rhythm of the music, which put the prophet into direct contact with God.

Perhaps one of the most interesting shamanic figures is Joseph, the seer who foretells the future and interprets dreams. We are told that he wore a "coat of many colors," and this may have been far more than a fancy robe given to a favorite son. The fact is, scholars are not exactly sure what kind of garment it was, and the Hebrew *k'tonet passim* has been variously translated as a "robe with sleeves," an "embroidered tunic," or a "patchwork coat." Louis Ginsberg, in his seven-volume work *Legends of the*

Jews, has collected many stories about this garment. Taken together, they suggest that it was indeed something special, perhaps some kind of priestly robe, or even an effeminate garment. According to one story, the cloth was so gossamer fine that it could be crumpled into one hand—more of a veil than a cloak. The *Anchor Bible Commentary* points out the linguistic similarity between *k'tonet passim* and the ancient Akkadian *kittinu pissanu,* a robe draped around statues of goddesses!

Was Joseph an androgyne shaman? Dressing in clothes of the opposite sex has often been associated with shamanism, and while later Judaism rejected this practice, we cannot totally deny the possibility that Joseph was cross-dressing. Other legends, also cited by Ginsberg, portray Joseph as curling his hair, painting his eyes, and walking with a mincing step. Compare this with stories about his macho brother Gad, who could swing a lion around by the tail, and an interesting possibility emerges. Could it be that the "sibling rivalry" centered around Joseph's shamanic role, with his brothers simultaneously despising him as a sissy while fearing him as a magician?

Be that as it may, it is clear from the Biblical story that Joseph can both receive and interpret prophetic dreams. Nor is he unique among Jews; the importance of dreams as a medium for divine guidance continues to be accepted throughout Jewish history. Our tradition teaches that "a dream goes according to its interpretation," and one should therefore try to find a positive meaning. Failing that, the negative effects of a bad dream can be averted by repentance, fasting, and giving charity. In addition, medieval Jews sometimes practiced the technique of "dream requests," asking God to reveal hidden knowledge, by writing down a specific question and placing it under the pillow. Even today many Jews take their dreams very seriously. It is probably no accident that Sigmund Freud, himself a Jew, placed such great importance on dreams as tools for exploring the subconscious.

During the Roman period there lived an interesting man known as Honi the Circle-Drawer, a Jewish rainmaker. When there was drought, the entire community would fast and pray for rain. If rain still did not come, they would call upon Honi, who would draw a circle on the ground, seat himself in the center, and tell God that he, Honi, would not leave this circle until it rained.

Once, when he did this, it began to drizzle. The people said, "Well, that gets you out of your vow, but it doesn't help much." Honi then said to God: "I do not want a rain that will merely release me from a vow, but a good hard rain." Thereupon, it began to pour so hard that the land was flooded, and the people again protested. Once more Honi prayed, "I do not want a drizzle, or flood, but a nice steady rain." And God answered his prayer. (Talmud, Tractate Taanit)

Such miracle-workers were quite common in Talmudic times; it comes as a shock to many Christians to learn that Jesus was not unique, nor even particularly unusual. There is a long discussion in the Talmud (Tractate Sanhedrin) concerning the difference between the kinds of magic that are permitted and those that are forbidden. Generally speaking, any practice that involved healing was permitted, even if it appeared to be outright superstition, so long as the practitioner called upon the name of YH'VH, and not some non-Jewish deity. Miracle stories were common; there are even legends of disciples who behaved irresponsibly and killed each other in a drunken brawl, then were resurrected by their teachers! (Such behavior was frowned upon, however.)

The historian Flavius Josephus, in his work *Antiquities of the Jews,* describes how magic incantations attributed to Solomon were used by Jews in his own day. He testifies to the power of a certain Eleazar who cast out demons in the presence of Vespasian, his sons, and Roman soldiers. The cure was effected through the use of a ring which contained a particular herb. When this was placed under the patient's nose, it drew the demon out through his nostrils. Eleazar then commanded the spirit never to return and, as proof to the witnesses that it really existed, instructed it to overturn a full basin of water on its way out the door.

With the destruction of the Second Temple by the Romans in 70 C.E., followed by 1900 years of exile, the focus of Judaism began to switch from the magical to the intellectual. When Moses Maimonides wrote his famous "Guide to the Perplexed" in the twelfth century, he was attempting to reconcile Judaism with Aristotelian philosophy. In the end, the rationalist school seemed to win out, but mystical practices continued secretly.

During the late Middle Ages, we find Jewish individuals with the title *Baal Shem*, meaning "Master of the Name." (It should be noted that the word *baal*, pronounced "bah-ahl," has no connection with the idol Baal mentioned in the Bible.) The "Name" was the Tetragrammaton, the secret, unpronounceable Name of God, written with the four Hebrew letters, Y-H-V-H. (Neither "Yahweh" nor "Jehovah" are true pronunciations of this Name; both were invented by Christian theologians, and have never been used by Jews.) A *baal shem* (plural: *baalei shem*) was someone who knew the pronunciation of the Name, and could vibrate it silently within an altered state of consciousness known as "the Great Voice." As the Name was never said out loud, it could only be learned by purifying oneself through fasting, prayer, and other austerities, under the guidance of an accomplished *baal shem*, until the secret was revealed by God. Often, the spirit messenger sent to initiate the seeker was Elijah the Prophet, who, because he was taken up alive into heaven (see II Kings chapter 2), was believed to live eternally. Elijah thus provided a link between the ancient schools of mysticism and the medieval seeker.

Once initiated, the *baal shem* was able to work miracles through the knowledge of the Name and other combinations of Hebrew letters, which were seen as the building blocks of the universe, representing the primal sounds used by God to "speak" Creation into existence. In addition, a *baal shem* often used amulets, herbs, and religious ceremonies, as well as the laying-on of hands. Careful observance of Jewish laws and taboos was essential; the greater one's power, the greater one's responsibility to live a saintly and moral life.

Baalei shem were especially effective as exorcists, known for their ability to cure insanity and cast out *dybbuks* (souls of the dead who return to possess a living person's body). The most common way of performing an exorcism was to assemble a *minyan* (quorum) of ten pious Jewish men who, after ritual purification, would chant psalms and prayers, then blow the *shofar* (ram's horn). The sound of the *shofar*, associated with Judgment Day, invoked the power of God, before Whom Satan-the-Opposer cannot stand. Thus, for a *baal shem* to "call upon the Name of the Lord (YH'VH)" was not merely to pray words, but to invoke the power of the Creator to help heal the people and defend them against evil. God was the *baal shem's* "helping spirit," so to speak.

Early descriptions of Israel Baal Shem Tov, the eighteenth-century founder of Hassidism, portray him in exactly this mode. There exists a letter attributed to him which describes how he first met his spirit teacher while immersing in the *mikveh* (ritual purification pool) at the age of eighteen. He was then instructed to go to a local cave between two mountains, where this angelic messenger taught him from a secret book. Later, the spirit revealed that he was Ahiyah the Shilonite, the teacher of Elijah the Prophet. In addition, the Baal Shem Tov often ascended to heaven in his dreams, where he studied with the great Jewish sages of the past. All of this was kept secret, however, until he was thirty-six, a number associated with hidden saints and teachers in Jewish folklore. When he reached that magic age, he was told by Ahiyah that he must "go public" and reveal his gifts, which he did.

Meyer Levin's compilation, *Classic Hassidic Tales,* contains stories about the Baal Shem Tov reading past incarnations, conjuring angels, and winning showdowns with a non-Jewish sorcerer. He was reputed to have the power of *k'fitzat haderech,* literally the "jumping of the road," by which he could cover hundreds of miles by horse and wagon in a single night. Later disciples played down these aspects of their founder, adding the word *Tov,* meaning "good," to his name, to distinguish him from the ordinary *baalei shem,* who were often suspected of being in league with evil spirits. Subsequent generations portrayed the Baal Shem Tov as a scholar, and strongly discouraged the practice of kabbalistic or magical techniques. The title *Baal Shem* became synonymous with Israel Baal Shem Tov, and it was then considered presumptuous for anyone else to be called a *baal shem.*

Today, the term *baal shem* is not generally used: the leader of a Hassidic sect is called a Rebbe (which is different from a rabbi). Early Hassidim did not choose their Rebbes according to scholarly achievements, but rather on the basis of saintliness and piety. Frequently, the Rebbe's vocation was revealed to him (or her: there was at least one female Rebbe, Hannah Rochel of Ludmir) by heavenly messenger in a dream or vision. By the late

1800s, however, the Hassidic movement had become institutionalized, and today the position of Rebbe is passed from father to
son. Some Jews feel that this has diluted the power of the movement; nevertheless, Hassidic Rebbes are still believed to have
healing powers, and among their followers, tales of miracles are
often told. In one recent story, an Israeli soldier was brought out
of a coma by touching his lips with wine sent by his Rebbe, who
apparently knew without having been told that the man was
wounded.

Another common theme in Hassidic stories is that of defending
a soul before the Heavenly Court. In this scenario, the soul of
a sincere but ignorant Jew is about to be sentenced to Gehenna
(purgatory), when the Rebbe, through his magical powers,
ascends to heaven to act on the defendant's behalf. Opposing the
Rebbe is Satan, who serves as the district attorney and tries to
get the soul convicted by enumerating all of its sins. The Rebbe,
however, is always able to find some saintly deed that outweighs
them all, and God, the Judge, rules in favor of the accused soul,
who is then free to enter the Garden of Eden (Paradise).

In addition to dynastic Hassidism, there is a more recent movement which we might term "neo-Hassidic," seeking to combine
the mysticism of Hassidic teachings with "New Age" consciousness. Among these neo-Hassidic Jews are individuals who might
legitimately be called *baalei shem,* practicing Jewish forms of
spiritual healing, often combined with transpersonal psychology
and other human potential disciplines. (I consider myself to be
among this group.)

In conclusion, we can say that although shamanic practices
have probably never been considered mainstream within
Judaism, nevertheless, there is a persistent and continuous thread
of teachings which weaves itself in and out of the Jewish tradition. From Abraham to Moses to the prophets to the *baalei shem*
to the Hassidic Rebbes, these teachings have been transmitted
from teacher to student for over 5000 years. Now it is for us to
pick up this thread, and carry it into the future.

12

The Way of the Adventurer

SERGE KING

The Two Paths of Shamanism

Whenever shamanism is discussed, it is good to remember that we are using a Russian/Tungusic word, "shaman," quite arbitrarily to designate people with a particular view of life. These people have played and continue to play a unique role in nearly every culture on earth. Most languages have their own term for such a person which clearly distinguishes him or her. Others in the same society may share some of the same functions and activities, but do not share the same viewpoint nor all of the same skills. English does not presently have its own word for this kind of person, and so we use the term "shaman," which is not the same as a magician, sorcerer, priest, healer, or psychic. Basically, very basically, the shaman uses altered states of consciousness to communicate with and influence the forces of nature and the universe for the benefit of society. In order to do this, the shaman everywhere practices the accumulation of inner power. These are the three most distinguishing features of the shaman, then: the use of altered states; influencing events for social benefit; and the accumulation of inner power.

Among all the shamanic traditions of the world, there are two main paths to inner power. The most widely known and practiced is the *Way of the Warrior,* characterized by an emphasis on danger, the development of hyper-alertness, an ascetic and harsh self-discipline, the destruction of enemies and cultivation of allies, the practice of survival/fighting skills, and an ethic of conquer or be conquered. This is the Way followed by the majority of American Indian shamans, for instance, and it is a good way because its intent is good. In the islands of the Pacific, however, out of Polynesian culture, there arose another path, the Way of the Adventurer. In contrast to that of the Warrior, this path emphasizes the seeking of adventure, the development of hyperawareness and a goal-oriented self-discipline, the cultivation of friendship and unity, the practice of survival/exploring skills, and an ethic of love and be loved. It is not a "better" way, since both paths of shamanism have healing in broad terms as their social purpose, and both can lead to the same realms of high personal development. But it is a different way, and the differences may have profound social and personal effects.

The typical ideal for the warrior shaman is to act impeccably, that is, without error, and there is a great emphasis on developing and maintaining the strength to protect oneself and others from enemies. Because of the outlook itself, both become necessary. On the other hand, the typical ideal for the Adventurer shaman is to act appropriately, or in such a way as to get the best results in a given situation, and the emphasis is on enjoyment and creating peace. These, in fact, were the main activities of the *Arioi*, a shaman group of traveling bards and dancers in the Society Islands, and of the original shamanic hula troupes of Hawaii.

The Hawaiian Shaman

The model for the Hawaiian shaman is the great culture hero, Maui, known and loved from one end of Polynesia to the other. That Maui was a shaman is clear from the epithets attached to his name—in Hawaii he was called "Maui Kupua" and in Western Polynesia he was called "Maui Tikitiki," both of which are usually translated as "Maui the Wonderworker"—and by his exploits as evidenced in legends. Among other things, Maui was known for such shamanistic practices as turning himself into various animals and birds, being helped by animals and birds, visiting the heavens to gain the secrets of fire and cultivation and sharing them with humankind, and exploring the underworld. Almost all the stories of Maui end with him going off to seek another adventure, just for the fun of it. While Maui does engage in fighting when necessary, the emphasis in all his legends is on his great strength, his wit, his skill at magic, his independence from outside authority, his sharing of beneficial knowledge, and his love of adventure.

Using Hawaiian shamanism as a model, it is important to distinguish first of all between a *kahuna* and a shaman. In present-day Hawaii the word *kahuna* is used indiscriminately for a priest, minister, sorcerer, psychic, healer, or shaman, but it actually refers to someone who has mastered the secrets of some field of knowledge, whether that field be mindpower, navigation, or surfing. A close equivalent would be the Japanese *sensei*, or "master." It is important to realize, therefore, that a *kahuna* is not per se a shaman, although a shaman might aspire to become a *kahuna*.

In this same context, it is also important to note that the Hawaiian religion and Hawaiian shamanism were not the same thing. The Hawaiian religion was a highly structured and stratified affair, full of prohibitions, sacrifices, and ceremonies, run by a hierarchy of priests known as *kahu akua,* or "those who attend the gods." The priesthood was highly visible in Hawaiian society and linked indissolubly with the political hierarchy. The shamans, on the other hand, had very little structure, used prohibitions *(kapu or tabu)* only when it benefitted a healing, used no sacrifice to speak of, and kept ritual and ceremony to a minimum. In addition, they were not very visible in the society (even in the old days one might have to trek deep into a hidden valley to find one), and they had little to do with politics unless a situation required their leadership. In that case, they would become chiefs, rather than priests. Probably one of the greatest differences between the priests and the shamans is that the former worshipped the "gods" or spirits at a distance, while the latter simply interacted with them in a personal way.

Nor did the shamans engage in sorcery, or what is popularly termed "black magic." Those who did this were called *ana-ana*, and were despised and feared by all Hawaiians. Unfortunately, the word *ana-ana* has fallen into disuse and has been replaced by the overworked word *kahuna,* so that today many Hawaiians automatically think of sorcerers whenever the word *kahuna* is mentioned.

The true shamans of Hawaii were called *kupua,* or *kalakupua,* words which have meanings related to the possession of and ability to release *mana,* inner or divine power, and they were generally trained within the structure of an order or guild maintained by certain families. They started out as apprentices, advanced to the equivalent of journeyman status, and, once they had demonstrated enough mastery of the shaman practices, they could be initiated as a *kahuna kalakupua,* or master shaman.

The shamans of Hawaii have two rather unique characteristics which set them apart from the shamans of most other cultures. First of all, they do not use drumming or rhythmic percussion or even chanting to help them enter into trance states for journeying through inner worlds. For that they use the mind alone. They do use percussion or chanting to produce various kinds of altered states in themselves and others, but not trance states. Secondly, they do not use masks of any kind, and this holds true for all Polynesians. In most cultures which have shamans, including those of Europe, masks or costumes representing gods or animal spirits have been used to enhance a sense of connection with such spiritual beings, but not in Polynesia. My attempts to obtain a reason for this among the Hawaiian shamans I have known have not met with much success. When I ask, "Why not?" they answer with, "Why?" Apparently they feel that the inner ability to make the connection obviates the use of special clothing or coverings, but it is nevertheless very curious that the whole culture has excluded masks.

The Divine Power and the Web

Central to the Hawaiian shaman's view of the universe is the concept of *mana,* which may be translated as inner or divine power and energy. The most common symbol for it in old Hawaii was a lightning bolt, and this is where the well-known surfer symbol came from.

In spite of numerous references in modern literature which equate *mana* with the Chinese *ch'i,* the Japanese *ki,* the Hindu *prana,* and Reich's *orgone,* the fact is that *mana* is not identical to any of these. It is not just energy in the physical or bioenergetic sense, for which the Hawaiians use the word *ki;* it is much more. The word "power" is a better rendering, in the sense of "effective energy." For the Hawaiian shaman, everything has *mana,* but some things have more *mana* than others, either naturally or because it has been imparted to them. During his interactions with spirits, nature and other human beings, the shaman takes their *mana* into account and seeks to work with it using his personal *mana.* He does not try to control it, because that would cause a conflict and be a waste of his own *mana.* Instead of force, then, he uses persuasion, and the more *mana* he has, the more persuasive he can be. The Hawaiian shaman's daily aim is to increase his *mana* in order to be more effective in everything he does.

Simply put, there are four kinds of *mana* that the shaman seeks to increase in himself or others: first is physical *mana* (equivalent to what is called bioenergy); next is emotional *mana* (which can be likened to a state of inner excitement); then mental *mana* (best described as high self-confidence); and spiritual *mana* (which includes self-esteem and a deep respect for or sense of connectedness with the object of attention).

Almost as important as *mana* for the Hawaiian shaman is the concept of *aka,* which is something like "etheric" matter. Like many other shamans, the *kupua* has the conception that everything is interconnected and that these connections can be perceived and acted upon by one who knows how to do it. That is, the connections are real and not abstract, and can be given form by consciousness. The two forms most widely used by the Hawaiian shaman are those of an etheric "web" and an etheric "net." In the web concept, the shaman sees himself as a spider at the center of a three-dimensional web stretching out in all directions to every part of the universe. Like a spider he can be aware of vibrations from activity anywhere along the web, ignoring or paying attention to whatever he chooses. And like a spider he can move along the web without getting caught in it. Unlike a spider but like a shaman, he can also send out vibrations along the web and consciously affect anything in the universe, according to the strength of his *mana.* In the net concept, the shaman sees himself as a weaver and a fisherman, able to weave and cast nets in order to capture ideas and events, symbolized by fish.

Becoming a Shaman

There are two ways to become a shaman in Hawaii. You can have a natural predilection for it and more or less stumble your way into it, learning from experience and what you can pick up from relatives and friends; or you can be selected by a member of a shaman guild and be guided into its mysteries as deeply as you dare to go. Usually the selection is done by an older family member, but in Hawaiian terms this can mean anyone of your parents' or grandparents' generation. This selection generally takes place when one is between the ages of seven and fourteen and is based on observation of the interests, skills, and potential shown by the candidate. The main factors looked for are general health, dexterity, a curiosity about nature, and psychic ability. In old Hawaii psychic ability was often revealed through popular children's "guessing" games like *kahikahi-ku-palala,* the object of which was to find an object hidden in the earth or sand. If a child were very good at that and selected for training, he might eventually be taught the art of *kuhikuhi-pu'u-one,* a form of geomancy that was taught in a special hut on the beach, and which dealt with what could best be termed "earth currents." In my own case, my father used to lead my siblings and me in various kinds of telepathic and clairvoyant guessing games for the same purpose.

By age seven a potential shaman would already be noticed, and for the next seven years he or she would be subtly tested and gradually be introduced to the notion of becoming a shaman. Around the age of fourteen the youngster selected would be apprenticed to a kahuna and could expect another seven to fourteen years of training before being accepted as a kahuna himself. In the old days this would most likely be a live-in arrangement with the apprentice exchanging his labor directly for the training, but in modern times the exchange is either by barter or money and live-in arrangements are rare. Also in modern times, more attention is paid to inclination than to age, and the formal training may not take as long because much of it has already been done by modern education and experience. For instance, few people realize how developed their skill of concentration is compared to that of most non-technological peoples, simply due to their skill of reading a book. Another important factor is the extremely abundant repertoire of inner imagery and experience available to those in modern society from books, movies, and television. The value of such resources for a potential shaman cannot be overemphasized. Because so much of the work has been done already by modern education and communication, a person so inclined can learn basic shaman skills in a fairly short time. What usually takes longer is learning the viewpoint.

The Viewpoint of the Adventurer

The most common viewpoint in modern times is that the world is a dangerous place. There is danger of death and disease, failure and rejection, tyranny and annihilation. The Warrior shaman builds his world upon this viewpoint, and includes more dangers from unseen forces such as evil or chaotic spirits. He seeks to increase his own powers to the point where he is unconquerable by man or spirit and to where he can help others and protect them from the dangers of the world. The great appeal of the Warrior Way is that it starts from where the common viewpoint leaves off. Yes, the world is dangerous, but I can obtain the power to overcome it. Yet, that leap from powerlessness to power is too great for many people who not only feel powerless, but fear power.

The Adventurer viewpoint does not even accept the first premise. It acknowledges that there are dangers in the world, but not that the world is a dangerous place. On the contrary, the world is an exciting place, full of opportunity to make it what you will. For the fundamental premise of the Adventurer is that we are the makers of our own world, and all dangers, indeed all pleasures and all experience, are self-generated. The Adventurer seeks power to create and change experience and to help others do the same. So Maui gave fire to man so he could cook his own food and see by his own light. This is a hard viewpoint to handle in a society brought up on the idea of objective experience because it gives us the ultimate power over our own lives, and for many this is more devastatingly fearful than the more objective power of the Warrior. It is a hard viewpoint to maintain in an objectively-oriented society, but for those who are able it is immensely rewarding, for in this viewpoint we create our own good and we create our own evil. Significantly, the only word in Hawaiian for evil is 'ino, which really means "harmful" and is based upon roots which mean "too intense." In the original language there aren't even any words for evil spirits or an evil being. The closest ideas to that are simply "harmful thoughts" or "harmful minds." No matter how much evil there is in the world, it is still not an evil world. And no matter how much evil there is in the world, it can all be changed to good by the right beliefs. However, the Adventurer ideal of the power of belief may be even harder to maintain in the modern world than the Warrior ideal of the power of strength. In an apparently objective and dangerous world, the value of strength is more easily recognized than the value of belief. Also, in such a world, the power of the mind is more likely to be feared than cultivated.

For the shaman, using mental abilities to communicate with and alter realities is as natural and easy as using physical abilities to play sports. In some cultures the shaman may surround the use of his abilities with ceremony and ritual when in a social context, but on his own he slips in and out of shamanic states with ease. It is here that the shaman differs so much from the ceremonial magician who believes that ceremony and ritual are essential to his craft. For the shaman they are merely useful. The term "shamanic states" may be better described as "frameworks of belief," with the understanding that shifting into different frameworks allows different potentials to manifest. Each framework constitutes a set of beliefs about reality. What a person does and is able to do at any given time depends upon the particular framework (alternatively, "mind set" or "viewpoint") that the person's mind is operating from. Everyone has a few frameworks that they move in and out of according to circumstances, such as a parent who is also a child of his own parents; a teacher who is also a student of someone else; a scientist who must shop for groceries; or a dancer who is also a novelist. The shaman simply acknowledges a wider range of frameworks than most people do and is able to move among them at will, and the Adventurer simply uses a somewhat different set of frameworks from the Warrior. In addition, the shaman has the ability known in Hawaiian as *maka'ike*, (literally, "knowing eye"), which is being aware of the frameworks themselves.

The Shaman as Healer

When I was being taught by my African mentors to move out of a modern American, scientific/objective view of health and into a shamanic one, it wasn't easy, even though I already had been trained for years in various mental arts. For what I was asked to accept was that good health is our natural state, that illness of any sort is due to a malevolent spirit interfering with the natural healing ability of the body, and that the role of the shaman was to cast out that malevolent spirit. The real problem was that it took me a long time to realize that what they meant by a malevolent spirit was some kind of negative idea or belief held by the person who was ill, and that what the shaman had to do was to find some way to change that idea. This was not a purely psychosomatic approach to illness because they recognized that certain physical conditions could bring on diseases such as malaria and cholera; but they could also see that not everyone exposed to the same conditions would get the disease, and this they attributed to the different "spirits" (ideas) dwelling in each person. They also knew that an input of energy in various forms—as emotions, herbs, or Western medicines, for instance—could be very helpful in changing the negative ideas (or "casting out the malevolent spirits"). Whatever the form of the energy input, it was always seen as an adjunctive tool for accomplishing the main objective because they could see as well that the energy application alone didn't always work. Actually, just working with changing ideas alone didn't always work either, but they attributed this to the strength of the negative idea and not the fault of the concept. Since they were often successful at curing even serious illnesses through a form of hypnosis, they reasoned that medicine and energy, however helpful, were not the essential factors in healing.

This shamanic concept of the relationship between health and ideas or beliefs is both important and difficult to grasp. It is not "positive thinking" as it is commonly understood, nor is it a denial of the physical aspects of health and illness. It is, instead, a recognition that what a person believes is true, *is* true for that person, and that when basic beliefs are changed so is experience. One of the most important shamanic skills, particularly in regard to healing, is that of influencing others to change their beliefs in such a way as to bring about desired results. In certain instances, then, depending on the person, the shaman might seek to instill a belief in the power of the shaman's energy to effect a cure, in the power of a particular herb, medicine or ritual, or in the power of the person to do it himself. When the change in belief is effective, the negative idea is neutralized and the body is free to heal itself.

Of course this can operate for oneself as well. In my experiments with this concept, I have done what some would consider quite remarkable things. In one instance I deliberately shifted my mental framework to one that I had when a young child, and "succeeded" in bringing on a full-blown recurrence of bronchial asthma symptoms, which a shift to a different framework eliminated within minutes. On another occasion I was in bed with a viral flu and shifted to another framework in which I used a visualization process that removed all traces of the illness in an hour. In the latter case you could say that my subconscious believed in the efficacy of the visualization, and therefore it allowed the body to heal. I didn't have to know what the negative idea was; I just had to focus on a believable idea that had a positive intent. In still another case I actually watched in a mirror as a cold sore formed on my lip after an incident in which I suppressed an emotional response, and continued to watch as it disappeared when I switched to a different emotional framework.

In the healing realm, as far as I can determine, both the Warrior and the Adventurer shamans use similar concepts and are more interested in results than methods. Apart from cultural variations, I have found no significant differences in their approaches to healing.

The Shaman as Seer

The whole area of what may be called psychic phenomena is both fascinating and frightening to many people in the modern Western world because it is treated as supernatural, superstitious and/or dangerous. Of course this is because they are, in the main, unfamiliar with it. The typical Western view, when such phenomena are admitted at all, is that this is an area beyond the reach of most people, and that in order to achieve psychic abilities one has to submit to grueling discipline, occult rituals and arcane practices, or else be specially chosen by a divinity, or born with the talent. The shaman, however, once entered into the shamanic way of life, treats all such phenomena as part of the whole spectrum of human experience. Western psychic investigators tend to divide the area into specific talents such as telepathy, clairvoyance, precognition, etc., but I think it would be fair to say that while the shamans have terms for specific skills the emphasis is on where the attention is being directed rather than on what skill is being used. A more convenient way to divide shamanic abilities would be in terms of awareness—past, present, future, inner and outer, and the special in-between state, called *maka'ike* in Hawaiian, from where the shaman moves his awareness.

Shamans have such a wide range of psychic expression that traditional Western categories become useless. Take fire-walking, for example. It might possibly be squeezed into the category of psychokinesis, but that term is woefully inadequate to cover all the various mental states in which it can be done. When I did a fire-walk in Tahiti over glowing lava rock, I did not use self-hypnosis, nor a high emotional motivation, nor any kind of "positive programming," though any of those may work for some people at certain times. What I did was shift to a state or framework called *ho'okahi*, which I can inadequately describe as a state of "unthinking oneness with the environment." In that state I had no resistance to the fire, and so I could walk on it without harm. And yet I also used that same state in a completely different context. After a friend had fallen off a jungle trail and lost his glasses, I entered the area, went into *ho'okahi*, and in a few moments the glasses became visible to me. And that certainly wasn't any form of psychokinesis. There are other shamanic skills too that defy traditional Western categories, such as journeying to the inner worlds to effect changes in the outer one, speaking with plants, animals and rocks, calming the winds, bringing rain, and on and on. Clearly the rise of shamanism in Western awareness can lead to brand new approaches in the study of how our minds interact with our environment.

The main difference between the Warrior and Adventurer use of seership is based on the same concepts brought out at the beginning of this discussion, namely that, in general, the Warrior is alert to dangers and the Adventurer is aware of connections. By not using frameworks that include enemies or evil spirits, the Adventurer does not have to deal with them except when entering another person's reality for some reason, and even then he does not have to fear them. Of course, I am speaking of the ideal Adventurer, because in a practical sense an individual Adventurer does have to deal with enemies and evil spirits until he can learn to shift completely into frameworks that are clear of them. Furthermore, at the higher psychic levels of both paths the Warrior and Adventurer are indistinguishable.

The Shaman as Dreamer

Where the shaman is concerned, the verb "to dream" is to be taken in a very active sense. In other words, what for most people is a passive experience is, for the shaman, an intentionally creative act. Furthermore, the shaman makes no essential distinctions between his inner life and his outer life. They are decidedly different but equally real, like oranges and apples. This has caused some anthropologists no end of problems as they try to fit shamanic experiences into the Western scheme of things. For instance, let us say, in an African village a shaman comes in from working in his fields (yes, shamans also do ordinary work) and tells the villagers that as he was planting the manioc a *boekin* (spirit) called out to him from the nearby sacred grove. He stopped and gave the *boekin* some tobacco, and in return it told him that the rainy season would come one week early this year. The villagers would have no problem with this. They could easily accept the shaman's experience as real, even though they themselves would not have been able to see or hear the spirit. But a Western anthropologist staying in the village might spend sleepless nights trying to ascertain whether the shaman was tricking the villagers, had a hallucination, or simply misinterpreted a natural event. And his task would not be made easier when the rains came a week early. The real problem for the anthropologist is that none of his categories fit the experience. In the shaman's framework of reality, he can communicate with spirits. The information he receives is effectively true in regard to physical experience and therefore the *ukin* (plural form) are real, whether the anthropologist likes it or not.

In a way, you could say that the shaman, with the help of his cultural framework and the acceptance of the villagers, dreams the spirits into existence. That does not make them any less real, however, because from the shamanic point of view the whole

United States has been dreamed into existence by the people who live there. This way of looking at life is rather difficult to communicate because the shaman treats all realities as subjective, much like some modern theoretical physicists are beginning to do. In such a viewpoint the question of whether an experience is real or not makes no sense, because the answer is yes and no, depending on your point of view.

The most widely-known shamanic dreaming skills are those of ascending to the Upper World and descending to the Under World, and using the experience to effect some kind of change in the outer world, whether individual, social, or environmental. As far as the experience itself goes, the closest correlation in modern experience is probably lucid dreaming, where the dreamer is aware that he is dreaming and can influence the events of the dream. Another close approximation is the process of active imagination, or active daydreaming, especially when the involvement is so deep as to produce a virtual trance state. The content of such inner journeying usually differs with Warrior and Adventurer shamans, as do their methods of reaching the inner state. Generally speaking, Warriors tend to resolve conflicts in the inner dimensions through combat of some kind, while Adventurers tend to use non-combat skills, and please notice the word *tend*. As mentioned, percussion or drumming seems to be more popular in the Warrior tradition as a means of inducing the shamanic trance, but the shamans of either path may use monotonous sound, a fixed visual focus, or sensory deprivation. Among the Adventurer traditions that I have studied, the most popular method is a shifting of the senses to an inward focus. While I am at it, I may as well explain that a shamanic trance is not a state of unconsciousness, but a highly focused, very active state of consciousness. No matter how deep the trance, the shaman almost always retains some awareness of what is going on around him in the outer world.

The effectiveness of the journeying for either Warrior or Adventurer, that is, its effectiveness in terms of influencing a change in an outer condition, depends almost entirely on the absolute conviction of the shaman that something substantial has actually been accomplished in the inner world. This sense of conviction or confidence is the shaman's greatest asset because by it he convinces others of his truth, and their joint belief creates a joint reality.

Less well known are the shamanic journeys to the Middle Worlds of human past, present and future. These are dream-worlds in which symbols *are* reality, inextricably linked to outer reality, in which interactions with the symbols *are* interactions with their counterparts in the outer world. This is an area in which more and more modern therapists are becoming involved under such names as "creative visualization" and "guided imagery." The modern therapists acknowledge the effectiveness of working with symbolic imagery, but I doubt whether many would acknowledge their intrinsic reality. In a way, this is unfortunate, because too many people who use this method have put their faith in the method itself. That is to say, they think the effectiveness stems from the process used, when it is the belief generated by the process that does the work. Visualization or guided imagery is completely ineffective if it does not stimulate a belief response in the subconscious, as every shaman knows. The reason it does work so well, when it does, is that use of symbols (from the ordinary point of view) often bypasses the critical, analytical, conscious mind and more easily reaches the non-judgmental subconscious mind. Even so, the most effective imagery has to be adapted to the general framework of the subject, and at this the shamans are expert.

This process of using the inner Middle Worlds to effect outer change is not limited to therapy, but can be applied to any area of human interest from personal success to weather modification. I find it very interesting that the oldest and most consistent use of this powerful tool in modern times has been in the higher levels of the business world. This is probably because the upper level business person, like the shaman, is vitally concerned with what works.

The Modern Shaman

I often tell my students that anyone can be a shaman in the wilderness. That is easy. What is really tough is being a shaman in the city; and yet that is where we really need shamans. Historically, the shaman has always been an integral part of the society he lived in, whenever he was allowed to operate. Today we have that freedom, and today we need to use it, within society and not outside of it. The world needs shamans who can function within the modern cultural context for helping with our modern problems. Wherever there is unhappiness or disharmony, the shaman can play a constructive role, and whenever new ideas are needed for solving human problems or advancing the frontiers of any field, the shaman can also lend his special skills. In areas of health, psychology, technology, and ecology the unique viewpoint and practice of the shaman has space to grow and prosper, thus enriching the race as a whole. And there is a kind of duty to the Earth as well that the shaman can perform as no other.

Although he was not writing about shamans as such, I would like to close with a very apt quote from Dr. Lawrence LeShan, author of the excellent book *Alternate Realities:*

> Our freedom is so much greater than we have comprehended. We can learn to shift from reality to reality, choosing the one that is most relevant to our needs and purposes at the moment and use our new approach...to nourish our being, love, cherish, and garden ourselves and each other, be at home in our universes, and help save ourselves and our planet.

13

The Native American Prayer Pipe: Ceremonial Object and Tool of Self-Realization

JOHN REDTAIL FREESOUL

The following are the words of Pte Ska Win (White Buffalo Maiden) as she appeared, walking from sky to earth, bringing the first of seven sacred gifts:

> With visible breath I am walking. I walk and my voice is heard. I am walking with visible breath. I am bringing this sacred pipe; with it I walk to you. For you I am walking with this pipe...so that the breath may become visible.

To many people the story of White Buffalo Calf Maiden and the two young warriors who beheld her in the far north is classified and categorized as "Indian myth" or "Native American legend." But the account of Moses on Sinai, with the manifestation of the Lord Creator as burning bush, and the experience of Arjuna with Lord Krishna are accepted and discussed as "sacred scripture." The weight and credibility of truth and wisdom implied in "sacred scripture" versus "myth" are obvious. Myths are generally classified as stories created by human beings in an attempt to bring about order in life, or solutions to the mystery of life's origin. Sacred scriptures, on the other hand, are accepted as knowledge from God, the Creator, the source of all existence, communicated to human beings by revelation in visions and dreams. No single civilization in history nor individual tribe of any continent has an exclusive monopoly on revealed visions from the source and origin of all life. Moses was of the Semitic tribe, Arjuna an East Indian, and Crazy Horse an Oglala

Sioux. They are all human beings, sons of Earth Mother and Sky Father.

Moses descended from Sinai with ten commandments; the warrior who respected Calf Maiden returned with the promise of seven gifts, the first gift—the sacred pipe—being the tool which would teach the use and meaning of all seven gifts. With the smoking of the first sacred pipe, the ancient Native American elders of this continent discovered in spiritual communion that to share "breath" was to share life. A pipe is breathed into, with puffs of smoke ascending from earth to sky, as well as smoked by taking smoke into the body. Inhaling the smoke calls attention and realization to that which in life is received or accepted, exhaling to that which must be released or transcended. The inhaling and exhaling of smoke is as the ebb and flow of life.

There are two basic levels of native American experience: acceptance and transcendence, earth and sky, the visible and the invisible, male and female. The source and center of all existence is pure spirit existing in all created things simultaneously as a "great spirit." The absolute, unchanging, unmanifested invisible spirit is Sky Father; the manifested, ever-changing spirit becomes visible as nature in Earth Mother. The creator source is male and female; all that which exists is male or female. There are male and female plants, animals, rocks, and winds. There are male and female human beings. That which exists is alive. All that which exists is related, sharing a common source, a common breath. Plants, animals, rocks, and people breathe. The winds breathe. The earth breathes. Earth Mother Nature is the Creator's breath made visible. When concentration, attention, and recognition to this reality are present while smoking a prayer pipe, a powerful transformation occurs: the smoke becomes sacred as breath; the spirit of God in us all becomes visible. The experience is not accepted in common belief, but rather perceived in collective or individual spiritual communion with one another and with the divine source itself. This is the beginning of the "making of medicine." The key in making medicine is acknowledgment of the connection of authentic communication with the spirit world, and the experience of authentic self-realization. Such phenomena are verified through individual experience.

The sacred pipe is many things. To the casual observer, all

prayer pipes are the proverbial "peace pipes." Although all pipes promote well-being, there are specific clan, society, personal, social, and council pipes. There are sundance pipes, marriage pipes, and war pipes. Usually a pipe is kept in a bundle or pipebag along with the things used in a pipe ceremony, such as tobacco and sweet grass. There are pipe dances. The prayer pipe is a ceremonial tool and a traveling altar. While leaning against a forked peg pressed and anchored in the earth, the pipe becomes an altar, a center of focus and concentration—similar to a mandala. When not smoked or used as such, the bowl and stem of a pipe are separated and wrapped individually, yet kept together in a pipe bundle or pipebag.. The owner of a pipe bundle is sometimes known as a "pipeholder" or "pipe carrier." Such a person must earn the privilege of owning a pipe bundle through instruction, preparation, tasks, and initiation. A pipeholder is respected as one whose priority in life is purity, and is thus requested by people to conduct ceremonies with the pipe. This is a sacred responsibility. A pipeholder is expected to observe a code of purity in feelings, words, and deeds.

The bowl of every pipe represents the female aspect of the Great Spirit; the stem represents the male aspect. The pipe bowl is Earth Mother, the pipe stem is Sky Father. The bowl is the earth while the stem is all that grows upon the earth. The bowl is each person's head, and the stem is his or her spine. These things are to be reflected and contemplated upon in the temple of silence on the altar of realization, not merely accepted and memorized in blind faith. So it is understood why the first of the seven gifts from White Buffalo Calf Maiden was the sacred prayer pipe. The pipe is used in all Plains Native American ceremonies. It is the center of all we do; it is the *axis mundi* which forms a bridge between earth and sky, the visible and the invisible, the physical and the spiritual. The pipe is a tool and a sacred object in itself. As a tool it is crucial in assisting an individual or a group in determining what is to be accepted or released in life. The pipe bowl aids in recalling to mind the acceptance of change in nature. Although we are in a sea of constant flux and change, there is warmth, order, and beauty in nature.

When our lives are in harmony with other life (our relatives), and if our will and behavior are in balance with the sustaining natural law (order) of the Creator, then we perceive and experience directly this warmth, order, and beauty. If not, we experience confusion, chaos, disharmony and imbalance. Furthermore, we can negatively affect other life along with ourselves in the whirlwinds of our confusion. This "other life" may be other people, the environment, an animal, or a plant. The pipe ceremonies during the phases of the sun, of the moon, and of the four seasons assist us in accepting change, and sustain us during constant flux by anchoring us in the unchanging, in the source, in the Great Spirit. This is power. There is medicine power in the four phases of the sun and moon, in each of the four seasons. Such is the rhythm of life: the day is regulated to the sun, the month regulated to the moon, and each year regulated to the seasons.

The pipe stem is Sky Father, that which is unchanging and absolute in life. In the wheel of life and in the hub of motion there is non-motion in the center. The center is a focus of concentration, of power of all directions in life. There is a time appropriate for each of us individually, and sometimes collectively as clans, families, societies, or an entire tribe, to withdraw from the hub of motion in life and go to the center of the circle to get centered, to become focused. While Earth Mother teaches acceptance and nourishes us, Sky Father teaches transcendence and liberation, to gain release from relationships, substances, or desires. This is the pipe; it is the bowl and it is the stem. Joined together it yields the power of this realization. Knowledge of it is not enough. Just as training is useless without the honing of practice, so too knowledge of the sacred pipe without its use and practice as a tool will render it a mere abstraction. Trying to grasp the power and meaning of the sacred pipe using only the rational mind is like attempting to lasso the wind with a rope. Intellectual concepts cannot carry us to our destination; they can only point the direction.

Ancient native sages and contemporary elders share with us in oral tradition that we two-leggeds, the human beings, were not created and then cast adrift in a sea of despair. Knowledge of the

Creator and of the great mystery of life is hidden in everything created. The power of the sun is in every atom. Every person, animal, plant, or rock has a message or lesson, its Medicine Power. The more our perception is sharpened and our sensitivity purified, the less this presence of the divine in all things created seems secret or hidden. As direct communication with spirit increases, we respect creation more and worship only the Source of creation. The purpose of ceremony is to celebrate life and to sharpen our perception and *shanta-ista* (intuition). Some things are observed with the two eyes of the mind; others are known with the single eye of the soul, the *shanta-ista*. By observation of nature and by vision-questing, the native seeker learns about life from its Source, which is more powerful than theology, doctrine, or dogma. The mind is a servant and a trickster. Ceremonial symbols are runways for the spirit from sky to earth. The sacred pipe is the central tool and guide for all ceremony and symbol.

The most basic ceremony using the sacred pipe is the Vision Quest. The purpose of the Vision Quest is twofold: to discover one's self, one's destiny, one's relationships on earth, one's medicine power, and also to contact God directly. The Vision Quest involves much preparation, and the preparation is as important as the doing. The quest begins with the discovery of self. The seeker goes out alone and naked, exposed to nature's elements, carrying only a pipe and a blanket. The length of time spent alone in the wilderness varies with an individual's pledge, usually one to four days of fasting and praying, "lamenting" for a vision because one seeks release from the alienation felt from nature, God, and oneself.

Generally we experience daily alienation from one another; we do not know ourselves, and we commonly view God as a distant creator on a throne, eager to wreak vengeance on us for breaking some law or restriction. Preoccupied with guilt, the usual tendency is to seek forgiveness or to attempt to forget about the whole situation by burying oneself in excessive pleasures and indulgence. Such a situation is present in every culture, among all peoples—in some more than others. Through the Vision Quest one can achieve liberation from the concept of a legalistic Lord and become open to a living relationship with an indwelling Spirit.

In the Vision Quest, a circle is drawn on the earth around the vision-seeker, and the four directions and center of the circle are noted. The circle is a symbol of God, and the movement of God is in all directions. The directions vary and commemorate the seasons and the phases of sun and moon. But the center of the circle, the eye of the Creator, is motionless and unchanging. That which changes is set in motion and initiated from that which is changeless. How is this? Such is the Great Mystery, to be continually reflected upon, from which come enlightenment and wisdom. Enlightenment is knowledge of the self; wisdom is knowledge of the world.

So for days and nights the seeker smokes, performs the rite, the ceremony of the making of sacred smoke within the circle, moving to each of the four directions yet spending most of the time in the center, and sleeping in the center, remaining inside the circle always. All that has been mentioned about the pipe—the meaning of the stem and bowl, the act of making breath visible, of sharing breath with all creation and with God—occurs in this vision circle. When not smoked, the pipe is held in hand or set in the circle as an altar and contemplated. In using the pipe, all elements are joined in communion: the stone bowl, wooden stem, fire, air, and breath. The plant, animal, and mineral kingdoms are represented. This is one of the many ways the sacred prayer pipe is used as both a ceremonial object of spiritual communion and a tool of self-realization. The sacred pipe is the "tool of tools," the most powerful and most cherished gift of all Native American Plains tribes. Today the use of the sacred pipe is being revived among all tribes, even those which traditionally did not use long-stemmed pipes. People of all races and ethnic backgrounds are journeying on Vision Quests, entering into sweat lodges, and gathering at sun dances—and the pipe is always present.

The sacred pipe is the center of the nation's hoop, and without it there is no life. This statement summarizes everything about the sacred pipe, and clarifies its relationship to ceremony and life. We raise our children with the pipe, counsel alcoholics and drug addicts, resolve differences, heal the afflicted with it, celebrate life at sun dances, and, most important. . .it is the only tool we bring with us when we meet the Great Mystery face to face on a Vision Quest.

Our ancient sages and contemporary elders assure us that the pipe and these sacred things associated with it are far from theoretical. The Great Spirit has specific principles manifested as natural order. The creator continually and consistently reveals instructions: "If you do this, then this will happen." These instructions are timeless, revealed in nature and manifested as order and laws as those governing motion, gravity, the phases of the sun and moon and the seasons. We are not interested in abstractions. We take our pipes out as instructed to determine if they work. They do.

The sacred pipe was brought to different tribes through different messengers, for the invisible spirit world is widely populated as is the visible world. To the Blackfoot it was Thunder who brought the pipe, to the Arapahoe it was Duck. To many tribes it was White Buffalo Calf Maiden. And then there was Moses, and Arjuna with Lord Krishna. So be it.

IV

Shamanism and the Perennial Philosophy

The world view of shamanism coincides with that of the Perennial Philosophy or the "Wisdom Tradition" in many respects, and in fact probably forms a strand in that many-textured perspective. Hinduism, Buddhism, yoga philosophy, alchemy, and other Western forms of esoteric knowledge, along with shamanism, hold in common a mystical and holistic view in which all things are interconnected and all inhere in a numinous background Source. Many other parallels with formerly secret esoteric and spiritual traditions are now evident and available for scrutiny in the West.

The inner experiences associated with such things as mystical journeys and rites of passage have commonalities across cultures, as Halifax makes clear. Absorption states described in Buddhist scriptures have counterparts in shamanism. The notions of change and impermanence are also prominent in both traditions, as are the concept of a spiritual path and the cultivation of such qualities as generosity. Also, the idea of human kinship with animals, trees, rocks, etc., can be found in Eastern religions as in shamanism. Halifax considers shamanism an "earth philosophy" which focuses on instinctual energies, while traditions such as Buddhism are "sky philosophies" that emphasize the mind.

Australian Aboriginals "journey in the dreamtime" to commune with spiritual powers, and conceive of mountains as places from which gods descend and to which the human spirit ascends. Thero explains that the divine plane is interconnected with the human plane in the

Aboriginals' view and therefore available to all, as is the case with Eastern traditions. The Aboriginals stress the expansion of consciousness rather than possession, and practice "sky gazing," staring into the sky to contact infinite knowledge. Thero likens this to the meditative and mystical experiences of Buddhists and Hindus. The Eastern focus on infinity within oneself may have roots in shamanism, which is far older even than the Eastern religions. Among other areas with parallels between the Wisdom Traditions and shamanism are life after death and stages of life in which one goes off alone for spiritual practice toward the end of one's life on earth.

Metzner distinguishes traditional systems from modern psychotherapy, but he sees ceremonies such as the sweat lodge as involving psychotherapy as well as healing and worship, as the older traditions consider body, mind, and spirit. Shamanism, alchemy, and yoga share many techniques for transformation including use of imagery, breathing exercises, sounds, and music. For example, the tree of life appears as a symbol in shamanism, the Hermetic tradition, and alchemy, and animals represent the chakras in yoga and are important in alchemy, as they are in shamanism. Metaphors such as that of the spiritual journey and dismemberment followed by reconstitution are also shared by all three disciplines, as is the concept of reconciling dualities like Sky Father and Earth Mother among shamans, and the harmonizing of solar and lunar spinal currents in some forms of yoga.

Ellwood compares shamanism with the world view of the Ancient Wisdom expressed in modern times through the Theosophical movement and its literature. Both shamanism and theosophy perceive the universe as permeated by spirit and matter, and seemingly miraculous feats depend on little known natural forces within this context. Theosophy (like yoga philosophy) depicts alternate realities as interpenetrating one another in a series of increasingly subtle and spiritual spheres of existence, which helps explain some of the feats of shamans and initiates, who can function at various levels of this superphysical continuum. Life after death and even reincarnation, prominent ideas in theosophy, are implicit in the notion of the shaman as a psychopomp or guide after death. Further, an ancient spiritual way involving initiations and mastering alternate realities is central to both shamanism and theosophy.

14
Shamanism, Mind, and No-Self

JOAN HALIFAX

A torrential rain thoroughly soaked me as I awkwardly climbed a slippery embankment on the way to the Cayapa shaman's dwelling. I had broken my right arm that morning, July 1980, in an accident on the Rio Cayapa in a remote jungle in northern Ecuador. The healing ceremony that was to take place that night was not for my benefit but for many who had traveled from far distances in canoes, and for the local sick.

The dwelling was less like a domestic space and more like a hospital with dozens of men, women, and children lying curled up on the split bamboo floor. Joining the ranks of the infirm, I realized that suffering united each of us with the other. I felt humbled by this knowledge and ceased to wait, as there was already a sense of motion and purpose in the human field around me.

Some fifteen hours later, in the early morning after the conclusion of the ceremony, I looked into the kind face of the shaman who had officiated at the ceremony, and the heat of recognition passed through me. I cannot describe even to myself in a wordless way the opening of compassion that seemed to happen between us. The spaciousness of that moment was ancient and familiar. I wished for all of humanity this dissolving of boundaries in an act of healing that transcended cultural differences.

I recognized that the stillness between us had been born in the bright darkness of his Ayahuasca trance after the candles had

213

been extinguished, and he had traveled uninvited into my dream. He came to me like a luminous body arriving in the ocean of my sleep. I knew he was there, although I had not been told that this was what he had to do in order to see my affliction and to be given the cure.

What can I say about the kindness of this stranger who was now so close to me? Without being asked, he had called my guardian spirits from far off. This he had done for all of us gathered in his jungle hospice. He enchanted the spirits with his song, whistling, and with the rustling of the dry leaves that he played like a rattle. He and his assistants had drunk the Caapi infusion and could thus travel the terrain of the spirit world. After the familiars were gathered, clans of the unseen, the candles were extinguished and a great silence fell upon all. I was curled up on a platform to the shaman's left, holding my throbbing arm, when I suddenly fell asleep. For the next hours I had the sensation of a compassionate presence joined by a Council of Others. At times, I awakened with the conviction that a lamp had been lit. But the night continued silent and dark. Hours passed, and then I heard the shaman singing and "working" on one person after another. Sucking sickness from the patient's body, blowing tobacco smoke to purify the field of the individual, playing the rattle of leaves, exhorting, crying out, cajoling, he went from one to another until his "job" was completed at dawn. Then, resting with his family around him, he ate and spoke briefly to me about the night.

I have thought often of this encounter in the Ecuadorian rain forest. As an anthropologist, I have spent many years working in the "field" with men and women who are especially gifted as healers. I have also worked as a medical anthropologist in conventional and unconventional medical settings. I have attempted in a sincere way to understand the deepest aspects of the healing process historically, culturally, psychologically, and parapsychologically. In all instances I have stumbled against the rock of credibility with regard to paranormal phenomena. Materialistic science was the basis for a pragmatic orientation in my attempts to analyze and comprehend the metaphysical and parapsychological. Friend and scholar Joseph Campbell once described this perspective as "groveling before mere facts!" My own belief system obstructed my view, made me doubt even that which not only I but others had observed.

After many years of questioning, with the need to "verify" my observations, I abandoned this approach at the suggestion of friend Hyemoyohsts Storm. One day he said to me, "Do not verify, only clarify!" I took these words to heart. So let us explore a possible clarification of the experience of the shaman.

It is not altogether surprising that the most archaic of mystical practices is of great interest to many today. As the cultures that are the ground for the shaman are overtaken by Western technology, more than an atavistic nostalgia for the past is directing our attention and scholarship to this phenomenon. I would like to offer in brief several reasons for this unusual situation.

For several decades, a growing number of Westerners have been drawn to various types of mysticism and mystical world views—for example, to Eastern spiritual paths such as Yoga, Taoism, and Buddhism. The attraction of shamanism as well as these other forms of mysticism appears to be connected for us in the West with the possibility of healing at both the individual and societal levels. It has become quite obvious that personal, social, and environmental disturbances pose a threat not only to the fabric of our culture but also to the existence of all sentient beings, plant and creature. The initiatory and visionary experiences of the shaman, as well as the practical methods used to achieve them, are thought by many to offer a possible key to psychophysical reintegration, while the shamanic world view appears to provide a possible basis for reharmonizing our now out-of-balance relationship with nature and the Earth.

The shaman has often been referred to as a "wounded healer," a "half-healed madman," a poorly integrated individual. Many shamans have indeed undergone a psychophysiological crisis of tremendous proportions prior to entering their vocation. The shamanic initiatory experience contains much that is similar to, if not identical with, certain states of mental illness such as schizophrenia. However, it is quite clear that the shaman has not only been psychically wounded or physically ill, but has also somehow been healed; that he or she is in fact a "healed healer." Such healing may sometimes occur spontaneously, as in the cases reported by psychologists of certain schizophrenics who have apparently experienced a full-blown shamanic initiatory crisis, complete with phenomena of the "Lower and Upper Worlds," and have emerged from it after a period of recovery. More often (and reliably), however, the shaman-to-be in tribal societies is helped through his or her initiatory crisis by a tradition of shamanic methods, teachings, and teachers that prepare the neophyte for the ordeal. This tradition is the legacy of those who have already traveled the same path and have to some extent charted the terrain and found ways of dealing with the phenomena likely to be encountered there.

The shaman is also one who has directly explored the realms of disease, decrepitude, mental suffering, and death. He or she is profoundly familiar with human affliction and the possibility of transcending human agony. Thus, the shaman's personal entry into the realm of suffering is the ground for compassionate action in the social domain. The shaman's painful rapture is, therefore, not a solipsistic pursuit, but an experience that is undergone on behalf of others. In this respect it has a close affinity with the emphasis on altruism found in Mahayana Buddhism.

The shaman's approach to healing and ritual is a contextual one. The individual is seen in relation to society, and society to nature—a nature infused with "beingness" or *sattva,* a nature also inhabited by spirits and ancestors. These realms are often found in a wider circle of a "Great Spirit," and this divine entity is in some cultures preceded and embraced by Great Grandmother Space, a primordial emptiness that gives birth to all phenomena. Hence, the seen and unseen, the social and spiritual, the cultural and natural, the ordinary and extraordinary inhabit one continuum of being that is not simply of opposites but is complementary, bonded, and interdependent inflections of a single extended unity. In effect, the shaman has a mystical world view in the tradition of the Perennial Philosophy, characterized by a numinous unity that underlies all forms and all appearances, while at the same time, the various worlds of form and appearances are seen as interdependent.

Turning to the discrete content of the shaman's initiatory ordeal, we discover an astounding consistency among the narratives of shamans the world over with regard to their inner experiences. We can extend this parallel to a number of other areas, including the mythical journeys of heroes, death-rebirth experiences in rites of passage and other rituals of initiation, the entry into ancient mystery religions, the posthumous journey of the soul, clinical death experiences, Yogic and Buddhist absorption states, and psychedelic drug experiences. The consistency in the themes of these diverse areas could well indicate common structures and processes within the deep psyche. That the shaman taps directly into the unconscious in the course of initiatory raptures and visionary experiences makes this individual a unique source of psychological and parapsychological information. The experiences of the shaman in an altered state of awareness reveal that the contents of consciousness are of an archaic and durable nature. The study of these experiences gives us a greater understanding not only of psychology, psychopathology, and parapsychology, but also of near-death and mystical experiences.

Regarding mystical experiences, interestingly enough there are a number of areas of significant overlap between shamanism and Mahayana Buddhism. It is, of course, not possible to *equate* these two traditions, as there are important areas of divergence which should not be glossed over. For example, in Zen Buddhism, or at least in Japanese Zen, there seems to be little or no interest in the sorts of visionary phenomena characteristic of shamanism. Nevertheless, there are other, more shamanic forms of Buddhism, such as the Tibetan Vajrayana or Korean Zen, in which such phenomena are investigated in detail. In Korean Zen, for instance, there is still in existence today a tradition of extreme ascetic practices—a tradition that corresponds in many ways with the Vision Quest in native North American shamanic tribes, where an aspirant for initiation goes alone into the wilderness to fast and meditate in order to attain realization and inspiration. It is also interesting that in Korean Zen there is a practice known as *kido,* where chanting with percussion instruments is done for twelve or more hours a day. This is a method for inducing a state of consciousness similar to those described in classical shamanism. In this state the chanter becomes one with the Bodhisattva of Compassion, Kwanseum Bosal in Korean. Native shamans in tribal cultures all over the world have their equivalent practices.

Indeed, it can be plausibly argued that many of the stages or levels of absorption and awareness described in Buddhist scriptures are in one way or another accessible to shamans. Certain

Tibetan Buddhists, for example, have spent months or years in isolation during practice. In the Bonpo religion, the native shamanism of Tibet which antedated the introduction of Buddhism into that country, the stages of absorption are described in imagery involving demonic and blissful appearances. From this perspective, we can say that the different traditions, whether shamanic or Buddhist, are each merely using different labels and metaphors in an attempt to describe or suggest what is fundamentally the same religious experience—an experience which is indescribable because it transcends the subject/object relationship upon which our languages, grammars, and discursive thought-processes are based.

The fact that we are able to compare shamanism and other spiritual paths in this way points to an interesting richness in our present cultural situation, namely, the availability now of nearly all the spiritual and esoteric traditions of the world—traditions formerly kept secret from those outside the particular society in which they originated. This is indeed fortunate since we as Westerners are faced with the very peculiar problem that we do not, for the most part, have a tradition appropriate for us to practice in our present situation. The contemplative practice of Christianity, for example, has traditionally been reserved for monks and nuns. Hence, in terms of a contemplative and mystical practice for ordinary people, shamanism, Buddhism, and a few other spiritual traditions provide us with methods.

This, however, is not to recommend that we become, for instance, Japanese Buddhists or Lakota shamans. If we were not raised in Japanese or Lakota society, we would find much in these traditions that could be confusing to us in our present situation. Many people today are interested in exploring Western Buddhism and neo-shamanism, in which elements from the older traditions relevant in today's world are combined—a kind of "Bodhishamanism." This is still very much of an experiment. Such a notion may sound contradictory if one has a concept of religion that is based on faith and obedience to authority. Nevertheless, the experiment continues; the ingredients from the different traditions are being put "in the same crucible," as it were, in order to see what will result from their encounter.

This is not to imply, of course, that shamanism and Buddhism make a perfect fit. This is hardly the case. For example, there are very concrete metaphysical differences, such as finding a way to reconcile the Buddhist doctrine of non-self (Skt. *anatma*) with the animistic world view of shamanism which posits many souls, e.g., in rocks, trees, rivers, animals, human beings, and so on. Buddhism is quite "naked" and pure in its logic—especially from the perspective of the Madhyamika philosophy which greatly shaped the Mahayana schools—and does not easily compare with other traditions in respect to metaphysics. Shamanism also deals much more with mind-display or phenomena, whereas Buddhism emphasizes "suchness" or emptiness. The latter concept is not very prevalent in shamanism except that, as we have noted, the primordial ground of being is perceived in some shamanic cultures as Great Grandmother Space, regarded as the feminine emptiness, the ground in which the creative matrix of all phenomenal manifestation is embedded. Nevertheless, the concept of emptiness may have a greater role in the new shamanism now arising in the West, for it is very useful during the crisis of shamanic initiation to hold the view that all the potentially terrifying phenomena encountered in the Lower World (the various "hells" of Tibetan Buddhism) are in some sense mind-stuff, fundamentally empty and certainly impermanent. The Australian Aboriginal experience of "the dreamtime" may have elements of this sort of recognition of fundamental emptiness. But for the most part, shamans do not try to analyze experiences in the way that Buddhists do. The shaman does not generally approach the mind in terms of emptiness or suchness as its foundation. The places of strong philosophical and practical convergence between shamanism and Buddhism are to be found in other areas; for instance, in the concept of impermanence, the Path of the Sacred Warrior, energy discipline, the practice of generosity, and so on.

For example, there is no doubt that both shamanism and Buddhism deal very artfully with the notion of change. Confronting death and the fear of death are central features of the practices of each. This convergence can be seen very clearly in the Shambhala Teachings of the Tibetans as given recently by Chogyam

Trungpa in his book *Shambhala: The Sacred Path of the War-rior*. Although Trungpa acknowledges the relationship of the Shambhala Teachings to Buddhist principles, the former seem to be derived from the shamanic warriorship tradition of the in-digenous Tibetan culture prior to Buddhism. In these teachings there is a great emphasis on working with fear—especially the fear of death—by transforming it into an *ally* (a particularly shamanic notion). The method used in this practice is that of gen-tle confrontation; that is, the absence of courage is viewed as a refusal to acknowledge reality, resulting in the invention of endless strategies to avoid facing fear or to deny its presence; whereas the presence of courage comes from facing fear with an open heart and keen awareness.

Shamanism and Buddhism also converge on the notion of in-terdependence. In shamanism this is the idea of the kinship of all life, the recognition that nothing can exist in and of itself without being in relationship to other things, and therefore that it is in-sane for us to consider ourselves as essentially unrelated parts of the whole Earth. From here we are led naturally to the concept of *sattva*, or "beingness," which in both shamanism and Bud-dhism is the idea that sentience is enjoyed not just by human be-ings but also by animals, trees, rocks, and so forth. Such a philosophical framework provides a very good foundation both for compassion and for a harmonious relationship with the natural environment, based on respect and reverence for every form of life.

In many ways shamanism and Buddhism complement each other. Shamanism tends to develop the instinctual side of one's being—the lower *chakras* in Tibetan Buddhist terms. Hence, in shamanism there is great importance attached to the cultivation of "life energy force." In Tibetan Buddhism, for example, there is emphasis on taking that energy up into the higher chakras for the development of compassion and wisdom. Turning again to Korean Zen, which is influenced by native Korean shamanism, we find that in this tradition too it is extremely important to cultivate energy, to center oneself in one's "energy garden," the region just below the navel corresponding to the *manipura* or third chakra. But there is also the idea that this instinctual energy or life force of the lower centers must be integrated with the higher centers—that there must be a joining of the instinctual with the spiritual.

From one point of view shamanism stresses the instinctual because one cannot be a shaman without first being psychophysically quite powerful. Due to the nature of the healing shaman's work with persons suffering from illness, one cannot be a poorly integrated individual and expect to be able to perform skillfully. Hence, the shaman has many practices for developing life energy force. Just as scar tissue over a wound ultimately gets tougher and stronger than the surrounding normal tissue, so the psychically wounded shaman who is healed may frequently become stronger and develop more energy than others. As in Zen, where the emphasis is on the "energy garden" below the navel, so in shamanism the same location is the focus of energy-building techniques. The whole practice of developing energy at this point in the body is to give a strong focus in the initiatory crisis, without which there might be a total shattering of the psyche, or even death during the initiatic ordeal. It has been my experience from living and working with native shamans as well as Buddhist teachers that through such methods an individual can become sufficiently vital that it is possible to develop compassion spontaneously, and to transcend neurotic defense mechanisms and societal roles.

It should not be forgotten, however, that energy in itself is neutral and can be used for beneficial or harmful purposes. From this point of view shamanism meshes interestingly with the teachings of Buddhism related to the "practice of virtue" and altruism. There are few cultures other than Buddhist ones where there has been a concerted effort to include within the teachings the idea, for example, that territorial or ideological war is wrong. "Justifiable warfare" seems to be very much a part of human culture except among very "primitive" people such as the Mbuti Pygmies or !Kung Bushmen of Africa. For this reason one of my reservations about shamanism has been that the psychological, philosophical, and ethical elaborations which would make shamanism relevant to people today do not exist in an accessible way for the most part. Tribal shamanism is appropriate for people living in tribal societies; but those who live in modern Western society would seem to need something generated from its own social ground. This is a further rationale for the approach I have described earlier; for weaving together the relevant elements from Earth philosophies such as shamanism, where instinctual energies are enhanced, and sky philosophies such as Buddhism which emphasize the mind.

Let us now return to the Cayapa ceremony in Ecuador. I have asked myself many times whose mind it was that created the shaman's presence in my dream, and where the boundary of this mind might be. My belief system did not allow for the cultural and psychological possibility of another or "outside" observer in my dream field. Yet recently I have begun to understand that the "I" who conceives of my mind as limited to my own experience is not necessarily the same self who looks past this world of appearances into the realms of dreams, visions, and mystical consciousness. The boundaries of this latter Self are more like limitless frontiers where all possibilities exist—a Greater Mind that contains many smaller minds. As I write this I am reminded of the words of the visionary Black Elk as he prayed on the summit of Mt. Harney: "While I stood there I saw more than I can tell, and I understood more than I saw; for I was seeing in a sacred manner the shape of all things in the spirit, and the shape of all shapes as they must live together as one being." This "seeing in a sacred manner" points past our materialistic science to a new science that embraces the Greater Mind. And from the Buddhist perspective of "no-self" this "relative mind" of vision emerges from the ground of the Absolute, the ground of emptiness.

15

The Dreamtime, Mysticism, and Liberation: Shamanism in Australia

VENERABLE DR. E. NANDISVARA NAYAKE THERO

The land mass of Australia is a very ancient one, being isolated from the other continents perhaps from the earliest ice age. Yet it is quite possible that the ethnic group now inhabiting Australia may have been part of the prehistoric or proto-African culture, for we speak of a community that existed in Africa long before the rise of Asiatic and European civilization, and also of the geological sinking of a crust of earth where one part of the Asiatic continent (or then macro-continent) disappeared. That portion was supposed to have been connected with Antarctica, and possibly joined what are now Asia and Africa with Australia.

Anthropologically, the color and features of the Australian natives, as well as some of the characteristics of their behavior, relate to the presumed ancient African culture as scientists have reconstructed it. The Aboriginals of Australia, however, are not so closely related to the present African societies, which developed away from the original proto-African community in ways that the Australians did not. In any case, the latter are an extremely ancient race whose way of life has not substantially changed for perhaps about 35,000 years.*

To those who judge the degree of culture by the degree of technological sophistication, the fact that the Australian natives live

---

*This article is written in the ethnographic present, although referring to pre-contact, pre-aculturation lifestyles. Today, most Aboriginals follow the way of life of their ancestors only part of the year, if at all.

in the same fashion now as they did thousands of years ago may imply that they are uncivilized or uncultured. However, I would like to present a few facts which suggest that if civilization be defined as the degree of polishing of an individual's mind and the building of his or her character, and if culture is the measure of self-discipline as well as the level of consciousness, then the Australian Aboriginals are actually one of the most civilized and highly cultured peoples in the world today.

It is of course true that the Aboriginals have very little technology. They do not wear a thread of clothing, nor do they farm, manufacture, or engage in commerce; and nearly the only tools they use are the boomerang and the spear for hunting game, as well as baskets woven from tree bark for catching fish. But this lack of technology allows them to maintain a deliberately uncomplicated life-style. I say *deliberately* because they know very well about our machines, gadgets, appliances, and so forth, but these they emphatically reject, saying that they prefer to live in the manner of their ancestors. Thus, through a conscious decision their way of life remains to this day the essence of simplicity and harmony with nature.

In a typical day they set out early in the morning just before dawn to gather and hunt food. They utilize every kind of animal in their diet, from kangaroos and emus down to lizards and grubs. In the rivers they fish and sometimes even snare crocodiles, roasting all their game over an open fire until the skin is burnt off. Every part of a killed animal is always used in some way. Nothing whatever is wasted, and hunting for sport would be unthinkable. They have great reverence for the natural powers that supply them with their needs, and they only kill animals because in the harsh environment where they make their homes there is not enough edible vegetable material to sustain their lives. Moreover, they always kill only as much as is necessary. Nearly the only vegetables they gather are various kinds of mushrooms and medicinal or sacred herbs. Yet despite their predominantly carnivorous diet, which would not seem conducive to great health and longevity, the Aboriginals often attain an age of over 100 years. In the wintertime they sleep around the open fire, and in the summer they lie under trees without any covering. This may sound like a very harsh and austere way of life to us, but what they lack in comforts and luxuries they appear to gain in serenity and peace of mind.

Our own criterion of civilization is always biased in favor of ourselves, for the ego always wants to feel itself superior. And so we tend to have the view that an archaic culture such as the Australian natives' must be "pagan," with no sophistication of religious belief. This, however, is certainly not the case, as anyone with a knowledge of the world's major religions would realize from talking to them about their spiritual life. In fact, from a number of such conversations with the shamans and elders, I have concluded that their spiritual tradition is highly advanced and that their religious beliefs are parallel with those found in the various branches of the Perennial Philosophy. Moreover, the states of consciousness known to them through their shamanic and mystical practices are in no way inferior to those described by Patanjali, the Buddha, St. John of the Cross, and other great mystics.

The Aboriginals believe that the spirits of their dead ancestors live on the peaks of rocky mountains. They especially revere rocky crevices and caves on these mountains because they say that their ancient ancestors dwell in them. Likewise, the hum of the wind in the mountains is very often associated for them with messages from the spirits. For this reason, they regularly perform a ceremony known as a Canburee, a type of ritual dance around the highest mountain for the purpose of propitiating the ancestral spirits who are thought to protect them.

This is essentially the practice of circumambulating a holy mountain, a practice found in many other religions. For it is a curious fact that mountains are associated with the sacred in most religions, including Hinduism, Christianity, Judaism, and Buddhism. God, in monotheistic faiths, was always seen on the summits of mountains, and this is where wandering holy men, ascetics, yogis, and so forth have always preferred to dwell. Moses, of course, received the Ten Commandments on the top of a mountain; and Muslims also favored the mountain peaks as places from which to approach God and where the angels communicated with humans. In Hinduism, Mount Kailash in particular is regarded as the seat of Brahma, but the entire Himalayan range has been sacred to them from time immemorial.

Buddhists have a similar respect for the mountains, and the ideal of many Buddhists in Asia is to be reborn in the wilds of the Himalayas among the holy men who have dedicated their lives to the enlightenment of humanity.

Thus, the mountain has always been a universal symbol of spiritual values and attainment. In the Aboriginal tradition, wisdom is always measured in terms of the mountain. People say "His wisdom is like the mountain," referring to the gradual descent of wisdom from the lofty summits where the spiritual beings dwell, and at the same time, an ascendance of the human spirit toward religious perfection.

The idea of reincarnation is also found in the Aboriginal culture. They believe that the spirits of their dead ancestors will again return to earth in human form. Moreover, they hold that when these dead ancestors return from the spirit world, they will come as great chiefs or leaders, thus indicating a belief not only in the immortal spirit or soul of a human being, but also the more sophisticated notion that this spirit can evolve and return to humanity for the purpose of guiding and helping other less-evolved souls.

Another significant area of interface between Aboriginal beliefs and those of the Ancient Wisdom tradition is in the idea that the spirit of a human being is always in contact with the higher spiritual realms of being (even if there may be no awareness of this contact in one's ordinary state of consciousness), and therefore that there can be direct communication between the human and divine planes without the need for any sort of ecclesiastical intermediary. In this respect, then, their beliefs are different from those theological schools which hold that there is a great impassable gulf between the human and the divine. In Australian shamanism there is no belief in such a gulf, because they have a direct, personal experience of the interconnection and intercommunication between these two domains through shamanic techniques of ecstasy. This is the main reason that no priestly hierarchy has evolved in their society. Anyone can be his or her own shaman if there is a strong enough intent, and hence anyone can directly receive inspiration and instruction from the spiritual world. Naturally, it is very difficult to develop an organized religion and priesthood under such conditions. What they have instead is a real spiritual egalitarianism.

Aboriginal methods of communing with the spiritual powers involve the use of various sacred herbs with psychotropic properties; and, as in nearly all shamanic societies, the drum and other percussion instruments play a key role in the peoples' religious life in general, and of the shaman's work in particular.

Probably there is no culture in the world where the drum is not utilized for religious purposes. In many sects of Buddhism, for example, drumming or other rhythmic percussion sound is employed in nearly all rituals; but the drum is clearly an importation from pre-Buddhistic, shamanic practices. In Aboriginal society, the drum is used both in good times and in adversity. When there is some problem in the community, they beat the drum to dispel the evil influences which are causing it, but in times of great joy they also beat the drum in order to invite the beneficent supernormal powers to the celebration.

Aboriginal drums are usually fashioned out of hollow logs rather than from stretched animal hides. They have other instruments too, such as the ancient bamboo or wooden trumpet known as the didgeridoo, as well as "click sticks," cylindrical pieces of hard wood that are struck together to produce a sharp, rapping sound. All these instruments are used by the shamans in conjunction with rhythmical dancing and inhalation of the smoke from the sacred herbs in order to induce a profound trance condition which they call *the dreamtime*. This type of trance, however, is not associated with possession by spiritual entities, but rather with an expansion of consciousness into the spiritual dimension (see below). In such a state they are able to bring back hidden knowledge for the use of the community and themselves.

In Aboriginal drumming it is the *echo* of the drumbeat that is important, for they say that the sound circulates around the mountaintops where the reverberation brings the spirits surviving on the cosmic planes around the mountain back to the human world. And of course it also helps the shaman to enter the expanded state of consciousness. Thus the drum is a tool for journeying in the dreamtime in order to perform certain kinds of work, whether this be to recover a lost soul or lost power for a member of the community who is ill, to consult with spiritual teachers about some problem, or to undergo shamanic initiation.

Shamanic work in Aboriginal society may also involve exploring the areas in the dreamtime world where human spirits go after death, and describing them in ways that are remarkably similar to descriptions given in religious thanatologies in other traditions, such as *The Tibetan Book of the Dead*. The human consciousness after death is described by the Australian shamans as "survival in infinity," implying that the individual point of contact with the infinitude of cosmic consciousness expands until it is co-extensive with the latter. The Hindu notion of liberation *(moksha)* as a merging of the limited individual consciousness with the Absolute seems very likely to have had its roots in earlier shamanic experiences such as those cultivated and described by the Aboriginals. These experiences can be called an awareness of the focus of infinity within one's own finite being. Thus the Vedantists say, very much like the Aboriginals, that after death the seemingly enclosed individual consciousness dissolves into the infinitude of space, which is Brahman. Hence, there is a significant overlap between these spiritual traditions. In fact, it can be said that the basic meditative and mystical experiences of the Australian shamans are the same as in these other traditions, although the terms used to describe the experiences will of course vary from culture to culture. For example, an Easterner will tend to use words like *samadhi* instead of *dreamtime;* but empirically or phenomenologically the states appear to be essentially the same.

Besides the shamanic work undertaken for the purposes described above, there is also a tradition of personal spiritual aspiration in Aboriginal society very similar to that found in Yoga. Thus during the last years of their lives, some of the elders secede from the community and go off alone into the mountains to engage in spiritual practices, much as in the last two stages of the so-called Four Stages of Life in the Hindu system, which are characterized by solitary retirement to the forest, a striving for spiritual understanding, and preparation for death.*

One of the techniques practiced by such renunciate elders in Aboriginal society is gazing at the sky with wide-open eyes. This practice may be connected with their idea that the universe is imbued with inspiration that awakens the human mind; that the cos-

---

The four Stages of Life in Hinduism are: *Brahmacharya*, unmarried student; *Grihastha*, householder; *Vanaprastha*, forest dweller; and *Sannyasa*, wanderer.

mos contains an infinitude of knowledge which can be learned. But their sky-gazing is not a type of astronomy or astrology. Rather, it is a meditative method used to obtain spiritual inspiration and intuition from the cosmos.

The close relationship with nature enjoyed by the Australian natives appears to be in no way different from that which characterized the Indo-gangetic civilization where both Yoga and Tantra originally developed. It has been said that Buddhism, Yoga, and other relatively recent religious systems contain "sky philosophies" in which sky deities or the concept of space are of greatest religious importance, as distinct from earlier religions in tribal societies having "Earth philosophies" where the Earth Mother and other female deities or fertility goddesses were the chief objects of reverence. In Aboriginal society, however, both types of philosophy are present. The Earth is implied as the basis for all studies during the first and intermediate stages of life. But when the basic Earth study is completed toward the end of life, there is an ascent of the spirit toward the boundless reaches of the sky. Thus the highest spirituality is associated for the Aboriginals not with the Earth but with the infinity of space. So, for the Australian shaman, as for the Hindu, the first and middle stages of life are connected with the Earth, with doing one's worldly duties—raising a family, taking part in the activities of the community, and so forth—while the last part of life is connected with an aspiration to the highest spiritual state, cosmic consciousness.

Along with the elders' renunciation of family life goes another universal religious phenomenon, the practice of celibacy during the last years of life. Even in a complex society such as the Islamic, where multiple marriages are permissible, the Sufis—the Islamic mystics—in their final years become celibate. In Hinduism, celibacy is also emphasized, as it is in both Buddhism and Jainism. Apparently the conservation and transmutation of sexual energy has been found to be a prerequisite of the attainment of the advanced stages of mystical meditation in all of these cultures.

Along the way to these higher states of consciousness, the shamans in Aboriginal society are able to develop various sorts of psychic powers. For example, they undoubtedly possess the capacity to travel through the sky in an altered state of consciousness, and to visit in this way any place they wish. This is one reason, perhaps, why they have so little interest in cars, airplanes, rockets, and other modern transportational "marvels." Travelers in the dreamtime can journey to the moon, or to any other planet quite easily any time they choose. Hence, they would not be likely to be awed by our clumsy machines which are very slow in comparison. Similarly, there is evidence for their ability to communicate telepathically, a fact that would explain their apathy concerning modern methods of "advanced" communication such as telephones, television sets, and so on.

The Aboriginals' travel in the dreamtime appears to be identical with the *siddhi* or psychic power of aerial flight described in ancient Yoga treatises like Patanjali's *Yoga Sutras*. This is a science which must be available to them, since they speak of aerial flight (as well as descent to a "lower Earth"), implying that there is something mysterious in the upper ether to which they can ascend in their spiritual development. A detailed knowledge of their practices is unfortunately precluded by their extreme reticence to speak of such things. On consideration, however, the occurrence of this phenomenon seems quite probable, for when a person aspires to a deeper insight into his or her mind, there is often—as the great Teachers in the Perennial Tradition tell us—an ascent of the soul or spirit to the cosmic plane, focused from the body.

From the standpoint of the Indic esoteric schools, such an ascent would be a form of *nirvikalpa samadhi* in which the mind passes beyond the level of discursive thought and merges with a "ray" that connects it to the infinity of cosmic consciousness. At this stage, both the body and the mind are absolutely still. There may or may not be detectable breathing, but in either case it is not prominent because the body in such a condition does not require as much breath, and because the thoughts, which usually agitate the breath, have been eliminated. This state is not associated with the *chakras* described in Kundalini Yoga and other schools of esoteric science because it is beyond such experiences. In fact, it is a withdrawal of energy from the chakras so that the latter no longer have an effect on the mind. This is the borderland between the mind that is connected to the world and the mind that is not connected to the world—which is absolutely free. An area of experience like this may seem frightening, especially if one is very much identified with and attached to one's thoughts; for then the absence of thoughts and other mental fluctuations will seem like death. Actually, it can be described as a form of temporary death, because the communication between the body and the mind has for the time being been cut off. The mind then drifts to the vastness of space and is reduced, as it were, to a small speck. And as a small speck, it can float in that infinitude.

From my conversations with them it appears that this is also the experience of the elders in Aboriginal society after they renounce their homes and go off to live in the mountains to practice gazing at the sky. Then they say that the mind is no longer in the body but is reflected out into the cosmos. Although their practice involves gazing at the sky, it is really the shaman's invitation to the spiritual cosmic force to embrace the focus of his mind. It can therefore be called a form of Yoga—in the essential meaning of a union or "yoking" of the mind with the Infinite.

It is, of course, possible to idealize shamanic cultures, perhaps out of a dissatisfaction with our own society and a longing for something better. And certainly many shamanic groups are far from perfect. Tribal envies, jealousies, and territorial rivalries have been the cause of frequent feuds in some native tribes, for instance in North and South America. But this has not been found to be true in the Australian Aboriginal culture. They have apparently never been a bellicose race. Warfare and tribalization have not been their "game," and their spears are used only for hunting food, never to shed the blood of their fellows. Perhaps this is due at least in part to the fact that they are an extremely well-disciplined and self-controlled group of people. For example, during all the time I stayed with them I never saw even so much as a family quarrel. In short, theirs is a society of beautiful human beings who practice the most perfect *ahimsa* or harmlessness toward each other without any indoctrination, external teaching, or coercion. It apparently develops naturally as a function of growing up in that culture.

The wonder and beauty of the Aboriginals, then, is that they are so perfectly peaceful and quiet, so harmoniously in tune with nature and the spiritual dimension, while in the rest of the world around them most of the so-called "civilized" races are running amok, killing each other on all sides, exploiting the environment and their fellow living beings, polluting the water and air, and threatening to destroy the entire planet in a nuclear holocaust. Is it therefore surprising that I have described the native Australians as one of the most civilized and cultured of all peoples in the world today?

16

Transformation Processes in Shamanism, Alchemy, and Yoga

RALPH METZNER

One possible definition of shamanism is that it is the disciplined approach to what has been variously called "non-ordinary reality," "the sacred," "the mystery," "the supernatural," "the inner world(s)," or "the other world." Psychologically speaking, one could say these expressions refer to realms of consciousness that lie outside the boundaries of our usual and ordinary perception. The depth psychologies derived from psychoanalysis refer to such normally inaccessible realms as "the unconscious," or "the collective unconscious." This would, however, be too limiting a definition for shamanism if "unconscious" is taken to refer to something within the individual, i.e., intrapsychic. Shamanic practice involves the exploration not only of unknown aspects of our own psyche, but also the unknown aspects of the world around us, the external as well as the internal mysteries.

I suggest that there are three traditional systems of consciousness transformation, of belief and practice, in which the exploration of these non-ordinary realms is pursued with discipline and intention: shamanism, alchemy, and yoga. Of these, shamanism is of course the oldest, and the one with the widest distribution all over the globe.[1] Alchemy, which developed independently in Europe, the Near East, India, and China, shares with shamanism the goal of consciousness transformation, the quest for healing, knowledge, and power, and profound respect for nature. Alchemy could in fact be regarded as being a development of a

233

certain type of shamanism, i.e., that practiced by miners, smiths, metalworkers, toolmakers, and their descendants. Mircea Eliade, in his work *The Forge and the Crucible,* on the historical origins of alchemy, has documented this connection very thoroughly.[2] The psychospiritual purposes and techniques of the alchemists came in time to be all but forgotten and overshadowed by its applications in the experimental physical sciences.

Yoga, like shamanism and alchemy, comprises a certain kind of world view and a systematic technology of changing consciousness. There is less emphasis on nature, animals, plants, minerals, the environment, and more focus on interior higher states of consciousness. In some of the Indian yoga teachings there is a kind of detachment from and transcendence of the realms of nature, matter, the earth, the physical body. Important exceptions to this general tendency are *tantra yoga* in India and Tibet, and Taoist yoga practices in China, which are closely allied to alchemy in those cultures. Alchemy in India and China, as well as Tantra and Taoism, emphasize the transmutation of the physical body and practices of regeneration and longevity, along with the seeking of higher, transcendent states of consciousness.

Modern schools of psychotherapy, especially those based on psychodynamic depth psychology and the newer so-called "experiential therapies," employ many of the methods and techniques of consciousness change that were known in the ancient systems of shamanism, alchemy, and yoga. In some instances, for example in both Freud's and Jung's borrowing of alchemical ideas, the derivation is quite conscious and deliberate; in other cases, for example the use of inner journeys of imagery sequences, psychologists are rediscovering or reinventing methods that have been known and practiced for centuries in these older traditions.

I propose, in this essay (1) to outline some of the *techniques of transformation* used in the traditional systems and their modern derivatives, and (2) to compare some of the key *metaphors of transformation* that are used in these systems both to describe and to activate a consciousness-transforming process. Before doing so, I would like to comment on two important differences in goals and values that distinguish traditional systems from modern psychotherapy.

The first difference is that shamanism, alchemy, and yoga are not focused only on solving psychological problems, as is most psychotherapy. Rather, these traditional systems operate from an integrated world view in which physical healing, psychological problem-solving, and conscious exploration of spiritual or sacred realms of being are all considered as aspects of the way, or work, or practice. A shamanic ritual such as the Native American sweat-lodge, for example, is simultaneously a healing, a psychological therapy, and a form of worship including prayer. Alchemy's interest in healing is evident in its quest for the *panacea*, the "cure-all"; and the deep spiritual commitment of the genuine alchemists, who sought to produce the *lapis*, the wisdom stone, is likewise apparent. Similarly, in yoga the spiritual purpose of the attainment of higher states of consciousness is paramount; physical or psychological problem-solving may occur but almost as a secondary effect.

The purpose of psychotherapy, in contrast, is generally not to bring about physical healing, nor does it concern itself normally with spiritual values or religious issues. The goal is usually framed in terms of psycho-social adjustment, or the resolution of intrapsychic conflicts, or interpersonal communication problems. The split in Western "civilized" consciousness between body, mind, and spirit is reflected in a rigid separation of roles between the physician, the therapist, and the priest. There are, however, encouraging signs that this situation may be changing: the contribution of psychological factors to the origins and the treatment of diseases is attracting increasing attention.[3] The work of C. G. Jung with archetypes, of Abraham Maslow with the notion of self-actualization, and of Roberto Assagioli with psychosynthesis has pointed the way toward greater recognition of spiritual factors; and the transpersonal psychology movement explicitly has attempted to integrate the spiritual dimensions into a comprehensive understanding of the human psyche.[4]

The second important difference in goals and values is that psychotherapy focuses on changing or helping the other—the patient, client, victim, sufferer—whereas in the traditional systems of shamanism, alchemy, and yoga, the emphasis is on self-transformation, self-healing, self-understanding. While it is true that the more sophisticated approaches to psychotherapy are well aware of the relevance of the therapist's own perceptions and feelings to the therapeutic process, these tend to be categorized as "countertransference" reactions, and seen as an impediment to the conduct of therapy, to be eliminated if possible. On the other hand, while it is true that helping or healing others is an important application of shamanic work (in healing shamanism especially, as distinct from power shamanism or sorcery), such work is always based on the shaman's own inner process. Typically, the healer shaman may contact his or her own power animal or ally, in order to facilitate a similar contact with inner sources of support and healing for the patient or sufferer.[5] The wide-spread concept of the "wounded healer"points to a direct personal engagement of the healer with the sickness or wound of the patient. The shaman may journey into the inner world in order to combat or destroy the "spirits" or "forces" that are manifesting as physical or psychic pathology.[6]

In so far as practitioners of shamanism, alchemy, or yoga are exploring inner or non-ordinary worlds in order to recover lost knowledge or gain insight into the workings of nature and cosmos, such work was traditionally seen as leading to healing abilities, as a derivative of the ability to understand and heal oneself. The alchemists who attained the philosophers' stone, which was also a tincture as well as a panacea, were able to free themselves completely from any disease, and then heal others simply by a kind of direct transfer of energy (as in Jesus Christ's healings described in the New Testament). Similar seemingly miraculous healing powers, or *siddhis,* have been recorded for advanced yogis, and the Buddha was recognized as the Great Physician, who showed the way to the alleviation of suffering.

A comparison of shamanism, alchemy, and yoga, as traditional systems of consciousness transformation, with modern psychotherapy, as a problem-solving approach that uses similar methods and similar metaphors, must be tempered by the awareness that the traditional systems see the human being as an integrated body-mind-spirit continuum. Their approach seeks to recover a way of knowledge that can not only heal and solve psychic problems, but lead to ultimate concerns of human destiny and the meaning of life.

Techniques of Transformation in Shamanism, Alchemy and Yoga

A crucial notion that grew out of the early research on psyche-delics was what became known as "the set-and-setting hypothe-sis." According to this hypothesis, widely accepted by conciousness researchers, the actual content of a psychedelic ex-perience is a function of the *set* (intention, beliefs, expectations, personality) and the *setting* (physical and social context), with the drug playing the role of trigger, or *catalyst*.[7] The same principle can be applied in other situations not involving drugs: the trigger or catalyst of an altered state might be hypnosis, special breathing, sound, sensory isolation, meditation, stress, and so on, and similar features of subjective experience can oc-cur across the different modalities.

Techniques of consciousness transformation then refer to the specific triggers and catalysts that are used to bring about altered states in which the healing, or insight, or vision, can occur. Fur-thermore, the systematic and continued use of a given technique to induce altered states constitutes *training* or *practice*. The shamanic, alchemical, or yogic initiate is, after all, not only interested in a one-time experience of heightened consciousness, but rather in a more or less permanent development of the capaci-ty to enter into such states at will, to gain knowledge from them, and to apply them in healing and problem-solving situations. Thus the psychologists' distinction between "state" and "trait" changes is important to keep in mind here also. The same stimuli or agents that function as triggers for altered states become, when used with the appropriate set and in the relevant context, ingredients in an integrated practice, discipline, or *sadhana*.

Techniques of directed imagery or visualization are very wide-spread. A recent work by Jeanne Achterberg reviews the use of imagery methods in traditional shamanism, and compares it to the role of imagery in contemporary medicine, such as the Simontons' application of visualization in the treatment of can-cer.[8] Achterberg distinguishes preverbal imagery, where "im-ages communicate with tissues and organs, even cells, to effect a change," and transpersonal imagery, where "information is transmitted from the consciousness of one person to the physical substrate of another.'' The shamanic practitioner in training is directed and prepared to "see" objects, plants, animals, spirits in the inner realm, the non-ordinary state. Such inner seeing, which may be intensified by drumming or hallucinogenic plants, is not regarded as "imagination" in the sense of something that is "made up," a constructed fantasy. Rather, it is regarded as seeing in non-ordinary reality, with perceptible results and impact in this reality (as, for example, if the patient is healed). Numerous accounts now exist of shamanic visionary experiences, both those collected from native informants,[9] and those gathered from modern Westerners who have taken up the practice of shamanic work.[10] Under this heading, we can also consider dreamwork as an important aspect of shamanic imagery technology. Images are explored and "amplified" (Jung's term) regardless of whether they occur in dream or waking states.

The use of imagery methods in alchemy is pervasive, so much so that Jung and his followers regard all of alchemy as primarily a system of symbolic imagery. Edward Edinger writes, "The great value of alchemical images is that they give us an *objective* basis from which to approach dreams and other unconscious material."[11] Alchemical literature is filled with engravings showing mythological figures and symbolic creatures and objects, suggesting that conscious contemplation of such images was an important aspect of the alchemical transformation process or *opus*. It is likely that alchemists systematically practiced visualization techniques as they performed experiments in their retorts and furnaces, looking for the symbolic images in the fire that the ancient books and pictures portray.[12] Jung wrote, "While working on his chemical experiments the operator had certain experiences which appeared to him as the particular behavior of the chemical process."[13] I would differ from Jung's view only in so far as he claims the alchemists projected the contents of their own unconscious into matter; it seems to me rather that they projected certain core mythic and symbolic images *consciously*, according to the prescribed tradition.

The use of imagery, both in waking and dreaming states, in the various branches of yoga is well-documented.[14] Especially in the Tantra traditions, both the Hindu and the Buddhist Vajrayana forms, visual symbolic images of the interior subtle-body anatomy are pervasive. The *chakras* and *nadis* are described in great detail, with all their associated colors, geometric shapes, animals, Sanskrit letters, and so on. The awakening energy of the root chakra, called *kundalini,* is visualized as a serpent rising up a central pillar, or two serpents coiling back and forth across the central axis. *Tantras,* or geometrical diagrams including the *mandala,* are constructed as external supports or expressions of the interior domains.[15] In Tibetan Buddhist yoga there is even an elaborate and sophisticated system for working consciously with dream images—an area Western research is only now beginning to explore with the concept of controlled lucid dreaming.[16]

The use of waking and dream imagery in psychotherapy is too well known to require much elaboration here. In the Freudian or Jungian depth psychological approaches, the emphasis is on letting unconscious images emerge into consciousness. In other systems such as psychosynthesis, Gestalt, or various newer forms of imagery therapy including hypnotherapy, the emphasis is more on consciously selected and developed sequences of images. In such approaches the guide or therapist typically may "set the scene" as it were, or suggest some initial framework, which the patient then explores, develops, or amplifies.[17]

The use of *breathing techniques* as means to develop special states of consciousness is well documented in the yoga traditions, although its use in shamanism or alchemy is more uncertain. In Patanjali's classic exposition of the *ashtanga* (eight-limbed) yoga, breath control *(pranayama)* is the fourth step, after various behavioral and moral restrictions, and *asanas* or the physical postures of hatha yoga.[18] Moreover, *prana* refers not only to the physical breath, but also to the breath-like subtle life force, that is accumulated, preserved and distributed throughout the body by the use of special breathing techniques.

Breathing techniques have not, to my knowledge, been documented in shamanic traditions nor in alchemy. However, the practice of certain kinds of chanting, such as the so-called "throat music" of the Inuit and other very rapid, rhythmic chants, appears to involve a kind of accelerated, rhythmic hyperventilation, which probably induces an altered state. The circular or continuous breathing that is required to play the *didjeridu* of the Australian Aborigines and the long curved horns of the Tibetans may have a similar function.

In modern psychotherapy breathing methods have not been employed in any systematic manner until fairly recent times. In Gestalt therapy as well as in Reichian and bioenergetic types of bodywork, attention to breathing and the deepening of normal breathing beyond the restrictive patterns of the "armored" individual play an important role. The primal therapy of Arthur Janov, the "rebirthing" method of Leonard Orr, and the holotropic breathing therapy of Stanislav Grof are examples of modern approaches in which controlled hyperventilation is used to facilitate the emergence of very deeply repressed unconscious material. [19]

The use of sound as a trigger or catalyst of heightened states of consciousness is also widespread in all traditional cultures. We leave aside the important role of group chanting, with or without dancing, in various kinds of tribal rituals, which probably also induces collective alterations of consciousness. For the induction of shamanic states of consciousness, inner journeys for healing, or the acquisition of knowledge, it appears that the method of rhythmic drumming is the most prevalent technique, besides hallucinogenic plants. [20] There is some evidence that this method involves "auditory driving" or entrainment of cerebral electrical rhythms. Shamans who employ this method often refer to the drum as their "horse" or "vehicle." The beat seems to carry the awareness naturally and effortlessly through various inner landscapes. Other sound techniques in shamanism include use of instruments like the already mentioned *didjeridu,* as well as various kinds of rattles, conches, and of course chanting or singing.

In alchemy methods of sound cannot with certainty be identified, partly because of the general secrecy and intentional concealment of the technical aspects of the alchemical art. However, in the Indian and Tibetan yoga traditions the use of *mantra,* or specific syllables and formulas that have definite psychic and spiritual power, is pervasive. Though there are some analogies to the role of prayer in the Western religious traditions, *mantras* are said to have definite effects on consciousness through their sound quality alone, quite apart from their meaning content. [21] Particular *mantras* are said to activate or energize certain *chakras,* for instance. In the Tibetan Buddhist tradition there are practices of overtone chanting, which also have quite definite consciousness-heightening effects on the listener, as well as, presumably, on the performer. It has been suggested by some that the practice of Gregorian chants in the European medieval churches and monasteries may also have had trance-like effects, but this has not as yet been proven.[22]

It cannot be said that sound or music plays any particularly important role in psychotherapy in the West. Certainly there are schools and teachers of music therapy, in which listening to selected pieces of symphonic music is used to "tune in" to and support various emotional states (with or without the use of psychedelic drugs); and some hypnotherapists or imagery therapists use music as accompaniment to their procedures. But the focused use of selected sounds for the induction of altered states has not been explored to any great extent, with the exception of music for relaxation or un-stressing, which is often little more than listening to a kind of New Age background music.[23]

The role of *psychoactive and hallucinogenic plants* in shamanic practices has been amply documented by Schultes and Hofmann, by Furst, Wasson, Dobkin de Rios, Harner, Weil and others.[24] Elsewhere, I have written on the use of psychedelics in the traditional systems of transformation. It appears to me that in the world view of traditional cultures, "The use of hallucinogenic plants, when it occurs, is part of an integrated complex of interrelationships between Nature, Spirit and human consciousness."[25]

Our knowledge of the possible use of hallucinogens in alchemy is much more limited than in the case of shamanism. However, the use of solanaceous (nightshade family) hallucinogens in European witchcraft, which is related to both shamanism and alchemy, has been documented by Harner.[26] Likewise, in Chinese Taoist alchemy, the use of botanical and mineral preparations to induce spirit-flight and other kinds of altered states has been discussed by Strickman.[27] The sparseness of the record on this subject may be due to the persecution and elimination of both alchemists and witches.

In the case of yoga, the classic theoretical statement on the role of hallucinogens is found in the fourth section of Patanjali's *Yoga Sutras.* Here, the author lists four causal factors that can lead to the development of *siddhis*, which are miraculous, magical, or psychic capacities: herbs *(ausadhi)*, sacred sounds *(mantras)*, the discipline of inner fire *(tapas)*, and meditative absorption *(samadhi)*.[28] In this work, which is not tantric, only the last of these four methods, meditation, is discussed any further. The use of hallucinogens as an adjunct to tantric yoga practice is known to this day in India, among certain tantric Shaivite sects in particular.[29]

It appears incontrovertible that hallucinogens played some role, of unknown extent, in the transformative traditions of shamanism, alchemy, and yoga. If we regard psychotherapy as, in some respects, the modern descendant of these traditional systems, then a similar application might be expected. This has in fact already occurred, as the various studies of psychedelics as adjuncts to therapy in alcoholism, terminal cancer, obsessional neurosis, depression, and other conditions testify.[30]

Metaphors of Transformation in Shamanism, Alchemy, and Yoga

In studying the various systems and techniques of consciousness transformation over the past twenty-five years, I have become aware that, while there are literally dozens if not hundreds of specific methods, there is a limited number of core metaphors that have been used to describe experiences of transformation. One such metaphor, to give an example, is "awakening," that our ordinary consciousness is a kind of dream-sleep state, and that a more awakened consciousness, an enhanced objective awareness, is possible. In *Opening to Inner Light* I describe ten of these basic metaphors of transformation, found in shamanic art and ritual, alchemical symbolism, yogic texts and the writings of mystics, in myth, legend, and fairy tale, and in the reports of modern individuals undergoing psychotherapy or having significant dreams and visionary experiences.[31]

Metaphors, symbols, and analogies are evidently indispensable for the description of the phenomenology of transformation and for the description of non-ordinary states of consciousness and entry into "other worlds" of reality. Presumably, this is because our ordinary language has evolved to accommodate ordinary reality and everyday life, not the complexities of these special states and experiences that are inherently rare and non-ordinary. I have come to appreciate that metaphors are not merely the literary devices of poets and mystics, but totally pervasive in our ordinary language as well. George Lakoff and Mark Johnson, in their seminal book *Metaphors to Live By*, give the linguistic evidence and philosophical argument for supposing that our language *and our thinking* are inherently and inescapably metaphorical, although often the metaphors are implicit in everyday language and not recognized as such.[32] The social psychologist M. Brewster Smith, starting from Lakoff and Johnson's work, has discussed the metaphorical nature of psychological concepts of self.[33] Gregory Bateson in *Mind and Nature* argues persuasively for the fundamental and unrecognized role of analogical thinking (for which he uses C. S. Pierce's term "abduction") in the natural and social sciences.[34]

The metaphor of "the journey" is widely used in at least two senses in discussions of shamanism. In the non-ordinary shamanic state induced by drumming or hallucinogens, the practitioner's awareness "leaves" the ordinary reality of time, space, and body for a limited period, exploring the "otherworld" to obtain healing or knowledge, and then returns to ordinary, body-based consciousness. This parallels the metaphor of the "trip," a term spontaneously created by users of psychedelic drugs in the sixties. Another metaphorical meaning of "journey" relates to a longer-lasting, ongoing process of personality transformation, in which concepts of self and world view may undergo a profound change as a result of guided practice, or *sadhana*. This kind of journey of self-transformation, which also involves a departure from the conventional world of home, family, and culture, parallels the mythic hero's journey, as described by Joseph Campbell in his *Hero With a Thousand Faces*.

As is well known, shamanic journeys may be one of three types: lower world, middle world, or upper world. Traveling downward, horizontally, or upward in space are the chosen *metaphors* for these kinds of altered states; no actual physical travel is of course involved (the physical body is usually lying on the ground). They are appropriately chosen metaphors because they aptly characterize the phenomenology of these states. In "lower world journeys" one feels and perceives oneself to be falling, sliding, or crawling down, into, or under the earth. In "upper world journeys" one feels and perceives oneself rising up, flying or floating through the air or sky, or climbing a mountain or the world tree. In "middle world journeys" one is traveling horizontally through an interior landscape that may be in many ways very different from exterior reality, but is somehow perceived as being on the same level. This metaphor of journey or travel is found equally in the traditional lore of shamanic cultures, and in the reports of modern individuals practicing shamanic methods.[35]

From the point of view of a psychology of consciousness that espouses a multidimensional model of the human constitution, such as is found in esoteric and theosophical teachings as well as Vedanta, one would say that a lower world journey is a movement of awareness to a level "lower" than the normal waking consciousness (also referred to sometimes as "sub-conscious"); and a higher world journey is movement to a level "higher" than the normal waking level. Theosophy and other esoteric teachings describe these levels as differing in vibratory rate, or frequency rate (as the notes of a musical scale). "Lower levels" are lower or slower in frequency, denser, more involved in matter, the physical body, and the "earth plane." "Higher levels" are higher or faster in frequency, subtler or less dense, more like the traditional "heavens" or etheric and astral planes.

The theme of ascent to higher levels of consciousness is of course central to the *raja* and *tantra* yoga traditions, where it is sometimes symbolized by the ascent of the *kundalini* energy up the physical body axis, and sometimes described as ascending through the levels or "sheaths" of successively finer substance. Processes of downward movement are rarely described in yoga and meditation teachings. This is one of the major differences between yoga and both the shamanic and alchemical work. In yoga there is more emphasis on transcendence, on rising up into higher states of absorption or *dhyana*—states progressively more devoid of form and content—to the pure and formless states of *samadhi* or *nirvana*. Only in the tantric tradition and the related alchemical way of *rasayana* do we find much concern with the transmutation of physical substance and form per se, the downward involvement into matter being for the purposes of refining it.

"The upper world journey" is one of a class of metaphors of ascent that can include, besides flying or floating through the air (such as can also occur in flying dreams), riding on a giant bird (eagle or wild goose) or a "magic carpet," and climbing a mountain, pillar, or tree. This connects with the very widespread *tree of life* symbolism found in shamanic cultures around the globe. Eliade has amply documented the tree of life or world tree motif in cultures all over the world.[36] The shaman typically reports that he has climbed the tree and obtained information for diagnosis or healing, perhaps by a certain leaf from the top of the tree. The tree is described as being at the center of the world, and sacred. The different branches represent stages in the ascent and subsequent descent; they are symbolically analogous to the planes or levels of consciousness in esoteric and occult lore. The trunk or axis of the tree is the axis through which we can ascend to the higher dimensions: it is therefore an interdimensional axis. And the individual axis and world axis are aligned, so that climbing one means climbing the other. Hence the prevalence of the *axis mundi* image in connection with the tree of life.

The tree of life symbolism is also prevalent in the hermetic tradition, where it is associated with regeneration. There are images of Hermes standing beneath the tree in two forms: as old man and as youth. An alchemical text advises that the old man should eat of the fruit of that tree until he becomes a youth. "For the alchemists, the tree of knowledge has little to do with the making of judgments—separating good from bad; it is more a symbol for inner 'seeing,' for insight into the inner structure of things, for seeing how everything hangs together. To them the tree symbol is a vast reservoir of imagery and psychic energy. The 'tree of the philosophers' is, to the alchemist, the axis of the transformational work, the unfolding *opus*. Significantly, the Old English root word for 'tree' and 'truth' is the same: it is *treow*."[38]

The shamanic metaphor of climbing the tree also appears in the Indian yoga traditions, especially Tantra, in the notion of the central axis, called *merudanda*, or staff of Meru, which is also the *sushumna* axis on which the *chakras* are aligned. The bottom chakra is called the "root chakra" *(muladhara)*, and the awareness of energy moving up this axis of transformation is symbolized by the ascent of the coiled *kundalini* serpent.

Another very widespread theme in shamanic training and apprenticeship is *dismemberment* or shamanic sickness or the wounded healer. Shamans in training often expect to become sick or wounded as part of their initiation, or voluntarily submit to the experience of feeling oneself being dismembered, cut open, broken into small pieces, and then reconstituted, often by the animal ally or other spirit guide. Psychologically, one could say that this is a metaphor for the psychic fragmentation that anyone may experience to a greater or lesser degree at various phases of life. The psychotic episode, with its shattered language and fragmented thinking, is perhaps an extreme (and involuntary) form of this kind of experience. In total contrast, the shamanic initiate who intentionally undergoes a dismemberment experience as part of his training "feels he is being delivered from the limitations of the ordinary world and empowered to perform visionary, healing, and protective work for himself and the members of the tribe."[39]

Dismemberment imagery occurs in the yoga traditions also, where the ability to separate the body into different pieces and reassemble them at will is recognized as one of the *siddhis* of an advanced yogi. There are eye-witness accounts of the 19th-century saint Sai Baba of Shirdi performing such practices, visibly to others. Likewise, in the Tibetan Vajrayana Buddhist teachings, admittedly strongly influenced by the indigenous Bon shamanism, there is the gruesome *chod,* or "cutting off" rite, in which the yogi invokes a demon to devour and transmute his body, with all its negative past karmic patterns.[40] The mythologies of Osiris and of Dionysus also feature stories of the god's dismemberment and reconstitution.

In alchemy the operation or process that most nearly corresponds to dismemberment is *separatio.* This is discriminative perception and attention, which carefully distinguishes, and analyzes the different aspects or elements of consciousness. It is akin in some ways to the discriminative wisdom of meditation and to the "taking apart" process of psychoanalysis. *Separatio* was seen as the necessary prerequisite to healing and new growth.[41] Transformation consists in first recognizing the degree of fragmentation that exists, through the methods of interior visualization, and then integrating and harmonizing these separated fragments and pieces. Discriminative separation precedes and prepares for integration and wholeness, as death precedes and prepares for rebirth.

Central and essential to all traditions of transformation is the notion of opposites or *dualities and their reconciliation.* There are at least three major pairs of opposites whose mutual balancing and integrating is important in shamanism, and in alchemy and yoga as well: the balance of male and female; the reconciliation of good and evil; and the integration of human and animal consciousness. In each case the task is to recognize the duality that exists within and then to find ways to transform the opposites from a state of divisiveness and antagonism to a state of complementarity or peaceful coexistence.

The ubiquity of the *androgyny* motif is well known. The central belief here is that all human beings are, in essence, of dual nature, though the sides may be unevenly developed. Shamans, alchemists, and yogis, as well as the mystics of almost all religious traditions, have concerned themselves with integrating these polarities. In shamanic cultures the mythology of Father Sky and Mother Earth is the cosmic dualism on which this integrative project is based. Shamans in some cultures may practice a ritual transvestism, or even live for long periods of time completely as the other sex does, in order to bring about a better balance of the masculine and feminine energies. In alchemy Sun and Moon, King and Queen are the symbolic representatives of the male and female energies. The "alchemical marriage" between fire and water is the union from which arises the new "philosophers' child." In yoga practice is also found the notion of solar and lunar currents of energy flow, the *ida* and *pingala,* which must be balanced for the yogi to attain liberation. And in Jungian psychotherapy, the process of individuation calls for integration with one's interior sexual opposite, the *anima* or *animus.*

Another very important duality is that of *good vs. evil.* In Jungian terms this is the notion of integrating the shadow, our unacceptable, destructive tendencies. There is an inner adversary (in Christian terms, the devil) that we have to know and recognize if we are to cease projecting this split-off enemy image onto

other people. "They" as the enemy, who gets blamed for everything that goes wrong in our life, is possibly the most pathetic
and the most dangerous of all our delusions. Shamanic warrior
training and practice, whether against sorcery spells or evil
spirits that are attacking the shaman or his or her client, become
most relevant here. In alchemical literature the dark, destructive
aspects of the psyche are symbolized by the *nigredo* (blackness),
that has to be transmuted and uplifted through the alchemical
fires of purification, and by various monsters and predatory
creatures that vampirize and cannibalize the pure life essence. In
the yoga traditions negative psychic complexes are described as
samskaras, the karmic binding patterns resulting from past actions, that keep us trapped in the same old negative attitudes.
These *samskaras* are dissolved and reduced through the practice
of meditation.[42]

The cultivation of balance and right relationship between
human and animal consciousness, the third of the dual pairs
mentioned above, is most important in shamanism. Shamanic
cultures speak of the soul or spirit of each species—Bear, Wolf,
Eagle—who represents and protects the individual members of
that species, and with whom the shaman can communicate on
altered-state journeys. People used to know the language of
animals and vice versa, according to ancient animistic and
shamanic belief systems. Through the practice of finding and
working with a "power animal" or animal ally or guide,
shamans re-establish in the inner realms the kind of communication and alliance that existed outwardly in earlier times. This can
be most relevant and helpful to humans in an age when so many
feel dispirited and cut off from their vital instincts.

Animal spirits and symbolic visions play a very important role
in alchemy also: the green lion that devours the sun, the black
crow emerging out of the earth, the pelican nursing its young, the
wolf (wild animal energy) and the dog (tamed animal energy)
fighting for dominance are only some of the alchemical metaphors found amply illustrated and discussed in alchemical texts.
Sometimes the animal images clearly symbolize the predatory,
aggressive, destructive aspects of all nature, including human
nature. At other times, they portray possibilities of transforma-

tion for the human, as when the serpent or the lion is shown with a crown, which signifies that the instinctual feelings have been raised up and dignified into a creative, nondestructive expression. In a psychology doctoral dissertation, Jose Stevens showed that individuals who regularly worked with animal imagery in their meditations and dreams scored higher on tests of self-actualization.[43]

In the yoga traditions animal spirits and animal consciousness play some role, though much less than in shamanism or alchemy. There are symbolic animals associated with each of the *chakras,* like the elephant with the foundation root *chakra.* And there are animal figures and composites portraying "wrathful deities" or threshold guardians in the intermediate *bardo* realms of Tibetan Buddhism. These figures appear to function primarily as symbolic meditation images, and are not treated as real inner animals as in shamanism. Nevertheless, such images play an important role in transformative processes, as has been demonstrated in some interesting research by the psychotherapist Eligio Gallegos.[44] In this work, significant improvement was observed in psychotherapy as a result of using guided meditations with animal images in each of the *chakras.* The yogic practitioner is learning, through such symbolic visualizations, to incorporate within himself or herself the strengths and qualities of that animal.

In all three of these ancient teachings of transformation, and in their modern derivative practices of psychotherapy to a limited extent, we find a recognition of the value of integrating animal consciousness. Shamanism in particular holds out to humanity the ancient wisdom and strength that come from a mutually supportive symbiosis between the animal and human kingdoms of life.[45]

Transmuting opposites from antagonism to complementarity is a common theme in these traditions of transformation. This is a kind of core metaphor, that, along with the other metaphors discussed, exemplifies a deep cognitive pattern that reflects the structure of the transformative experience. Such core metaphors can provide a conceptual framework or guidepost to individuals in contemporary society who may be undergoing such transformative crises, and who are looking to the ancient Earth Wisdom teachings for insight into the dilemmas and challenges of *homo sapiens* in our time.

References

1. Eliade, Mircea. *Shamanism: Archaic Techniques of Ecstasy.* Bollingen Series LXXVI. Princeton: Princeton University Press, 1972. Halifax, Joan. *Shaman—The Wounded Healer.* New York: Crossroads Publishing, 1982.
2. Eliade, Mircea. *The Forge and the Crucible.* New York: Harper & Row, 1962.
3. Pelletier, Kenneth. *Mind as Healer, Mind as Slayer.* New York: Delta Books, 1977.
4. Walsh, Roger & Vaughan, Frances (eds.). *Beyond Ego: Transpersonal Dimensions in Psychology.* Los Angeles: J. P. Tarcher, 1980. Boorstein, Seymour, ed. *Transpersonal Psychotherapy.* Palo Alto: Science & Behavior Books, 1981.
5. Harner, Michael. *The Way of the Shaman.* San Francisco: Harper & Row, 1980.
6. Halifax, Joan. op. cit.
7. Weil, Andrew. *The Natural Mind.* Boston: Houghton Mifflin, 1986. Metzner, Ralph, ed. *The Ecstatic Adventure.* New York: Macmillan, 1968.
8. Achterberg, Jeanne. *Imagery in Healing: Shamanism and Modern Medicine.* Boston: Shambhala, 1985.
9. Halifax, Joan. *Shamanic Voices: A Survey of Visionary Narratives.* New York: E. P. Dutton, 1979.
10. Harner, Michael, op. cit.
11. Edinger, Edward. *Anatomy of the Psyche.* La Salle, Illinois: Open Court Publishing, 1985.
12. Metzner, Ralph. *Maps of Consciousness.* New York: Collier/Macmillan, 1971. pp. 83 ff.
13. Jung, C. G. *Psychology and Alchemy.* C. W. Vol. 12. Bollingen Series XX. Princeton University Press, 1968. paras. 345 ff.
14. Eliade, Mircea. *Yoga—Immortality and Freedom.* Princeton University Press, 1969.
15. Metzner, Ralph. op. cit. pp. 30 ff.
16. For the original texts describing the Yoga of the Dream State, see Evans-Wentz, W. Y. *Tibetan Yoga and Secret Doctrines.* New York: Oxford University Press, 1928. For an account of various approaches to dreamwork, including the Buddhist, see Garfield,

Patricia. *Creative Dreaming.* New York: Ballantine, 1974. For an account of controlled lucid dreaming, see LaBerge, Stephen. *Lucid Dreaming.* Los Angeles: J. P. Tarcher, 1985.

17. Lazarus, Arnold. *In the Mind's Eye.* New York: The Guilford Press, 1984. Sheikh, Anees (ed.) *Imagination and Healing.* Farmingdale, NY: Baywood Publishing Co., 1984. Watkins, Mary. *Waking Dreams.* New York: Harper & Row, 1976.

18. Taimni, I. K. *The Science of Yoga* (Yoga Sutras of Patanjali). Wheaton, IL: Theosophical Publishing House (Quest Books), 1975.

19. Grof, Stanislav. *Beyond the Brain.* Birth, Death and Transcendence in Psychotherapy. Albany, NY: State University of New York Press, 1986.

20. Harner, Michael. op.cit.

21. Eliade, Mircea. op. cit. pp. 305 ff.

22. Hamel, Peter Michael. *Through Music to the Self.* Boulder, Co.: Shambhala, 1979.

23. Halpern, Steve, and Savary, Louis. *Sound Health: The Music and Sounds That Make Us Whole.* San Francisco: Harper & Row, 1985.

24. Schultes, R. E., & Hofmann, A. *Plants of the Gods.* Origins of Hallucinogenic Use. New York: McGraw-Hill, 1979; Furst, Peter T. *Hallucinogens and Culture.* San Francisco: Chandler & Sharp, 1976; Wasson, R. Gordon. *The Wondrous Mushroom: Mycolatry in Mesoamerica.* New York: McGraw-Hill, 1980; Dobkin de Rios, Marlene. *Hallucinogens: Cross-Cultural Perspectives.* Albuquerque: University of New Mexico Press, 1984; Harner, Michael (ed.) *Hallucinogens and Shamanism.* New York: Oxford University Press, 1973.

25. Metzner, Ralph. "Molecular Mysticism: The Role of Psychoactive Substances in the Transformation of Consciousness." In Ratsch, Christian (ed.) *Das Tor zum Inneren Raum.* Festschrift fur Albert Hofmann. In Press, 1986.

26. Harner, Michael. "The Role of Hallucinogenic Plants in European Witchcraft," in Harner, M. (ed.) op. cit.

27. Strickmann, Michel. "On the Alchemy of T'ao Hung-ching" in Welch, Holmes & Seidel, Anna (eds.) *Facets of Taoism.* New Haven: Yale University Press, 1979; see also my *Maps of Consciousness,* where in the chapter on alchemy some possible alchemical psychedelics are mentioned.

28. Taimni, I. K., (Patanjali), op. cit. p. 377.

29. Aldrich, Michael. "Tantric Cannabis Use in India." *Journal of Psychedelic Drugs* Vol. 9 (No. 3) Jul-Sept. 1977.

30. Grof, Stanislav, op cit.; also Grinspoon, Lester, & Bakalar, James. *Psychedelic Drugs Reconsidered.* New York: Basic Books, 1979.

31. Metzner, Ralph. *Opening to Inner Light. The Transformation of Human Nature and Consciousness.* Los Angeles: J. P. Tarcher, 1986.
32. Lakoff, George, & Johnson, Mark. *Metaphors We Live By.* Chicago: University of Chicago Press, 1980.
33. Smith, M. Brewster. "The Metaphorical Basis of Selfhood" in Marsell, A., Devos, G., & Hsu, F. L. K. (eds.) *Culture and Self: Asian and Western Perspectives.* New York: Tavistock Publications, 1985.
34. Bateson, Gregory. *Mind and Nature: A Necessary Unity.* New York: E. P. Dutton, 1979.
35. Harner, Michael. *The Way of the Shaman.* San Francisco: Harper & Row, 1980.
36. Eliade, Mircea. *Shamanism: Archaic Techniques of Ecstasy.* op. cit. chapter 4, pp. 110-144, chapter 8, pp. 259-287. See also Cook, Roger. *The Tree of Life: Image for the Cosmos.* New York: Avon Books, 1974.
37. Metzner, Ralph. op. cit. chapter 10, "Unfolding the Tree of Our Life," pp. 161-179. An earlier version of this essay was published as "The Tree of Life as a Symbol of Self-Unfoldment" in *The American Theosophist* Vol. 69 (No. 10), Nov. 1981.
38. Ibid., p. 179.
39. Ibid., p. 96.
40. Ibid., p. 97.
41. Ibid., p. 100.
42. Ibid., chapter 4, "Purification by Inner Fire." pp. 59-74; also, Metzner, Ralph. "On Getting to Know One's Inner Enemy" *Revision* Vol. 8, No. 1, Summer/Fall 1985.
43. Stevens, Jose. "Power Animals, Animal Imagery and Self-Actualization." Ph.D. Dissertation, California Institute of Integral Studies, San Francisco, 1981. For a brilliant discussion of animal and other imagery in alchemy, see Edinger, Edward. *Anatomy of the Psyche.* op. cit.
44. Gallegos, Eligio S. "Animal Imagery, the Chakra System and Psychotherapy." *Journal of Transpersonal Psychology* Vol. 15, No. 2, 1983.
45. Metzner, Ralph. "On the Integration of Human and Animal Consciousness." *Unpublished Paper, 1985.*

17
Shamanism and Theosophy

ROBERT ELLWOOD

In *Isis Unveiled* Helena Blavatsky refers repeatedly to shamanism and shamanistic phenomena. The book offers numerous accounts of wizards and men of power in many traditions and out-of-the-way places who display remarkable powers. Tibetan adepts walk on air, and Siberian shamans trace the lost and strayed through their thoughts, as we flip the pages of this extraordinary work. These feats are depicted, however, not as the product of any capricious and irrational sorcery, but as dependent upon the employment of little-known but natural forces and laws of nature, which indeed have revealed themselves, though tenuously, in the West as well as in spiritualism and psychic phenomena.

Ultimately, the power of the ancient adept and the modern psychic alike derive from the same reality as does religion. Blavatsky sums it up in this sentence: "Truth remains one, and there is not a religion, whether Christian or heathen, that is not firmly built upon the rock of ages—God and immortal spirit."[1] If by "God" we understand the universal Principle underlying the manifested universe, and by "immortal spirit" its presence in the individual, we, like the shaman and adept, are affirming the reality of more than "ordinary" matter and natural law. We are implying that knowledge of that "more" can, with training and skill, become the knowledge that is power.

Blavatsky suggests as much in another passage in *Isis Unveiled* in which she speaks of shamanism as "one of the oldest religions of India" and elsewhere, reporting that

> It is spirit-worship, or belief in the immortality of the souls, and that the latter are still the same men they were on earth, though their bodies have lost their objective form, and man has exchanged his physical for a spiritual nature. In its present shape, it is an offshoot of primitive theurgy, and a practical blending of the visible with the invisible world.[2]

We must assume these exchanges are worked by that subtle energy of which Blavatsky says, "There has been an infinite confusion of names to express one and the same thing": the sacred fire, the astral light, akasa, od, vril, magnetism. The basic point, which comes through as the fundamental theme of *Isis Unveiled,* is that the universe is permeated by two substances, spirit and matter. Both derive from the same source, God or Universal Mind. Consciousness derives from the union of spirit and matter, and so reflects God, the unity from which both stem. Spirit generates the sacred energy, the sacred fire or odic force, and matter the raw material; all apparent existence is the combination of both, though in varying degrees.

Much in *Isis Unveiled* and other theosophical classics suggests that shamans, knowingly or not, have in effect perceived and worked the universe in a fundamentally comparable way. Four interrelated basic premises of theosophy are particularly relevant to the interpretation of shamanism: 1) There are several planes or realms of existence besides the ordinary material in the universe in which we live and move. 2) A human life is part of a continuum that extends before birth and after death. 3) Through intensive training and initiation a person can obtain power to transcend the ordinary limits of experience. 4) There is a universal ancient wisdom and spiritual path which precedes and underlies the great religions, as well as standing in a critical relationship with modern philosophy and science.

Inner Realms

First let us consider the planes of existence. Mircea Eliade, in the chapter from his *Shamanism* reprinted in this volume, indicates that in shamanistic societies the sense of cosmological complexity engendered by the adept's flights and ecstasies is typically expressed concretely through a "layered" universe. Beneath "our" world lies an Underworld, and above it the heavens of gods and mythical beings, often many of them stacked one on top of another. The Altaic (Mongolian) shaman, for example, performs a scenario in which he, in ecstatic trance, proceeds up a series of ten steps attached to an upright tree trunk. Each represents a supernatural world, and from each he calls down to the assembled tribesmen a narrative of the adventurous encounters he is experiencing there. With a fine sense of dramatic pace, he may combine laments about his effort and his weariness with solemn conversations with high gods about the future of the world, mixed with comic elements such as a burlesque hare-hunt on the sixth level. Finally, when he has ascended as far as he can go, the performer addresses a lofty prayer to Bai Ulgan, the supreme deity. He then descends and collapses, exhausted, only later to rub his eyes and greet those present as if awakening from a deep sleep.[3]

The theosophical world view conceptualizes the several planes or realms of existence as interpenetrating rather than stacked in layers. Since they are comprised of different qualities or "densities" of matter, they may coexist in the same space and time, like salt and air in sea-water or, better, like the "subtle matter" of an electric current and free electrons in a metallic conductor. The finer and finer gradations of the space-time-matter stuff of the universe in interaction with consciousness may be cited as ordinary physical matter, etheric, astral, mental, intuitive, and atmic levels, though variations in terminology and arrangement obtain. These might be thought of as both localized fields or "sheaths" in each person and universal fields that extend throughout space and are the substrate of nature, with all the levels mutually interpenetrating.

The implication is that a person of wisdom and skill could experience his or her own reality on various levels, and also "travel" on different levels to perceive and even manipulate their structures, just as the shaman can move through the several layers of his cosmos. This world view gives a reasonable context for accounts in theosophical literature of clairvoyants able to see, for example, human auras and "thought-forms" on the etheric, astral, or mental planes, superphysical beings such as nature spirits and invisible helpers, or even journeys into nonphysical planes in which, we are told, we may sojourn after death before we are reborn. This is not the place to assess these accounts; we wish only to note the fundamental similarity to the shamanistic world view. Both presuppose a universe of several coexistent realms of varying ontological nature, with all accessible to the person of wisdom and power. Further, cause and effect can, in both views, work from one plane to another, so that the adept could well make causes on one plane that would find their outlet on another. Those effects would appear to the untutored eye as magic, yet in fact would involve only what in the theosophical view is the scientific use of little-known laws of nature and the manipulation of subtle forces.

This multilayered world view is apparent in Larry Peters' experience of a healing. While studying as an anthropologist/disciple under a Nepalese shaman named Bhirendra, he was hospitalized with a serious illness. At the heights of his sickness, he dreamed that he was pursued down a street by a black bull. A stick in his hand was transformed into a bright yellow and black snake. He used it as a whip to chase the bull away, cracking it over his head. Then he heard a mantram being chanted and turned to see the shaman Bhirendra. From that hour the course of the illness reversed and Peters steadily grew better.

Later, when he told Bhirendra of the dream, the shaman's eyes gleamed. The latter said that his spirit had come to Peters in the dream and uttered the mantram that cured him. The bull, representing the sickness, was an evil spirit sent by a jealous shaman, Bhirendra alleged.[4] Here the shaman was apparently able to operate on a plane other than the physical, and thereby to work an effect, healing, on the physical level. Contacts with masters and initiations in dreams or other subjective experiences are not unknown to theosophical lore as well.

Likewise, such feats as the "earth-diving" of the Eskimo shaman to contact gods underground or under the sea, or the scenarios by which other shamans cross over to the land of the dead to recover lost souls, are not to be taken as literal, physical events, but adventures on a plane of being other than the physical. The classic shaman, indeed, is a specialist in such transitions from one plane to another under fully conscious control and with a definite purpose. He knows the "short cuts" from this world to the other; he has the strength and wisdom to overcome the guardians of those dread paths; he can go there to converse with the gods or the departed spirits, to recover the lost, to gain invisible allies.

Before Birth and After Death

A second related theme linking shamanism and theosophy is the idea that there is more to human life than that which lies between the birth and death of one's present existence. The present has been influenced by an endless chain of previous existences, which have helped determine the basic conditions and problems to be dealt with in the current lifespan. That life in turn will reverberate down the chain of subsequent existences, whether on the inner planes, astral and devachanic, or in subsequent embodiments, until all its loose ends are gathered up. Shamanistic societies characteristically do not elaborate concepts like karma and reincarnation in systematic detail. Yet these concepts are implied when the shaman is considered a psychopomp or guide of the soul after physical death; or a traveller between this world and the land of the dead; or as being reborn time and time again in his lineage, as are the souls of some great shamans. An account of the road to the soul's world, as conceived by the Thompson River Indians of British Columbia, tells us:

> The country of the souls is underneath us, toward the sunset;
> the trail leads through a dim twilight. Tracks of the people
> who last went over it, and of their dogs, are visible. The path
> winds along until it meets another road which is a short cut
> used by the shamans when trying to intercept a departed soul.[5]

In fact, the entire practice of shamans depends upon the reality of such an alternative land, to which they have free access. Shamans of the Salish Indians enacted an elaborate healing rite involving the common belief that a person is sick because the soul has been stolen and taken to the land of the dead, from which it must be recovered. A crew of ten shamans, captained by the officiator, embarks on a journey in a boat which crosses the River of the Dead. Making paddling gestures, the company actually enacts this voyage dramatically. On the other side, the officiating shaman must overcome further obstacles. He crosses a raging torrent, struggles with a guardian who attempts to refuse him entrance to the Land of the Dead, and finally must battle spirits who throw blazing torches at him. The last are played by boys of the tribe, and the torches are real and sometimes dangerous. Finally the heroic shaman succeeds in taking the desired soul, and leaving the Other World, ceremoniously closes its door so that more spirits cannot get out. Making the return journey by boat, he sings the song of the sick man's soul. Hearing it, we are told the invalid leaps up cured.[6]

One is not unwilling to believe this. Imagine the impact on a sick person of such a performance on one's behalf—a perilous journey, mortal combat, victory, and finally the joyous sound of one's own song as one's soul is triumphantly returned home! Like all shamanistic and medical healing that successfully integrates itself with its culture, this performance accomplishes two things: it interprets the cause of the illness in terms consistent with the world view (i.e., that the patient's soul has been taken to the Land of the Dead), and then corrects the dysfunction in the same terms (by returning the soul dramatically). Thus a shamanistic world view which clearly posits a postexistence in the Land of the Dead serves to undergird healing in this world.

Initiation

Now let us consider the third theme, the role of the shaman as a person of power. By strong dedication and intensive training, he has attained at least a portion of the power implied by the two previous themes, ability to operate on more than one plane of existence, and to travel or communicate between this world and the realms of gods and departed spirits.

An Eskimo shaman said to Rasmussen: "All true wisdom is only found far from men, out in the great solitude, and it can be acquired only through suffering. Privations and suffering are the only things that can open a man's mind to that which is hidden from others."[7] The idea that loneliness and suffering are the anvil upon which great shamans are forged runs deep. In shamanistic cultures, one finds time and again the notion that the greater the preparatory suffering, the greater the shaman, and the initiations some have passed through are indeed horrendous. This is the case whether the sufferings are from outward causes or appear to be only subjective, passed through in fevered dream or vision, and characteristically we are at a loss to know on which level to impute them. What are we to make, for example, of the claim of Australian shamans that their internal organs have been removed and replaced by organs of quartz?[8] Or what of the perhaps happier case of the Siberian Goldi shaman whose initiation centered on his forced marriage to a female tutelary spirit, who appeared to him when he was on a sick-bed, and which he says was consummated like any ordinary marriage?[9]

It is clear which side some instances fall on. *Miko,* or Japanese shamans such as one this writer visited in 1967, are female and moreover are all blind or nearly so. They are apprenticed to a senior shamaness as a child—in traditional society, probably as good a fate as could be hoped for a blind girl whose marriage prospects would not be bright. After training in shamaness songs and trance techniques for several years the day comes for initiation. The *miko* wears a white robe. She sits facing her mistress and other shamanesses who sing and chant. Suddenly the mistress cries, "What deity possessed you?" Giving the name of a Shinto or Buddhist deity, she answers. The initiating shamaness then throws a rice cake at her, at which she faints. The elders dash cold water over her many times, and finally revive her with their body heat. When she comes to, she is said to be reborn as a shamaness; she exchanges her white robe for a wedding dress, and a traditional Japanese wedding is conducted—but with the deity as bridegroom. Here we see, in an appealing ritual, the traditional initiatory themes of death, rebirth, and *hieros gamos* or sacred marriage.[10]

Other initiations seem to be quite inward. A Siberian shaman reported an elaborate ordeal of journeys to faraway lands replete with such symbols as cosmic trees and mountains, and being dismembered by a mysterious blacksmith and reforged as a shaman, with letters on the inside of his head to tell him what to say while shamanizing. But it all happened while he way lying in his tent near death from smallpox.[11]

Whether subjective or objective, we see the shaman's initiatory ordeal as basically the undergoing of suffering, alone and often in a deserted place. It is seen as a remaking of the man of power, in a way which recreates him so that he is able to *see* and to travel between two worlds. The process can be compared to the agony and illumination associated with classic mystical experience, as in the enlightenment of the Buddha, and with the descriptions of initiations in such theosophical sources as C.W. Leadbeater's *The Masters and the Path.* In the latter is a striking account of the "Fourth Initiation," a "Dark Night of the Soul" type of ordeal, which the author compares to the crucifixion of Christ. Aloneness is a key element of this trial:

> . . . he has also to experience for a moment the condition called Avichi, which means "the waveless," that which is without vibration. The state of Avichi is not, as has been popularly supposed, some kind of hell, but it is a condition in which the man stands absolutely alone in space, and feels cut off from all life, even from that of the Logos; and it is without doubt the most ghastly experience that it is possible for any human being to have. It is said to last only for a moment, but to those who have felt its supreme horror it seemed an eternity, for at that level time and space do not exist.[12]

The Ancient Way

The shaman, then, can be seen not only as an important figure in tribal societies, but also as prototypical of the spiritual, initiatory course followed by all those down through the ages who have set foot on the great path, and followed it far enough to know something of its tribulations and awesome vistas. This perception brings us to the fourth great theme shared by shamanism and theosophy, that there is a universal ancient spiritual way, and one which still can be found by those who seek.[13] Prior to the primal light breaking into the spectrum of several great religions beginning around the pivotal fifth century BCE, religions were more similar from one continent to another than they have been since. For despite almost infinite local variations in ritual performance and the names of the gods, the religious world of, say, 1000 BCE in England, Egypt, and Japan would have presented more of a common face than do Anglican Christianity, Sunna Islam, and Mahayana Buddhism today. All would have worshipped a variety of polytheistic gods associated with particular shrines and places, in priestly rites involving sacrifice, the evocation of the deity, and shamanistic or prophetic communication from the realm of the gods and spirits. Indeed, shamanism un-doubtedly goes back many, many more thousands of years to serve as the earliest known exemplar of most of the great themes of personalized, experiential religion. The shaman is the first of many types which have since taken different tracks: the initiate, the mystic, the psychopomp, the suffering savior, the medium, the physician, the psychotherapist, the custodian of tribal lore. The primordial unity of all these functions hints at the theosoph-ical theme of an ancient unbroken wisdom known to the wise, founded on Blavatsky's "God and immortal spirit," though the-osophy gives it even deeper roots than those known to ordinary human history.

The lineage did not stop, however, when tribalism gave way to the ancient empires, and finally to modern monarchies and republics, or when the shaman's muttering was replaced by scrolls, books, television, and computers. According to theoso-phy, the shaman's role as initiated loremaster merely took new forms. Such figures important to theosophical tradition as Apol-lonius of Tyana, Saint-Germain, or Helena Blavatsky herself may be thought of as magi, the magus being, so to speak, a "sha-man in civilization."[14] Parallels can easily be found between the typical career of the magus and that of the shaman: call, ini-tiatory psychopathology, ordeal, illumination, mission. Not sel-dom characteristic ancillary features arise in both as well: extraordinary, even supernatural, travel to bring wisdom from far away; commerce with supernatural allies and masters; episodes or periods in one's life which are shrouded in mystery; a special relationship with animals; ability to gather a circle of disciples.

The shaman and the magus also share certain ambiguities. In some though not all instances of both, the adept seems capable of engaging in a certain amount of deception on one level as a means to the greater ends of faith and healing in which he prob-ably does genuinely believe. Sometimes he may even double-cross himself on this treacherous terrain. The famous anthropol-ogist Franz Boas told of a Kwakiutl Indian shaman named Quesalid he talked with, who said that he had started as a skeptic and associated with shamans as a novice only to learn their tricks and expose them. He learned plenty: not only shaman songs and trance techniques, but also how to produce seeming magic through sleight-of-hand. His reputation spread nonetheless, and he was invited to do healings. He knew that the "sickness" he pretended to suck out of the ill person's body was actually down concealed in his mouth. But rather to his surprise, the healings were successful and he became a famous miracle worker. Finally, he came to feel that the healings worked because the sick person "believed strongly in his dream about me," and apparently he felt the deceptions were justifiable insofar as they helped people believe.[15]

Nonetheless, just as we should not approach the shaman or the magus with total credulity, neither should we take such protestations without a grain of salt. These are complex figures who may well erect blinds before their inner secrets and couch their answers on a level appropriate to the questioner, the rationalistic scientist getting no more than what he expects to hear. The shaman and the magus, who were among other things the first fathers of poetry, song, and riddle, know well the allusive but elusive nature of words. They are masters of that verbal indirection which can lead to realizations greater than can language alone, while safeguarding mysteries from the profane. All this is summed up in the qualities of lightness, charm, and enigma reported in the greatest of shamans and magi.

The shaman, and the shaman's path, then, have not utterly vanished from our electronic and paved-over modern world. One can hear its call and, if one dares, undergo its transformative ordeals and assume the burden of its power in high-rise apartments as well as in primordial forests, for it is ultimately inward. The theosophical tradition, with its custodianship of the names and narratives of magi in all ages who have found that path and, one way or another, been initiated into the ancient wisdom behind it, has done much to keep awareness of it alive in our own day.

Notes

1. Helena P. Blavatsky, *Isis Unveiled.* New York, 1877; Wheaton, IL: Theosophical Publishing House, 1972, vol. I, p. 467.
2. Blavatsky, *Isis Unveiled*, vol. II, p. 615.

3. Mircea Eliade, *Shamanism: Archaic Techniques of Ecstasy*, trans. Willard R. Trask. Bollingen Series LXXVI. New York: Pantheon Books, 1964, pp. 190-97.

4. Larry G. Peters, "An Experiential Study of Nepalese Shamanism," *The Journal of Transpersonal Psychology*, vol. 13, No. 1 (1981), pp. 15-16.

5. H. B. Alexander, *North American Mythology*, Boston, 1916, pp. 147-49. Reprinted in Mircea Eliade, *From Primitives to Zen: A Thematic Sourcebook of the History of Religions*. New York: Harper and Row, 1967, pp. 366-67.

6. Andreas Lommel, *The World of the Early Hunters*. London: Evelyn, Adams, and Mackay, 1967, pp. 84, 97.

7. Cited in Lommel, *World of the Early Hunters*, p. 151.

8. A.W. Howitt, *The Native Tribes of South-East Australia*, London, 1904, pp. 406-08. Cited in Eliade, *From Primitives to Zen*, pp. 424-26.

9. Eliade, *Shamanism*, pp. 72-73.

10. See Ichiro Hori, *Folk Religion in Japan*. Chicago: University of Chicago Press, 1968, pp. 203-06.

11. Eliade, *Shamanism*, pp. 38-42.

12. C.W. Leadbeater, *The Masters and the Path*. Adyar, Madras, India: Theosophical Publishing House, 1965 [1925], p. 220.

13. That theosophical classic by "Alcyone," *At the Feet of the Master* (1910), suggests four qualities which must be possessed by one who would quest for this path: Discrimination, Desirelessness, Good Conduct, and Love.

14. See the discussion of the magus in my *Religious and Spiritual Groups in Modern America*. Englewood Cliffs, NJ: Prentice-Hall, 1973, pp. 49-52. See also Eliza M. Butler, *The Myth of the Magus*. New York: Macmillan, 1948.

15. Franz Boas, *The Religion of the Kwakiutl*, Columbia University Contributions to Anthropology X, part II. New York, 1930, pp. 1-41. Summarized in Claude Levi-Strauss, *Structural Anthropology*. Garden City, NY: Doubleday, 1967, pp. 169-173.

V

Shamanism in a Changing World

There is a renewed interest in shamanism today—in its world view, its altered state, its practices. Anthropologists and psychologists are combining shamanism with contemporary disciplines such as psychology to explore the possibilities of the human mind. Shamanism is better understood today than at any previous time because of all we have learned through modern psychology. The ancient way of the shaman is being adapted to life in today's world and is further enriching our knowledge. This development points to the necessity of integrating primordial instinctual levels of consciousness, which have largely been cut off in Western society because of the "Cartesian split" between mind and body.

Cultivating the "shaman within" is the aim of workshops developed by Krippner and Feinstein, which seek to integrate mythology with current trends in psychology. Feinstein explains that these sessions include techniques to induce altered states such as progresssive relaxation, visualization, dreamwork, chanting, and meditation, as well as didactic instruction. Participants learn to identify the personal myths by which they live and also to discover whether these are becoming outmoded and being challenged by conflicting myths that are emerging. There is a session in which they commit to the new mythic vision. Techniques are also taught for applying mythic wisdom to everyday life.

Brooke Medicine Eagle focuses on Native American wisdom and points to recent dark times when the traditional ways were being threatened. She feels that now the dawn is returning for the Wisdom tradition. The Sundance has always been common to Indian peoples, and now they are beginning to dance together. Modern shamans are healing not only individuals but also Mother Earth. They are not being chosen by family ties as in the past, but by "inner lineage" or calling. She feels that we are now being given a harmonious tone, but we must resonate to it in our lives for it to make a difference in the world. It signifies the rise of the feminine principle and must be worked out through deep caring for all peoples.

Two Black Elks of the Lakota tribe illustrate the changing times. Both power shamans, they considered the sacred pipe as central to their work. Both felt that power for their shamanistic work comes from the other world, not from themselves. Nick Black Elk, who died in 1950, was Wallace Black Elk's "grandfather," by adoption if not by blood. Both worked beyond the boundaries of the reservation, though Nick lived on it while Wallace's home is in Denver. Nick worked only with his own people, while Wallace works for all people regardless of race. Nick died brokenhearted because of the loss of the sacred ways. He felt that "the sacred hoop [of the nations] was broken and scattered." Wallace is more hopeful and sees shamanism on the upswing. He was first to speak in public about the sacred pipe. He has been influential in improving the condition of American Indians, especially through his successful lobbying for the American Indian Religious Freedom Act of 1977. He feels that "the tree of life will unify all the people."

18

The Shaman Within: Cultivating a Sacred Personal Mythology

DAVID FEINSTEIN

> Knowledge dwells
> In heads replete with thoughts of other men,
> Wisdom in minds attentive to their own.
> H. P. Blavatsky

A subtle but essential role of the shaman was to serve as a technician of the culture's guiding mythology. This paper will consider ways that modern individuals can cultivate "the shaman within" as an adept curator of their own mythic constructions of reality.

Creating myths is as natural to the human mind as learning a language, and like language, myths shape the way reality is constructed. This takes the notion of "myth" out of its contemporary vernacular usage—which is roughly the equivalent of a falsehood—and revitalizes its sacred significance. This powerful, ancient concept appropriately reflects the hypothetical nature of any construct of reality. In this light, myth has been defined as "the ever changing mask that the mind of the beholder fits over a reality he has never truly seen" (Larsen 1976, p. 16).

The essential function of the shaman was no less than to guard, transmit, and cultivate changes in the culture's inherent mythology (Campbell, 1969). The very foundations of the manner by which reality was construed might be renewed or challenged by the shaman's ecstatic vision. Mircea Eliade noted that the

267

shaman has "played an essential role in the defense of the psychic integrity of the community" (1964, 508), and this was accomplished through the use of shamanic powers to defend "life, health, fertility, [and] the world of 'light' " (p. 509). Shamans were "not only spiritual leaders but also judges and politicians, the repositories of the knowledge of the culture's history, both sacred and secular" (Halifax 1979, 4).

The shaman's profession was, in fact, "precisely the relationship between the mythic imagination," which touches the realm of inner, primary meaning, "and ordinary consciousness" (Larsen 1976, 59). For every society in which shamans have been known, they "have been the particular guardians and reciters of the chants and traditions of their people...the guardians of the mythological lore of mankind during the period of some five or six thousand years" (Campbell 1968, 250-251). One of their essential skills involved "influencing others to change their beliefs in such a way as to bring about desired results" (King 1987). By fostering the group's beliefs and practices, the shaman was a vital force in influencing the fundamental aspects of individual and community life which are the purview of mythology.

"The Shaman Within" as Curator of the Modern Individual's Personal Mythology

The historical record suggests that the self-reflecting individual is a relatively recent development in humanity's history, having emerged as a mass phenomenon perhaps only as recently as within the past 3500 years (Wilber 1981). This individualizing required a completely new way of thinking: a self-observing aspect of the psyche had come into being. This led to differentiation of a separate ego, and the individual's identity burst forth from its total immersion in the community and into the anxious solitude that characterizes many modern individuals.

The emergence of the individual ego allowed the previously unimagined possibilities embodied in the great hero myths—the capacities for psychological autonomy, self-reflection, and a measure of objectivity—but it did not come without substantial costs. As consciousness split off from the instinctive life of the body and became distinguished from that of the social group, the

Cartesian dualism that has plagued modern society had become full-blown. Erich Neumann has noted that "our cultural unease or dis-ease is due to the fact that the separation of the systems [ego and instinct]—in itself a necessary product of evolution—has degenerated into a schism and thus precipitated a psychic crisis whose catastrophic effects are reflected in contemporary history" (Neumann 1954, 363).

The alienation of ego from instinct has seen the Western world identify with the ego's side of the dualism, leaving the primordial side to its unconscious roots. While the Western ego has served to tend the individual's personal mythology, generally it has made a poor shepherd. The ego has identified its own rationality as the final arbitrator of reality, and personal mythologies have thus operated largely outside the realms of the individual's conscious awareness. Stanton Marlan (1981) has pointed out that it "is not that modern man has become any less mythic, but that he has unconsciously lived the myths of logic and science. These myths unduly restrict the deepening of human consciousness and help to foster the feelings of alienation and 'exile' so common in modern times" (p. 227).

Shamanism flourished when people were immersed in what might be termed a "pre-Cartesian mythology," where the cleavages between the self and the body, between ego and instinct, and between the individual and the group had not yet fully developed. Modern society has been caught in a dualism, a "Cartesian mythology" which negates instinct for rationality and negates community for individualism. In this atmosphere, the functions served by the shaman have been neglected and belittled. The forces of history, however, seem to be pushing toward an integration of the dualism, toward what might be called a "post-Cartesian mythology" in which the individual ego and the primordial nature from which it emerged will be reunited at a higher level of integration. For this to occur, the individual ego will need to expand its purview to incorporate the very territory that had been consigned to the ancient shaman.

Cultivating *the shaman within* is to develop an observing ego which, like the ancient shaman, is able to use altered states, rituals, and dreams to embrace more primordial forms of experiencing, peek behind the mythology that is operating, assess its limitations, and push on in new, considered, inspiring directions. In the remainder of this essay, I will describe a system that draws from a blend of shamanism and modern psychology for helping individuals develop the shaman within.

Cultivating the Shaman Within

The bestowal of shamanic initiation is traditionally reserved for those who inherit the profession along familial lines or are obeying a "call" from the gods or the spirits (Eliade 1964). Cultivating the shaman within, on the other hand, is the birthright of all modern individuals. It does, however, require an inner call to more actively participate in the implementation and evolution of areas of one's personal mythology that had been operating outside of conscious awareness. In modern times, this call comes frequently, as the requirements for adjusting and thriving are changing exponentially faster than in any previous sustained period of history. The guiding myths of the parents' generation are not even remotely fitting for the needs of the day. Individuals are increasingly challenged to participate consciously in charting new and more vital guiding mythologies. Developing the skills associated with what we are calling "the shaman within" provides a capacity for more effective participation in that process.

Shamanic initiation traditionally involved two kinds of experience: the ecstatic (e.g., trances, dreams) and the didactic (Eliade 1964). My colleagues and I (Feinstein 1979; Feinstein & Krippner, in press) have developed a workshop format that provides both an experiential base for entering and utilizing altered states of consciousness and an instructional framework for working with one's guiding mythology. This workshop often serves as a personal initiation for awakening a conscious relationship with the shaman within, and thus greater active participation in one's evolving personal mythology.

The conceptual groundwork for this approach has been nicely synthesized by Stephen Larsen (1976) in *The Shaman's Doorway: Opening the Mythic Imagination to Contemporary Consciousness*. Michael Harner (1980) has made shamanic principles and practices particularly accessible to Westerners. Our own focus has emphasized an integration of mythological thought with current trends in cognitive psychology and psychotherapy.

By thinking of myths cognitively, mythology may be treated in a more rational, systematic, and scientific fashion. By thinking of cognition mythically, the scientific study of consciousness may be approached in a holistic manner, embracing even the most profound and elusive dimensions of human nature. Recognizing the cognitive properties of personal myths provides access to the understanding offered by the cognitive sciences for mapping the terrain which must be mastered by the shaman within.

Psychologists use the term "cognitive schema" when speaking of the mental representations by which people construct their realities. Cognitive schemas assume mythic proportions as they begin to address four issues identified by Joseph Campbell (1968, 1983) as the primary domains in which mythic thought functions. These include: the longing to achieve a sense of participation in the vast wonder and mystery of the universe; the desire to comprehend that universe in a meaningful way; the need to establish fulfilling relationships within a social and cultural milieu; and the search for a pathway to carry oneself through the succeeding epochs of human life. Personal myths, as a class of cognitive schema, can be understood in terms of the properties by which cognitive schemas operate. Cognitive schemas, for instance, may be coded verbally or pictorially; operate at the conscious and preconscious levels of awareness; have their basis in biological structures as well as experience; govern perception, understanding, and action; and function at atomistic as well as molar levels of the individual's life (Feinstein 1979). These statements are descriptive of personal myths as well.

Based on such understandings, it is possible to establish a set of principles that pertain to the way mythological life functions at the personal level, and such information can be transmitted to individuals desiring to cultivate the shaman within. The principles that we have found to be of the greatest value to the individuals with whom we have worked focus particularly on the manner by which personal myths evolve. The core dynamic, in our view, is that when a prevailing personal myth becomes outdated or otherwise dysfunctional, it tends to be challenged by a new compensatory myth. This emerging myth is produced by the psyche and may be revealed in dreams, trance, or moments of lucidity, or it may not break into conscious awareness at all. In either case, the old myth and the emerging myth engage in a dialectic struggle which plays itself out in the joint arenas of the person's inner life and external circumstances. This underlying conflict is often a source of pain, regressive decisions, and other difficulties whose solutions seem beyond the person's grasp. Bringing the conflict into the light of conscious awareness provides an opportunity to participate in the process more meaningfully and more effectively. The skills of the shaman, adapted to the inner journey, can provide new pathways toward that end.

Shamans possessed a practical knowledge regarding the psychology of their people and its relationship to the culture's guiding mythology. The shaman within must also be versed in the inner psychology that affects the personal myths that govern an individual's perceptions, understandings, and actions. Our workshops provide a forum for offering instruction on such practical knowledge. These principles have been derived from our observations working with people's guiding mythologies in educational, clinical, and community settings. We have identified three essential responsibilites of the shaman within and developed a workshop format for unfolding the capacity to effectively discharge those responsibilities.

The Responsibilities of the Shaman Within

The first responsibility of the shaman within is to insure that a conduit be maintained between waking consciousness and the mythic underworld that operates in every human being. Just as shamans regularly enter the underworld and re-emerge with new visions and directions for their people, the shaman within is charged with using dreams and taking periodic inward journeys to stay conversant with the personal mythic underworld. The ability to take such inward journeys can be developed, and a central feature of our workshops involves practice in accessing and utilizing altered states of consciousness that may be reached through progressive relaxation, guided visualization, rituals, self-hypnosis, dream work, chanting, and meditation.

Among the procedures shamans have used to induce altered states are visualization, chanting, drumming, dancing, jumping, running, fasting, concentrating, ingesting mind-altering plants, engaging in sexual activities, and going without sleep (Krippner & Scott, in press). In a study of forty-two societies from four different cultural areas, L. G. Peters and David Price-Williams (1980) indentified three commonalities among shamanic altered states of consciousness. The shamans in their sample were able to 1) voluntarily enter and control the duration of the altered state; 2) communicate with others during the altered state; and 3) remember the experience at the conclusion of the altered state. Each of these abilities is also important for the shaman within.

A second responsibility of the shaman within is to empower the individual to effectively apply inner mythic wisdom to the circumstances that arise in daily life. This requires the close contact with the inner world discussed above, and further involves a dynamic and discriminating application of the appropriate guiding myth to the outer situation. Visions and insights encountered in altered states do not necessarily constitute sound mythic guidance, and informed, mature judgment must be developed. Just as traditional shamans used their shamanic powers to influence physical and social events toward outcomes that were harmonious with the guiding mythology, the shaman within evokes inner powers for joining the wisdom of underlying myths to the demands and opportunities of situations that must be faced. Westerners brought up in the Cartesian mold with a bias toward ego and away from myth and instinct can begin to heal that schism with journeys to their own mythic underworlds and with a commitment to utilize what is found there.

A third responsibility is to shepherd the evolution of the existing mythology. Sometimes in carrying out the second responsibility, it becomes clear that the guiding myth is dysfunctional or at least no longer appropriate. At other times, a visit to the underworld results in a new and inspiring vision that seems charged to replace the existing mythic guidance. Either development will tend to result in discomfort as the conflict between established ways and new directions begins to manifest. The shaman also lived at the fulcrum between established tradition and cultural innovation, serving as guardian while new mythic visions were being translated into social practice. The most useful interventions can be made at the points where the existing mythology is in conflict, and it is here that the motivation for formulating those interventions is the highest. We thus focus our workshop on this third responsibility, recognizing that the skills required for meeting the first two responsibilities must also be taught if the third is to be addressed successfully.

A Five-Stage Model for Fostering a Revitalized Personal Mythology

Our workshops begin by establishing a context for exploring one's own personal mythology. Personal rituals, didactic instruction, altered states, and ceremonies which utilize the group to empower the individual's quest will be found throughout the program. Early in the workshop, for instance, each participant creates a personal shield with drawings on four quadrants. Each quadrant represents a specific aspect of the person's inner journey. Participants contact the symbolism to be drawn on the shield by entering an altered state through the combined use of deep relaxation and guided imagery. As the personal shields are ceremoniously shared and their meanings explored, a commitment is made by the group to use its collective influence for empowering each of the participants on the next steps of the personal journey. The shield is later used in personal rituals, such as for protection if the inner work becomes too frightening or too painful.

In setting the context for the subsequent intense exploration, early in the workshop we have participants go on an inner journey to visit several of their ancestors. Guided visualization is accompanied by facilitative music and physical movement where each participant takes on a posture representing the ancestor being visited. They open their imaginations to envision the mythologies each ancestor lived out, and they consider the consequences each of these scenarios might have had upon subsequent generations. The sequence takes them in a direct line to their own birth, and they begin to apprehend the mythic ecology into which they were born.

The central focus of the workshop involves the identification of one area of dysfunction in each participant's guiding mythology and the transformation of that difficulty through the same procedures which a seasoned shaman within might guide the person to use. We have found that successfully completing this process even one time can awaken the ability to evoke the shaman within in subsequent situations. The workshop is organized around a five-stage model which we believe can escort the shaman within who has learned to enter and utilize altered states to effectively assist the person in responsibly encountering the mythic dimensions of ongoing experience. These stages are congruent with our cognitive formulation of mythology (Feinstein, 1979), and they have been developed and refined with over 2000 workshop participants. A brief description of each of these stages follows.

1. *First Stage—Recognizing When a Guiding Myth Is No Longer an Ally.* The first task of the shaman within in this model is to monitor the existing guiding mythology and recognize areas of conflict within it, as well as in areas of mythic guidance that no longer serve as allies. Myths, functioning properly, may be seen as allies that organize experience in a manner that empowers their holders. People and circumstances change, however, and myths that once served as the most effective guidance available in given situations may have become dysfunctional or even destructive. When a personal myth is causing trouble, the psyche will generate alternative cognitive schemas which begin to compete with it. As this occurs, evidence of the conflict will emerge, manifesting in anxieties, phobias, physical symptoms, puzzling dreams, self-contradictions, or feelings of confusion, ambivalence, or dissatisfaction. We view the conflict between an old prevailing myth and an emerging counter-myth as the cutting edge of personal growth.

While the psyche reflexively works to bring conflicting myths toward resolution, with or without conscious attention, the conflict will be more destructive and more likely to engender detrimental defenses when it occurs outside of awareness. Conversely, it is more likely to reach a harmonious and economical resolution that is in line with the person's deeper values when the conflict is worked through with conscious assistance. In this first stage of the workshop, a series of personal rituals is presented for systematically identifying areas of mythic conflict that might lend themselves to constructive resolution. For instance, the symbolism of the shield is examined for areas of mythic tension, a dream is requested which reveals areas of underlying conflict, behavior is ritualistically reviewed for evidence of mythic conflict, and symbolism is finally generated to represent the area of conflict that was ultimately chosen for further focus.

2. *Second Stage—Bringing Conflicting Myths into Focus.* The tasks for the shaman within in this stage are to examine the roots and the consequences of the prevailing, dysfunctional myth and to explore further the emerging counter-myth. The dysfunctional myth that was identified in the first stage had perhaps been the best guidance available in earlier life circumstances, but it now perpetuates a tired theme in the person's life. Its roots will be found in some combination of temperament, early conditioning, experiences with betrayal, trauma, and success, and a unique synthesis of the myths held by family and culture. The counter-myth that challenges the old order may be imaginative, inspiring, and forward-looking, but it will also often lack a practical realism that allows it to be lived out just as the psyche has formulated it.

Bringing focused attention to the conflict between the old myth and the emerging myth allows conscious participation in reaching a resolution that is attuned to the person's developmental needs and best interests. Among the guided instructions offered for productively focusing on both sides of the conflict is a journey back in time to a real or hypothetical instance that may have inaugurated the old myth. The old myth is also transformed into the first chapter of a three-part personal fairy tale. The emerging myth, which is further examined through dreams and structured imagery experiences, then serves as the basis of the second chapter. A final step in this stage involves ritually mapping the respective effects of the conflicting myths.

3. *Third Stage—Spawning a New Mythic Vision.* The task of the shaman within during this stage is to mediate the conflict as the opposing myths push toward a natural synthesis. After having identified an era of conflict in one's mythic construction of reality, and having come to understand the roots and the purposes of both sides of that conflict, images of integration become possible. The shaman within recognizes that facing one's inconsistencies without a retreat into the old or a flight into the emerging may be as difficult as it could be valuable. Sacrificing the familiarity, comfort, and identification with a prevailing though outdated myth can be so painful that some people fight dearly to

reject the emerging myth. For others, recognizing areas of dysfunction that are associated with the old myth may be so distressing that they totally disidentify with it and fully embrace the emerging myth.

The challenge for the shaman within in this stage of the work is to give adequate recognition to the messages and purposes of both sides of the conflict. At the same time one must foster a new guiding mythic image. The structured activities during this phase of the workshop are designed to create an integration that preserves the most beneficial elements of the prevailing myth and blends them with those of the counter-myth. Among the structured experiences designed toward these ends is a personification of both myths and the enactment of a dialogue between them. Various other techniques, using visual as well as bodily representations of the conflict and its possible resolution, are also used.

4. Fourth Stage—From Vision to Commitment. In this stage of the work, the shaman within is called upon to examine the new mythic vision that was synthesized from the dialectic described above and to refine it to the point where a commitment to that vision may be entered maturely. While it is necessary to allow the natural dialectic between the old myth and the counter-myth to take its course, the process may be never-ending, and a time does come when choosing to identify with a carefully refined version of the emerging mythic image can facilitate personal development.

A series of structured experiences leads workshop participants into altered states of consciousness where deeper sources of knowledge become available for examining and crystallizing this emerging mythic image. This may set the directions in which participants consciously begin to reshape their lives. Among the personal rituals that comprise this stage of the workshop are invoking the shaman within to heal emotional wounds that may be impeding one's development, consulting a power object regarding the new guiding image and its refinement, and consulting one's own dreams. The final chapter of the personal fairy tale, which embodies the newly synthesized guiding myth, is also created during this stage.

5. Fifth Stage—Weaving a Renewed Mythology into Daily Life.

The fifth stage extends beyond the workshop. It requires the shaman within to be a practical and vigilant monitor of the person's commitment to achieve a harmony between daily life and the renewed guiding mythology that was formulated during the workshop. The old Hassidic saying that "everyone should carefully observe what way his heart draws him and then choose that way with all his strength" summarizes this final phase. The proverb recognizes that old behavioral patterns, conditioning, and character armoring which were associated with the old myth will tend to persist. Focused attention is required for anchoring even an inspiring new myth that has been wisely formulated.

The workshop closes with a series of structured experiences that lay the groundwork for success in this transition. This final phase draws particularly from techniques that have been developed by cognitive and behavioral psychotherapists for bringing about changes in perception and functioning. Bodily representations and visual imagery are used to stengthen the chosen myth as a thought-form. Self-statements that support the new myth are formulated, and self-statements that might unwittingly promote the old myth or the counter-myth are identified. Role-plays allow the person to act upon the new myth under simulated conditions. Behavioral contracts with other group members or with the shaman within are also entered. These contracts focus on changes in the areas of participants' lives that still reinforce the myth they are wanting to transform, as well as on changes in areas that do not yet reinforce the mythic image they are wanting to pursue. Back-home ceremonies that inaugurate the new myth and daily rituals that reinforce it and re-establish contact with the mythic underworld are also suggested.

This five-stage model, paired as it is with training in entering and utilizing altered states of consciousness, has served as an initiation of the shaman within for many participants in our workshops. The framework, as presented in this chapter, integrates the model offered by traditional shamanism with contemporary scientific understanding of cognitive processes and psychological development. Cultivating the shaman within comprises one approach by which modern individuals may participate in unfolding a more incisive and sacred personal mythology.

References

Campbell, Joseph. (1968). *The Masks of God: Creative Mythology.* New York: Viking.

Campbell, Joseph. (1969). *The Masks of God: Primitive Mythology* (Rev.). New York: Viking.

Campbell, Joseph. (1983). *Historical Atlas of World Mythology* (Vol. 1). San Francisco: Harper & Row.

Eliade, Mircea. (1964). *Shamanism: Archaic Techniques of Ecstasy.* Princeton, NJ: Princeton University Press.

Feinstein, David. (1979). Personal Mythology as a Paradigm for a Holistic Public Psychology. *American Journal of Orthopsychiatry, 49,* 198-217.

Feinstein, David, & Krippner, Stanley. (in press). *Personal Mythology: The Inner Journey* (tentative title). Los Angeles: J. P. Tarcher, Inc.

Halifax, Joan. (1979). *Shamanic Voices: A Survey of Visionary Narratives.* New York: E. P. Dutton.

Harner, Michael. (1980). *The Way of the Shaman: A Guide to Power and Healing.* New York: Bantam.

King, Serge. (1987). "The Way of the Adventurer." *The Ancient Wisdom in Shamanic Cultures. Shamanism,* Shirley Nicholson (comp.). Wheaton, IL: Theosophical Publishing House.

Krippner, Stanley, & Scott, Patrick. (in press). *Spiritual Healing in North America.* Dusslingen: Chiron-Verlag.

Larsen, Stephen. (1976). *The Shaman's Doorway: Opening the Mythic Imagination to Contemporary Consciousness.* New York: Harper & Row.

Marlan, Stanton. (1981). Depth Consciousness. In Ronald S. Valle and Rolf von Eckartsberg (Eds.), *The Metaphors of Consciousness.* New York: Plenum.

Neumann, Erich, (1954). *The Origins and History of Consciousness.* Princeton, NJ: Princeton University Press.

Peters, L.G., & Price-Williams, David. (1980). Towards an Experiential Analysis of Shamanism. *American Ethnologist, 7,* 397-418.

Wilber, Ken. (1981). *Up from Eden: A Transpersonal View of Human Evolution.* Garden City, NY: Anchor.

19

The Lineage of the Sun

BROOKE MEDICINE EAGLE

Many people say that two thousand years or so ago, a Being of Light came walking across the water to the Americas from Polynesia. He traveled on the great white-sailed ships that plied the seas at that time. Rather than having a dinghy bring him to shore, it is said that he walked across the water to the people. He brought them a Lineage of Light, a tradition of allowing the Light of Spirit, the Light of Life, to shine down through the heart, unrestricted, on its way to others. He demonstrated his Truth by talking with the animals, healing the sick, curing the blind, stopping the winds, and walking on water. His compassion shone through to the people from his heart, and he was greatly loved. When the tribes asked his name, he replied, "Call me as you will." So they called him Healer, Lord of the Wind and Water, Elder Brother, and many other names of beauty and power. As he rose each morning with the new day, they called him Dawn Star. He took his twelve chosen apprentices and greeted the sun in silent and joyful meditation. He had coppery hair and blue-green eyes that changed like the sea. He wore a long white robe which had crosses embroidered on the hem. He wore a pair of golden sandals that were not really gold but were made of a substance strong and wonderful that never wore out. When his apprentices had become teachers, he left the Way with them, though the people sorrowed at his leaving.

Dawn Star came at a time when the tribes worshipped an angry father god or gods. These deities demanded sacrifice, even of human lives. He came teaching Light and Love, and he traveled all through the Americas, coming up from the South into Turtle Island, the native people's name for North America. He came as far as my Northern Plains country, and I am told by my elders that the highest teachers in our sacred lineage ran to him for their initiation. One of our northern tribes called him Wohogus, Light of the World. He left behind a pan-native web of Light, supported by twelve apprentices in each tribe who carried the Way. This Being of Light saw that the people would continue to travel through many stages, being crushed and buried and then returning to the angry gods of sacrifice. It sorrowed him greatly to leave, having begun an awakening among our people. It was an awakening that we ourselves in these modern times must strive to renew.

Today, our Sundance is said to be a remnant of the dance to the renewing power of the Light. To this day, the Sundance connects all native people throughout the Americas. At last, through this connection, we are beginning to dance with one another again so that the web of Light, spun so long ago by Wohogus, may be rewoven.

The various Lineages of Light that carried the way are known as the *nagual* lines, and they have gone through many changes over the centuries. In some cultures, the tradition faded totally because of a lack of understanding and commitment. Sometimes the teachings disappeared because of persecution. In other instances, those who carried the tradition tried to use the power to gain control over others. They became the dark sorcerers. Still others carried the Light and passed it down through the ages, showing themselves to be white sorcerers, shamans, and medicine people.

Now Native Americans are emerging from a time of darkness on this planet, a time when invading European people, wanting to subjugate us with their political and religious ideas, persecuted or murdered the shamans and sorcerers, forcing them underground. As Don Juan of the Carlos Castaneda books says, medicine people were required to fine-tune themselves against their worthy adversaries in order to survive. These powerful carriers of the tradition became very strong during the times of repression. Because of the intense secrecy with which they had to live, the once-connected web began to disintegrate. Distrust grew rampant. This underground time I call the hidden time, the time of the night and the moon, the time of the "House of Silverado." Yet today the dawn is returning. The laws of this land are finally in line with the acceptance of the ways of native people. No longer are we jailed for practicing our spiritual ways. It is time for the Lineage of Light to shine again. Those of us who represent the re-emergence of the Light are "bringing Gold to the House of Silverado."

The function of the modern shaman in the largest sense is to bring Light not only to individuals, but also to our Mother, the Earth. The dawn of this Light is inevitable. Its first rays may soon break over the horizon. As apprentices, we are told by our Native American elders, "We have been together since the time of the ancient mystery schools. For thousands of years the priesthood held and carried the Way. It is now time to share the ancient mystical knowledge, so that everyone may benefit."

If we think of ourselves emerging from the darkness of a thunderstorm into the clarity of a new day, we may be lucky enough to spot a rainbow. The rainbow medicine comes with the dawn and is a symbol for this time of all colors coming together to create a bridge into the new and golden time. It is a time of brotherhood and sisterhood, not only of the two-leggeds, but also of the four-leggeds, the wingeds, those who swim and crawl and wiggle, the rock people and the green growing ones. Our sacred pipe law reminds us of this oneness with all things. Whatever we do to any other being, we do to ourselves. The deepest truths of the ancient ways are re-emerging and connecting with all the myriad forms that exist on this Earth. A Light bridge is being formed among all spiritual practices.

During the storm though, a testing has taken place. Some lineages were outwardly broken, old ways were lost, forms were rigidified, some teachings degenerated. When one of my grandmothers, a keeper of the Light for her Northern Plains people and a guardian of the sacred lodge, died, she buried her medicine bundle. Rather than passing these objects—symbols of her acquired powers—on to someone else, she let them die with her. No one of her tribe was prepared to carry on. This same circumstance is recurring in many cases across the land. The loss of the old knowledge grieves me, and yet as I meditate more deeply upon it, it seems to be part of the testing that Mother-Father-Source is giving us right now. The power that grandmother held in her medicine bundle had come from the great Source in the first place. In this day and time, that Source is still available. The question is whether the new shamans are connected enough to It to bring back the Light once more. If we are not sufficiently connected, it is just as well that the bundle is not passed on. But if we are deeply in touch with the Source, we have broken through form into Spirit.

On the West Coast there was a powerful and well-known shaman and healer who conducted her Way in a round lodge that was a sacred center for her people. She was a sucking shaman and a hand-trembler who assisted her people in many ways. Yet when she was ready to pass on there was no one to take the round lodge, and so she closed it. Because the lodge had been a healing focus for the community, the fabric of the society around it began to unravel. Increasing drunkenness became a symbol for the disintegration. Then a young man, himself a drinker, was given a vision—a vision of restoring the sacred center, the round lodge of the people. Never having been trained in the ways of the shaman, he was disbelieving. He denied his vision, yet it returned again and again, showing him all that was to be done. When he was finally convinced and began expressing his intentions, he met with derision and obstruction. He continued, though, beginning in a simple way; and when people saw that he was keeping the old ways, that many of the forms looked the same, they began to gather around him. Gradually, the circle was reformed and today these West Coast people have their sacred lodge once more. This young man had not received the outward lineage, but the inward lineage of Spirit. He had received his information on "the left side," as we say. Both he and the lineage had successfully met the test.

It is now said that the inward lineage is being given to a rainbow mix of men and women of all races. For each of us, there is an inward lineage, if we are willing to honor that voice and that vision. As Rainbow Warriors, our challenge is to make that dream real, as the young drinker did—to quiet ourselves so that we may listen and see, and then to move ourselves to action.

I am told of a whole new vibration being given to Earth, a harmonious tone being set. This tone is coming to us freely as the dawn breaks. Yet this gift can be thought of as a "matching grant." We must match this tone, this harmonious song, with our own voices, our own lives, in order truly to receive it.

This harmony with all things is the *yin* or feminine side of the balance. There are many wobbles and bumps in our present song. To balance it we must bring about a deep caring for all peoples. This caring is the energy of Buffalo Woman, the symbol of the nurturing of the people, especially the nurturing of the spirit of the people. The philosophies of "any means to an end" and "progress at any cost" have thrown us into a dangerous imbalance. When Creator created the world, the only law given was "You shall be in good relationship to all things and all beings." This law has been given especially to the female, to she who holds creation within herself. She shall uphold and nurture and teach her whole family the ways. As native people say, "A woman must be strong in her discipline and gentle in her teaching." This law must live within the heart of each of us, for to be truly human the masculine and feminine must be balanced within.

We have heard the Father, the Mother and the Son in our time. Now it is the time of the daughter. The blessings of the daughter will bring us into a time of exquisite balance. It is said, in fact, that the Creator promised that when all dark sorcerers again became Light Warriors, the Source will give the hand of the daughter, the hand of Buffalo Woman or Earth Woman, in symbolic marriage to the Dawn Star, Elder Brother, Man of Spirit. Thus will Grandmother Spider again weave her medicine web, joining together the Earth and Sky, spirit and body, to create enlightenment on Mother Earth.

This is how these stories have come to me. Take them as you will, as we have taken them from our twisted-hairs, our storytellers, and passed them down through the generations. May this serve All-Our-Relations. Ho!

20

Black Elk: Then and Now

WILLIAM S. LYON

> now that I can see it all
> as from a lonely hilltop
> I know it was the story of a mighty vision
> given to a man
> too weak to use it
> of a holy tree that should have flourished
> in a people's heart
> with flowers and singing birds
> and now is withered
> "Nick" Black Elk

Wallace Black Elk is a pipe-bearing descendant of the renowned "Nick" Black Elk of John Niehardt's *Black Elk Speaks* fame. He is one of the few remaining shamans in North America who was raised in the traditional ways of his people to follow the "sacred red road" and is a leading elder among the Lakota people. As such, Wallace speaks with an authenticity rarely found among today's living shamans.

Wallace has lectured extensively throughout the U.S., as well as in Europe and Japan, educating people from the inner eye of shamanism. He has also played a major role in the political struggle for freedom among Native Americans. He often acts as "scout," operating on the forefront of current Native American developments.

Foremost, Wallace Black Elk is a healer and a traditional ceremonial leader in the Lakota sun dance, vision/quest, Yuwipi, Inipi, and other such rituals. Through the sacred pipe, he communicates directly with spirit helpers in order to bring health and help to individuals in all races of mankind.

285

In North America the ancient wisdom of shamanism still lives among many of the Native American cultures. The forms of this practice will vary from culture to culture due to their different historical roots, woven deep into the fabric of the language and experiences of the people of different times and places. For many years, professional anthropologists have concentrated on these differences, for they tell a story of the coming, spreading, and going of these different practices over time and space. This story is read in the shape of drums, symbols on a rattle, carvings on a pipe, words of a song. Basically it is a search into the history of the different forms of shamanism.

However, the overt forms of shamanism from culture to culture are only the tip of the iceberg. Beneath these myriad expressions lies an ancient and powerful form of human knowledge. We once thought this knowledge to be nothing more than childish superstition. The literature of the 19th Century is replete with examples from the Navajo, Cherokee, Cheyenne, Iroquois, and others of their "barbaric" state of being and "degraded" religious practices. However, late in the 19th century we "discovered" psychology, and now many years later, having developed a fair amount of psychological sophistication, we are beginning to see that shamanism contains a greater depth than heretofore imagined. For example, there were no students of psychology in the 1870s to explain why Wovoka was spreading the Ghost Dance among the Paiutes. Our ability to understand shamanism has been historically limited by the degree to which we understand the workings of the human mind. As we come to understand more about the mind, we in turn begin to understand more about the practice of shamanism. I firmly believe that we have learned more about the nature of shamanism in the past forty years than in all the previous years of study.

What is beginning to emerge is a cross-cultural core to shamanism which I refer to as the "shamanic complex"—a specific set of psychological and social factors woven together in a specific manner. Many believe that the first major contributor to this understanding was Mircea Eliade whose work on shamanism during the 1940s is seen as a classic study (Eliade 1964). Eliade referred to shamanism as an "archaic technique of ecstasy," thus clearly associating shamanism for the first time with the use of trance states. Eliade's study was limited, however, by his own disbelief in the efficacy of shamanism and his lack of direct field studies. Today scholars agree not only on the shamans' use of this excited state of being, but also on their ability to enter and leave this trance state at will. The goal of the shaman is to enter a state of consciousness that will enable him or her to communicate with spirits in what Nick Black Elk called the "outer" or "other world." This communication with spirits allows the shaman in turn to return to this space/timeframe with what is referred to in North America as "medicine powers."

We are finding that shamans from very different cultures, at different times in history, share many abilities such as communication with spirits. My own studies of Lakota shamanism show a decided continuity through time between two famous Lakota shamans, namely "Nick" Black Elk and Wallace Black Elk. Nick Black Elk became famous from the book *Black Elk Speaks* (Neihardt 1972), which was first published in 1932, and was recognized again later in *The Sacred Pipe* (Brown 1963). He passed away at Manderson, South Dakota, on the Pine Ridge Reservation in August of 1950. Wallace Black Elk was born in 1921, also in South Dakota, and as a youth met and knew Nick Black Elk. Although their exact genetic relationship is obscured due to the way in which the Lakota acquired names and the Bureau of Indian Affairs in turn assigned them names, Wallace refers to Nick as his "grandfather." This, of course, is a spiritual relationship centered on their mutual use of the sacred pipe. For the Lakota the sacred pipe is the most holy object in the universe, and nothing surpasses its power. All of their pipes are seen to be the offspring of the original sacred buffalo calf pipe that was brought to the Lakota by the White Buffalo Woman. They still have this pipe in their possession. The use of the sacred pipe forms the core of Lakota shamanism, around which all of their rituals revolve. Nick Black Elk was told by the spirits that "with this pipe you shall walk upon the earth, and whatever sickens there you shall make well" (Neihardt 1972:23). To us it appears merely a piece of stone and a stick. To the Lakota shamans it is an instrument that can never be fully fathomed during a lifetime of use— so deep is its inner meaning. For them its power has no limits.

In 1930 John G. Niehardt, poet and professor, traveled to

South Dakota to inquire about the Ghost Dance ceremony for an epic poem ("A Cycle of the West") he was writing about the westward expansion of civilization in America. In particular, he was unclear as to the deeper meaning of the term "medicine power." On the Pine Ridge Reservation he was eventually directed to Nick Black Elk, who in turn announced that he (Neihardt) had been sent to save Black Elk's great vision for mankind. There was an immediate rapport between the two that developed into a lifelong friendship, although Nick spoke no English. This rapport was not accidental inasmuch as both men had powerful transcendental experiences—Nick through his vision quests and Neihardt spontaneously while sitting one day in an orchard (recorded in his poem "April Theology"). There can be little doubt that they each recognized a kindred spirit in the other, and in 1931 Neihardt set to the task of recording Black Elk's words via a translator.

In May of 1931 Nick Black Elk, Neihardt, and company climbed to the top of Harney Peak near Sylvan Lake in the Black Hills of South Dakota to conduct a pipe ceremony. In one account of this adventure Neihardt wrote:

> On the way up he told his son that if he [Nick] had any power left, surely there would be a little thunder and some rain while he was on the Peak. This is a curious thing and equally interesting... but at the time we were going up and after we were on the Peak, the day was bright and clear. During his prayer on the summit, clouds came up and there was a low thunder and a scant, chill rain fell, but the old man seemed sad and broken. (DeMallie 1984:48)

Neihardt came to be convinced that Nick had supernatural powers (Neihardt 1972:x).

Niehardt's daughter Enid, also on the trip as stenographer, recorded the incident in her notes as follows:

> Before reaching the top of the peak, Black Elk told his son, Ben, that if he had power with the spirits that it would rain a little sprinkle when he gave this ceremony. It did rain out of a perfectly bright sky and then it cleared up immediately afterward. (DeMallie 1984:296)

I mention this incident only because my first encounter with Wallace Black Elk was similar, but slightly more dramatic. I first met Wallace when he came to Southern Oregon State College in August of 1978 where I was a professor of anthropology. He had come upon invitation to conduct an experimental class in which college students were to receive credit for conducting an "inipi" ceremony. These are popularly referred to as "sweat-lodge" ceremonies, but Wallace prefers the term "stone-people-lodge" ceremony.

Southern Oregon receives little to no rain during the summer months. Consequently, by August there is an extreme fire danger in this area, which is surrounded by national forests, and all burning must be done by permit. The fire permit was one of the many things I forgot to obtain prior to our class. When the time came to heat the "stone-people," we set fire to a circle of wood five feet in diameter that surrounded the stones. Since it was to take at least one hour before the stones were heated, I made a quick run back to the college located about four miles away. It was a sunny day with intermittent clouds. As I left the area a large and visible column of smoke rose from the valley floor.

Within minutes a call came from a nearby ranger tower to their local headquarters, inquiring if a fire permit had been issued for our area. Of course there was none, so two rangers left the tower to investigate the situation. Driving up to the site, they were rather startled to see over fifty half-naked youths wandering about. One ranger left the vehicle to investigate the matter, instructing the other ranger to stand by near the radio in the vehicle. As the first ranger approached the group, he asked who was in charge, and the students immediately pointed to Wallace Black Elk. The ranger then approached Wallace and asked to see his fire permit. Wallace responded with a "What that for?" The ranger then proceeded to explain that it was to help protect the surrounding forests from fire danger.

Wallace's world view could not comprehend any danger. He proceeded to tell the ranger that this was not an ordinary fire, but that it was a sacred fire watched over by the Thunder Beings from whom he derived much of his power. He then invited the ranger to join them in the ceremony. The ranger was not moved and began to insist that Wallace immediately drive to the forest service headquarters and fill out a fire permit request form. At this point Wallace assumed one of his classic defense postures, which was to act very dumb. Soon the ranger was being confronted with questions like, "Permit? What that word mean?"

After about twenty minutes of haggling, the ranger gave in and issued a "temporary permit." However, by this time the Thunder Beings had moved in. A cloud had formed over the site in a nearly cloudless sky, and rain began to pour down. The ranger, unable to write out the permit in the downpour, was forced to seek refuge underneath a sheet of plastic held up by the students in order to fill it out. Needless to say, the students found great delight in this scene. Unfortunately, the ranger was somewhat terrified, and I subsequently discovered that he never reported the incident or even told his wife, who at the time happened to be working as the radio receiver at the forest service headquarters. All she remembers is his calling in from the site and saying, "You wouldn't believe what just happened to me out here." By the time he reached the headquarters, he simply reported that things had been taken care of. When I returned, the surrounding area was soaking wet from the rain. There were no clouds overhead, and it had not rained in town only a few miles away. Wallace simply smiled in silence.

Lakota shamanism, of course, follows a particular cultural pattern. Within that pattern both Black Elks came to be aided by the powerful Thunder-Beings (Wakinyam). In addition, they both received their first power vision at the age of nine, although Wallace reports that he was being visited by spirits as early as age five. As one listens to Wallace and reads the accounts of Nick, one is struck by the tremendous similarity between these two great shamans.

Perhaps one of the most striking similarities has to do with both Nick's and Wallace's ability to leave the reservation boundaries. As a youth Nick traveled as far away as Europe with Buffalo Bill's Wild West Show. Among other things, he wanted to discover what secret powers the white race had that had allowed them to conquer the Lakota people. Although he spoke no English, he remained in Europe from the spring of 1887 to the spring of 1889. According to published accounts, "Black Elk became separated from the main party" and remained "stranded" until Buffalo Bill returned to Paris (DeMallie 1984:9). According to the unofficial account, he chose to remain in Paris with his then French girlfriend.

Wallace Black Elk has also taken Lakota shamanism to other parts of the world. Besides extensive touring in this country, he has traveled to Japan and to Europe. For example, he spent a great deal of effort to help people in Germany to find their own traditional ties to nature, Catholicism having eradicated most of the shamanic traditions in Europe. Both of these shamans see two basic paths to life—the sacred red path (or road) and the materialistic black path. For Wallace, those who follow the red path of life, no matter what their race, are referred to by him as "earth people." He refers to himself as an "earth man." Perhaps the major difference here between these two shamans is that Nick returned to spend the rest of his life on the reservation, while Wallace has resided in Denver, Colorado, for many years now. Of course, the reservation is only eight hours by car away from his home, and he goes there frequently.

As mentioned, the Lakota shamans gain their power by going *hanbleceya* (literally "to cry for a vision") (Powers 1977:61). First they go to an *inipi* ceremony, and then are "put up on the hill" to receive the *wakan* (holy) beings. Whatever power the shaman receives during this vision quest, it is expected to be manifested here on earth for the health and help of all people. Again, this can take many forms. For example, Nick performed the Horse Dance after which,

> It seemed that I was above the ground and did not touch it when I walked. I felt very happy, for I could see that my people were all happier. Many crowded around me and said that they or their relatives who had been feeling sick were well again, and these gave me many gifts. Even the horses seemed to be healthier and happier after the dance. (Neihardt 1972:147).

As Nick gained power, he performed many such cures. The medicine power comes in other forms as well. The concept of "medicine" is not limited to the curing of illness but includes anything that brings health or help to people. For example, I have heard Wallace speak of using their powers to find the body of a boy who had drowned in a river; to get the license number of a car that had been driven by some youths who beat up an elderly couple; and to find out what was being said in certain "secret" meetings or what was written on certain "secret" documents. The form of aid that is mediated through the sacred pipe seems limited only by the human imagination.

Because both shamans saw more and more of their people take up the black road, they both have a great deal of concern for our contemporary way of life. Among the Lakota people, it is customary to consider the effect of one's decision-making on "seven generations to come." That translates into, How will what we do now affect our children's future? Neihardt reported that Nick was saddened by the fact that the "flowering tree," their symbol of life, was withering. His hope was that maybe a small root of it still remained alive, but he lived at a time when fewer and fewer young people were taking up the sacred pipe. He stated:

> I kept on curing the sick for three years more, and many came to me and were made over, but when I thought of my great vision, which was to save the nation's hoop and make the holy tree to bloom in the center of it, I felt like crying, for the sacred hoop was broken and scattered. The life of the people was in the hoop, and what are many little lives if the life of those lives be gone? (Neihardt 1972:182)

Wallace has the same basic attitude when he speaks of this "tree of life" or "tree of knowledge." Both shamans point out that one's life is incomplete if one has not tapped into the "outer world" from which one can receive sound advice and help. A life without knowledge of the spirit is not a life at all. It is a wasted life. The major difference here between the two is that Nick was concerned mainly with his own Lakota people, while Wallace concerns himself with all of mankind, regardless of race. Wallace is quick to point out that the sacred pipe does not racially discriminate, and that when a spirit enters the "stone-people-lodge" it certainly doesn't announce what race it belongs to. I suspect this difference is due to the fact that Wallace speaks English, while Nick did not.

Unlike Nick, however, Wallace is filled with hope about the blooming of the sacred tree of life. He is living in a time when shamanism is not only on the upswing, but the use of the sacred pipe is spreading to all races of mankind. He said:

We aren't going any place, we're going to stay here. If you study a little deeper, you'll find only the humble meek shall inherit the earth. And we are related to it. The world purification will come, and everything will turn green like the way it was back in the beginning. And all the flying creatures will come back, us two-legged creatures will come back, and it'll be forever. That's unification. So this tree of life will unify all the people together here, one branch will be white men, one branch will be black people, one branch will be yellow. We all come from the same root, for this is a tree of knowledge, a tree of life. (From personal field notes)

Both Black Elks also clearly carry the attitude that they are not really healers, but that the power of the other world works through them. Because it is the power of the spirits that brings about changes in this world, it is common for true shamans to give credit where credit is due. As such, I am always suspect of anyone who claims to be a shaman while in the same breath taking personal credit for all that transpires. Humbleness and humility are general characteristics of the true shaman. Nick clearly revealed this when he told Neihardt:

Of course it was not I who cured. It was the power from the outer world, and the visions and ceremonies had only made me like a hole through which the power could come to the two leggeds. If I thought that I was doing it myself, the hole would close up and no power could come through. (Neihardt 1972:174)

Wallace is also clear about not taking the credit himself:

A lot of times people call me a medicine man, but I'm not a medicine man. It's that Spirit, he's truly the medicine man. Right now, in the world, we have cancer, polio, tuberculosis, heart disease. People don't understand these things. If I can take something, some medicine, and give it to someone who is sick, they want to see the plant. They want to analyze it. And if it cures them, they'll offer me a million dollars for it. But you can't put the Spirit in a capsule. (From personal field notes)

It is certain that Nick lived in more desperate times. Wallace tells of how they used to have to meet in secret to do their rituals, and that if discovered, the reservation police would descend on them, smashing their pipes. Nick's appeals to both Neihardt and

Brown were last-ditch attempts to save the red road path of life. It is somewhat ironic that Neihardt felt a tremendous sense of duty to Nick, but was never able to clearly formulate a plan of action. For one thing, although given a sacred pipe by Nick, Neihardt never seemed to fathom its depth and put it to use. Nick clearly saw that it was "in the darkness of their eyes that men get lost" (Neihardt 1972:2), and so in the winter of 1947, sixteen years after his work with Neihardt, he once again, via Joseph E. Brown, attempted to save the old way of life. Wallace, however, about this same time began to step forth in public, and dared to speak of the power of the sacred pipe. For this he was, at first, institutionalized as insane. But with perseverance and strength gained from the sacred pipe, he fought a long battle uphill to achieve freedom for all North American shamans. His major triumph has been the passage of the American Indian Religious Freedom Act in 1977, for which he lobbied for over seven years before it went before Congress. The Act virtually guaranteed the right of all Native Americans to practice their natural "religions," putting a stop to all efforts to wipe out shamanism in North America.

One could easily say that Wallace is a living extension of Nick. One has a difficult time distinguishing between the visions of Wallace today and those of Nick from yesteryears. For myself, I feel that the sacred tree has once again begun to bloom for these sacred shamans of North America. I wish them well on their renewed adventures into a world filled with misery and suffering. The key for both Nick and Wallace was to remain true to the teachings of the sacred pipe. At one point Nick was forced, due to his public notoriety, to denounce the pipe in favor of Catholicism. Of course, when backs were turned both he and Wallace sat together in the "stone-people-lodge." Nick remained, in secret, true to the sacred pipe until his death. Thus the vision of his people was not lost, for as Wallace says they "both spoke the same mind."

> purification will come
> and grandma will cradle us
>   in her arms
>   and wipe our tears
>   and grandpa will walk among us

it will be this generation
you people
will make it a reality
and the hoop
will come together again
                    Wallace Black Elk

References

Brown, Joseph Epes. 1953. *The Sacred Pipe: Black Elk's Account of the Seven Rites of the Oglala Sioux.* University of Oklahoma Press. Norman, Oklahoma.

DeMallie, Raymond J. 1984. *The Sixth Grandfather.* University of Nebraska Press. Lincoln, Nebraska.

Eliade, Mircea. 1972. *Shamanism: Archaic Techniques of Ecstasy.* Princeton University Press. Princeton, New Jersey.

Neihardt, John G. 1972. *Black Elk Speaks.* Pocket Books. New York, New York.

Powers, William K. 1977. *Oglala Religion.* University of Nebraska Press. Lincoln, Nebraska.

Quest Books
encourages open-minded inquiry into
world religions, philosophy, science, and the arts
in order to understand the wisdom of the ages,
respect the unity of all life, and help people explore
individual spiritual self-transformation.

Its publications are generously supported by
The Kern Foundation,
a trust committed to Theosophical education.

Quest Books is the imprint of
the Theosophical Publishing House,
a division of the Theosophical Society in America.
For information about programs, literature,
on-line study, membership benefits, and international centers,
see www.theosophical.org
or call 800-669-1571 or (outside the U.S.) 630-668-1571.

To order books or a complete Quest catalog,
call 800-669-9425 or (outside the U.S.) 630-665-0130.